SOVIET POLITICS FROM BREZHNEV TO GORBACHEV

SOVIET POLITICS FROM BREZHNEV TO GORBACHEV

DONALD R. KELLEY

PRAEGER

New York
Westport, Connecticut
London

Library of Congress Cataloging-in-Publication Data

Kelley, Donald R., 1943–
    Soviet politics from Brezhnev to Gorbachev.

    Bibliography: p.
    Includes index.
    1. Soviet Union—Politics and government—1953–
I. Title.
DK274.K44 1987   320.947   87-11677
ISBN 0-275-92522-6 (alk. paper)
ISBN 0-275-92732-6 (pbk. : alk. paper)

Library of Congress Catalog Card Number: 87-11677
ISBN: 0-275-92522-6
       0-275-92732-6 (pb)

First published in 1987

Praeger Publishers, One Madison Avenue, New York, NY 10010
A division of Greenwood Press, Inc.

Printed in the United States of America

The paper used in this book complies with the
Permanent Paper Standard issued by the National
Information Standards Organization (Z39.48-1984).

10 9 8 7 6 5 4 3 2 1

To Sally and Jean

Contents

SOVIET POLITICS

FROM

BREZHNEV

TO

GORBACHEV

1   The Brezhnev Legacy

Any assessment of the politics of the post-Brezhnev era must begin with an understanding of the 18 year tenure in office of the man who was elevated to power in October 1964. Unlike his volatile predecessor, Leonid Ilich Brezhnev brought relative stability and cautious leadership to the Kremlin. But like Khrushchev, he sought to make his mark on Soviet history and to forge a series of policy initiatives that not only dealt with the major economic and social problems facing the nation but also disarmed or coopted his critics and enemies.

Our retrospective assessment of the Brezhnev years must also begin with a reminder about the danger of last impressions. The rumors concerning the General Secretary's ill health, which began in the mid-1970s, the repeated and publicly-lamented policy failures at home and abroad, the growing sense of immobilism and malaise that characterized the last half decade of his rule, and the grim deathwatch of his final years should not obscure the fact that his tenure in office was also marked by major new policy initiatives and the formulation of a new vision of the Soviet future that were designed to lead the USSR through the second industrial revolution and into the further maturation of "developed socialism," as the brave new world of technological advances, an improved standard of living, and the "scientific management of society" was to be known.

We must also avoid the misleading conclusion that the Brezhnev years were devoid of political struggle at the highest echelons of power. Like all Soviet leaders of the post-Stalin era, Brezhnev assembled a coalition of powerful institutional interests that backed him through the use of selective appeals to their vested economic and political interests. His policy initiatives and the inevitable tactical retreats that followed setbacks in agriculture, the economy, or in foreign policy were always double-edged swords; while they offered Brezhnev's conventional wisdom of the day concerning the direction of policy, they also were intended to shape the nature of his own coalition and undercut his critics. To be sure, his style was different from that of his volatile predecessor; confrontation and constant institutional tinkering were replaced by a more cautious manipulation of the role of the party vis-à-vis other political actors and by attempts to redefine political and economic issues to his advantage. When clashes occurred, they were more often resolved by efforts to coopt and buy off opponents with policy rewards in other areas than by the neutralization and dismissal of his critics.[1]

THE COUP AGAINST KHRUSHCHEV: A MANDATE FOR NEW LEADERSHIP

Many of the political realities that shaped the Brezhnev years and set the parameters within which the General Secretary could exercise discretionary leadership were implicit in the nature of the coup against Khrushchev in October 1964. While the critical Politburo majority that assembled against the First Secretary (as the leading party post was known under Khrushchev) was concerned with his multiple policy failures and with his flawed vision of the communist future, their immediate actions were motivated more by their assessment of his style of leadership and by his efforts to escape the boundaries of collective leadership. The October coup was quintessentially about leadership and the relationship between the First Secretary and the senior echelons of party and state. (Khrushchev's title, First

Secretary, was changed to General Secretary when Brezhnev took over the post.) Khrushchev fell from power because his opponents throughout the party and state bureaucracies feared his incessant attempts to change the very nature of the major institutions of power and to force an already aging and conservative elite to accept the need for extensive changes in their own style of leadership.

The nature of party rule was also at issue in the coup. Consistent with his own new-found belief that the party must change its style of leadership if it were to cope with the emergence of an advanced industrial society in the USSR, Khrushchev called upon party and state officials both to shed the rough-hewn mechanisms of command and coercion of the Stalin era and to master the tools of modern management. Not only were they told that the style of leadership that had carried them through the early years of industrialization and into the 1960s was now increasingly outdated and irrelevant, they could also see the next generation of better trained and educated party officials and managers being groomed by a First Secretary who was quite willing to push them aside if they failed to heed his call for reforms.

The pace of social and political change, and especially the rate of progress toward the emergence of the beginning stages of communism itself, also were issues that troubled those who removed Khrushchev from power. Impatient to implement his reforms and anxious to score quick political victories against his opponents, the First Secretary forced the pace of change against the opposition of more cautious skeptics. Always in search of a seeming quick fix to a complex problem such as agriculture or consumer goods production, or quick to reject half-implemented policy initiatives for the latest "panaceas," Khrushchev acquired the reputation of an inconstant leader who shot from the hip. Even at the theoretical level, his new party program introduced at the 22nd Party Congress in 1961 boldly promised rapid progress toward the construction of the initial stages of communism by the early 1980s.

The plotters who assembled the hostile Politburo majority that ousted Khrushchev and chose Brezhnev and Kosygin to divide the mantles of party and state leadership — and there is no convincing evidence that either was the principal architect of his own elevation — had a clear vision of the sort of leadership they wanted: careful and systematic policy planning would replace ill-thought-out schemes and panaceas; realism about the pace of change and the ability of the system to deal simultaneously with its myriad economic and social problems would replace utopian promises about the attainment of communism in their lifetime; capricious reorganizations of the party and state bureaucracies would yield to a desire for routinization and stability; and, above all, the threat to the prerogatives and even the careers of senior officials of party and state would be replaced by a return to consultative forms of collective leadership and, as the catchword of the day soon foretold, to a healthy "respect for cadres."[2]

BREZHNEV AS LEADER: A MAN OF CAUTIOUS VISION

Viewed in retrospect, Brezhnev's years in power emerge as nearly two decades of cautious political and policy initiatives designed both to consolidate the General Secretary's hold on power and to implement economic and social reforms that would improve the standard of living and move the Soviet Union gently through the second industrial revolution. While the political style of the new regime was far different from that of its predecessor, the durability of the major policy issues that bedeviled Khrushchev and rose quickly to haunt his successor is striking. The modernization of the Soviet economy, the formulation of managerial reforms, the growing restiveness of consumers who had long been promised a higher standard of living, and the need to force the party itself to reconceptualize its role in society — all quickly emerged on the Brezhnev agenda.

On the central political question of the role of the communist party and its interface with other major institutional players, Brezhnev pursued a balanced course that combined strong insistence that the CPSU (Communist Party of the Soviet Union) maintain its leading role vis-à-vis the economic bureaucracy with increasingly strident demands that the party itself accept new challenges and put its internal house in order. The initial opportunity to define that role in ways that favored the institutional prerogatives of the party and that won support from among party cadres concerned with defending their powers came in connection with the economic reforms advocated by Alexei Kosygin in the mid-1960s, which halfheartedly offered greater powers and independence to enterprise-level personnel. In contrast, Brezhnev's initial response stressed the traditional prerogatives of the party and demanded continued reliance on party control and supervision in the economy. Rather than countenance the emergence of even the weakest of independent market relationships, the General Secretary argued for continuing party intervention and coordination as the keys to improved performance. In its initial guise, such continued party dominance offered the reassuring prospect of greater institutional stability within an administrative system that had been rocked by Khrushchev's constant reorganizations and that feared the unfamiliar world of even partial reforms.

In the longer perspective, Brezhnev's defense of party prerogatives carried with it increasingly strident demands for improved performance. Even as he defended the powers of the CPSU against Kosygin's decentralization proposals, he called for party committees within the economic ministries to assume greater responsibility for the success of their host institutions. They were to take the lead in fostering technological modernization and innovation, in cutting through administrative bottlenecks, and in coordinating the activities of their sprawling agencies. The party was clearly to play a greater interventionist role, yet one different from the capricious interference that had characterized its activities under Khrushchev. Rather its new-found activism was to be rooted in its own growing technological and managerial sophistication and in its ability to reconcile narrow departmental interests with the broader perspective.[3]

Brezhnev's reconceptualization of the role of the party acquired increasing force as a consequence of the emergence of developed socialism as the theoretical centerpiece of his tenure in office. Although he had backed away from the sweeping commitments to the rapid emergence of communism contained in Khrushchev's 1961 party program, Brezhnev offered his own more cautious vision of the future. As theory, developed socialism described the emergence of the USSR as a mature industrial system whose further evolution was dependent upon the application of what Soviet theorists termed "the scientific and technological revolution" to the nation's economic and social problems. While it was to be marked by the gradual and politically untraumatic transition to higher dialectical forms, it nonetheless demanded that the party both take an activist role in fostering the modernization of the economy and that the CPSU itself radically alter its own workstyle. In short, the party was expected to internalize the values and operationalize the workstyle of Brezhnev's brave new world of developed socialism. In the best of worlds, it was to be willing to accept the need for thorough internal reform and to lead other agencies through the transition.[4]

BREZHNEV AS LEADER: POLICY REFORMS

Despite the obvious tone of caution that marked his rule, Brezhnev nonetheless authored significant policy reforms. Like Khrushchev, he sought to make his mark by bold initiatives in agriculture, consumer goods production, and foreign policy, but unlike his predecessor, he moved with caution, seeking to balance bold initiatives in one area with concessions in another or to coopt his critics and their programs rather than opting for confrontation. Brezhnev emerged as a clear policy initiator rather than merely as a balancer of major Kremlin interests, although he was quick to moderate his new programs in light of policy failures or in the face of opposition.

Brezhnev's astute sense of balance can be seen in his handling of the issue of economic reform. While virtually everyone within the Kremlin leadership agreed that change was necessary, the new General Secretary of the Party (Brezhnev) and the chairman of the Council of Ministers (Kosygin) initially opted for different solutions. Kosygin's proposals focused on the decentralization of industrial management and on vesting greater powers into the hands of factory-level personnel, who were expected to utilize new methods of measuring enterprise performance to improve efficiency, encourage technological modernization, and produce goods more in demand by other industrial and private consumers. Politically his reforms smacked of limited "marketization" and shifted greater decision-making powers away from party supervisors at all levels into the hands of an increasingly autonomous economic bureaucracy. Both because they promised to upset deeply rooted prerogatives and because the timid and watered down reforms themselves failed to produce dramatic positive results, Brezhnev was able to paint Kosygin's initiatives as both politically dangerous and ineffectual.

But with the neutralization of Kosygin's challenge on economic issues, Brezhnev himself took up the mantle of reform, albeit in different form. In the early 1970s, he proposed that reform efforts focus not on the individual enterprise level — where resistance had been met from factory directors unwilling to assume new responsibilities and which provided too small an economic unit to deal with large-scale problems — but rather on the creation of multi-factory "associations" (*obedinenie*). These new units were to combine different enterprises that performed related tasks, to link weaker and less efficient factories with stronger counterparts that could foster their modernization, and to establish ties between enterprises and research and development operations. Patterned in part after the Western experience with vertical and horizontal integration of complex corporations, these associations were to take the lead in the introduction of new technology and in freeing up redundant elements of the work force for reassignment elsewhere.

In political terms, the redefinition of economic reform along these lines permitted Brezhnev both to seize the issue from Kosygin and to opt for a greater role for party leadership at the association level, where inter-factory party committees would assume important coordinating roles, and to press his case for a redefinition and "scientific" rationalization of the role of the party itself, which was called upon to exercise sophisticated managerial leadership commensurate with the growing technological maturity and institutional complexity of the system. While Brezhnev's vigor in pressing for such reforms waxed and waned with his political fortunes on other issues, the central premise of limited decentralization coupled with an improved quality of leadership remained at the core of his program for managerial reforms.[5]

Balanced against these economic initiatives was the tacit promise to senior party and state officials that their tenure in office and the prerogatives of leadership would not be capriciously challenged for the sake of breakneck reform. While the administrative mechanisms and the workstyle of economic officials in both the party and the state apparatus was to be revamped, the individuals themselves could rest assured that the Brezhnev administration would refrain from the sort of "hare-brained" reorganizations and sweeping reforms that had been undertaken by Khrushchev. Clearly the deal being tacitly offered combined elements of reform and stability, linking limited deconcentration of administrative power with intra-elite stability and increased powers for planners and managers who were willing to play by the new rules.

A similar balanced approach occurred in terms of investment priorities. While his first initiatives were for agricultural reforms, Brezhnev was quick to coopt the issue of increased consumer goods production and to link it with a demand that the heavy industrial sector play a role in meeting the nation's needs for a better standard of living. Yet his commitment to these priorities was not absolute and not immune to adjustment in light of the prevailing fortunes of other aspects of his program. Brezhnev periodically shifted new investment into favored technologically advanced branches of heavy industry, launched a dramatic program to develop the East by tapping its mineral and fuel resources and by shifting new industry from European Russia, and provided increasing investment for the Soviet military — which had a favorable impact on important segments of heavy industry.

In tactical terms, Brezhnev's political strategy also embodied a careful balance of institutional forces. Unlike his predecessor, who frequently shifted alliances and played important interests off against one another, Brezhnev sought to maintain a balance of supporters from all politically important segments of the Soviet establishment. In part because his policy initiatives were less threatening to the interests of such actors, in part because he pursued a strategy of compromise and adjustment rather than confrontation, and in part because he coopted representatives of the most important power blocs into the Politburo itself, Brezhnev was able to maintain a style of leadership that stressed consensus building and tacit negotiation. As first among equals, his task was to define his own policy initiatives in ways acceptable to the major institutional forces and to foster the emergence of a consensus among them. The fact that he was able to secure the adoption of most of his major innovations testifies to the wisdom of his cautious strategy and to his skills as a politician rather than to his ability to dictate to his colleagues.

BREZHNEV AS LEADER: PARTY POLITICS

Despite his vision of a modernized and more "scientific" party that would rule through its successful management of the scientific and technological revolution, Brezhnev moved cautiously in terms of internal party affairs. Quickly signaling nervous party officials that Khrushchev's efforts to destabilize the party machinery would be ended, he abolished the so-called rotation rule, which forbade the reelection of a portion of higher party bodies at each successive election, and reunited the party's industrial and agricultural committees, which were split in the bifurcation of 1962. He also deemphasized the vaguely populist role of Khrushchev's

Party/State Control Committee, which had played a threatening watchdog role.

To the party as a whole, Brezhnev's message was clear: institutional stability and internal reform were linked in a fashion that promised to exchange the General Secretary's willingness to forgo constant reorganization for a positive response to the call to upgrade the level of performance. The carrot of both a greater role for the party and a modern redefinition of its legitimacy in light of the scientific and technological revolution was to replace Khrushchev's stick of threatened reorganization and dismissal. While politically tempting, the proffered deal was flawed in implementation, as party leaders soon found the new regime unwilling to apply even modest sanctions against party officials who accepted the much desired promise of stability but resisted any alteration in their long-established workstyle and prerogatives.[6]

At the highest echelons of party rule, remarkable stability persisted throughout Brezhnev's rule. In part as a result of his strategy to coopt major institutional forces and in part as a product of his own censensus-oriented style of leadership, this stability provided an inner core of Kremlin leadership and sent a clear signal to lower-level cadres. For virtually the entire 18 years of Brezhnev's administration, that inner core was composed of Brezhnev himself, Kosygin as chairman of the Council of Ministers (the equivalent of "prime minister"), Suslov as senior party secretary for ideology, Kirilenko as general overseer of the critically important cadres office and heavy industry, and, in the later years, Chernenko as Brezhnev's aide and alter ego. This is not to say, of course, that the five were of a single mind on policy issues. Kosygin's differences with the General Secretary on the issues of management reform and consumer goods production have already been detailed, and Kirilenko's fall from grace as heir apparent shortly before Brezhnev's death will be described below.

In 1973, Foreign Minister Andrei Gromyko, Defense Minister Andrei Grechko, and KGB chief Yuri Andropov were elevated to Politburo status. When Grechko died in 1976, Dmitrii Ustinov, already a Politburo member and in charge of defense production, took his place and remained there until his own demise in 1984. Their elevation underscored the growing tendency to transform the Politburo into a functionally representative microcosm of the Soviet establishment. The 1971 appointment to the Politburo of Fyodor Kulakov, a member of the secretariat in charge of agriculture, also confirmed the trend toward balancing regional representation with the presence of policy specialists, as did Mikhail Gorbachev's assumption of the agriculture portfolio after Kulakov's death in 1978.

Similar caution was also reflected in Brezhnev's handling of the Central Committee. There was no wholesale dismissal of Khrushchev's appointees, perhaps in part because such action would have violated the tacit mandate for intraparty stability that governed the general secretary's rise to power but also perhaps because the coup in 1964 demonstrated that a genuine majority had already abandoned Khrushchev and shifted their allegiance to the new leadership. Once a member of that body, there was little likelihood that an individual would be dropped either for blatant failures or as a result of choosing the losing side in intraparty squabbling. This is not to say, however, that Brezhnev did not have an impact on the Central Committee. Rather, that influence was achieved through the politically more cautious strategy of enlarging both full and candidate membership. Each successive party congress during the Brezhnev era expanded the Central Committee, in part signaling Brezhnev's own ability to bring additional supporters forward but also in part further confirming the top leadership's willingness to continue to coopt important leadership elements.[7]

To observe, however, that Brezhnev pursued a cautious strategy vis-à-vis other important elements of the party and that his own style of leadership stressed consensus building rather than confrontation does not obscure the fact that there were obvious, politically-motivated dismissals from the Politburo during his tenure in office. Nikolai Podgornyi, an apparent challenger in the first years after Khrushchev's fall, was neutralized late in 1965 through his transfer from the politically important Secretariat to the essentially ceremonial post of chairman of the Presidium of the Supreme Soviet (the "president" of the Soviet Union), and then dropped from the Politburo altogether in 1977 when he apparently resisted Brezhnev's attempts to assume that post.

A similar fate befell Alexander Shelepin, who was also regarded as a contender for higher office in the mid-1960s. From his background as head of the KGB he was initially appointed by the new leadership to head the Party/State Control Committee, a post which he held until it was restructured as the less threatening People's Control Committee in December, 1965, at which time he also lost his position as deputy chairman of the Council of Ministers. Another telling blow came in the summer of 1967, when he was removed from the Secretariat altogether and appointed to the far less significant post of chairman of the All-Union Central Trade Union Council. Despite these obvious demotions, he remained a member of the Politburo for a full decade until 1975. Other lesser figures were removed from the Politburo in the 1970s. Petr Shelest, the Ukrainian party chief, and Gennadii Voronov, chairman of the Russian Republic Council of Ministers, both fell in 1973 amid rumors that they had opposed the General Secretary's willingness to pursue detente with the United States even in the face of Washington's escalation of the Vietnam War. Dmitrii Polianskii, the minister of agriculture, was removed in 1976 after severe criticism at the 25th Party Congress of his performance in office.

Brezhnev's final sally against potential pretenders to his position came in November, 1978, with the removal from the Politburo of Kiril Mazurov, first deputy chairman of the Council of Ministers. At the same time, Konstantin Chernenko was elevated to full membership in that body, and another Brezhnev crony, Nikolai Tikhonov, was advanced to candidate membership to await further advancement to the chairmanship of the Council of Ministers with the death of Kosygin.[8]

THE FINAL YEARS

We began by cautioning against the danger that final impressions might obscure the positive and reformist aspects of the Brezhnev era. We must end by giving proper weight to the palpable sense of immobilism and stagnation that characterized the last years of the general secretary's rule. Even setting aside the rumors of ill health and the morbid deathwatch, we must recall that the numerous and seemingly insoluble problems that confronted the aging Soviet leadership created a feeling that the nation was beset by a profound malaise; if the best intentioned reforms failed and were reduced to mere slogans in the mouths of conservative party and state officials who blocked their implementation, then the top leadership itself tacitly acquiesced in their demise.

An equally corrosive sense of purposelessness and corruption permeated the final years of Brezhnev's rule. Having shed Khrushchev's bold image of the communist future attainable within this century and substituted the more technocratic vision of developed socialism as the blueprint of the future, the general secretary found it difficult to sustain a sense of forward motion. To the extent that the Soviet intelligentsia or the man in the street thought about the incongruity between the promise and the reality, they were more likely to resent the failure of reforms and the lethargic leadership of the aging generation than to seek a sense of new direction. The widespread corruption that cut through all levels of society also added a demoralizing presence. Whether it was the high-level corruption of officials caught in the act of diverting public resources to their own private gain or the mundane transgressions of common citizens who bent the rules or turned to the so-called "second economy" to make their lives a little easier, the sense that everyone was involved — and that everyone looked the other way — was virtually universal.

The last half decade of Brezhnev's rule was marked by policy failures at home and abroad that lent credence to the notion that Soviet leaders had lost control of events. In the economy, the much-touted reforms to introduce new technology and restructure management along lines suggested by Western corporate structures did not have the desired effect. The technological level of Soviet industry grew more slowly than had been hoped, and the limited availability of advanced Western techniques did little to alter the situation. The problem was not only that domestic research and development efforts failed to produce viable practical innovations but also that the implementation of any innovations was resisted by managers who feared change. Nor did the managerial reforms lead to creation of economically viable units. In part because factory personnel received conflicting signals concerning the evaluation of their efforts, and in part because ministry officials reimposed centralized controls, the associations never emerged as the cutting edge of the modernization effort.

Other economic difficulties beset the nation. The rate of growth of the economy continued to drop during the final years of Brezhnev's rule, and efforts to revitalize production through a call for greater efficiency and a more rational use of a declining work force had little impact. Growing energy shortages occurred despite programs to develop the extensive resources of West Siberia and the Far East. Agriculture also added to the list of economic woes. Despite Brezhnev's massive investment program, repeated crop failures forced Soviet leaders to import grain and to launch a massive "food program" to deal with growing shortages.[9]

In the latter years of Brezhnev's rule Soviet foreign policy met with a series of disappointments and reversals. Soviet–U.S. relations worsened even before the inauguration of the Reagan administration, and Washington's new tone after 1980 led to a further deterioration of ties. The failure of SALT II and the American arms build-up forced Soviet leaders to rethink their assumptions about parity with the United States. Ties with Western Europe also were strained over arms control and security issues, and the failure to block U.S. plans to deploy Pershing II and cruise missiles was a major setback for Soviet diplomatic efforts. Involvement in Angola and Afghanistan as well as other parts of the Third World brought no clear diplomatic or military victories and only further served to complicate relations with Washington. Relations with Eastern Europe, which had been quiescent since the Soviet-led invasion of Czechoslovakia in 1968, once again occupied Kremlin leaders as a result of events in Poland. Even on the economic level, Soviet efforts to improve foreign trade to obtain advanced technology or to encourage foreign investment in the development of the vast resources of Siberia were undercut by political tensions or by the lack of confidence on the part of investors, and technologically primitive Soviet exports found a viable market only in the Third World.[10]

A sense of stagnation also permeated the Communist party itself. Despite Brezhnev's call for the party to lead in fostering economic and social change and to revitalize its own style of leadership by adopting modern managerial techniques, the old guard held firm against such reforms. Jealous of their own institutional and personal prerogatives and reluctant to accept the conclusion that the new age of developed socialism had perhaps passed them by, they resisted the general secretary's call for reforms. The lack of turnover at the highest echelons of party and state also contributed to the perceived lack of motion, and even though new and younger cadres were moving up to secondary posts in the provinces, the regime's propensity to fill top posts with members of their own generation frustrated the hopes of more junior cadres.

THE FINAL YEARS: A COMPROMISE GONE SOUR

In no small part the frustrations that Brezhnev must have felt in his final years were of his own making — or, perhaps more correctly, of the political compromises that had brought him to power almost two decades earlier. Like his predecessor, he had accepted the notion that extensive reforms were needed not only in the economy and society in general but also within the Communist party itself. But also like Khrushchev, his reform efforts had run headlong into the opposition of entrenched bureaucratic interests who resisted any threat to their power or any hint that their leadership was inappropriate in an advanced industrial society. But the very nature of the understandings that were reached when he rose to power militated against any effective reform. The "respect for cadres" policy that had governed party affairs since 1964 meant that the General Secretary could neither resort to widespread dismissals of uncooperative party and state officials, nor shake up the conservative bureaucracies through extensive reorganizations. He was left with the decidedly less productive strategies of touting the reformist implications of developed socialism and the scientific and technological revolution and exhorting always suspicious officials to change their ways in the interests of economic efficiency and a better standard of living. Some sense of the growing frustration Brezhnev must have felt was conveyed in his comments to the November 1978 Central Committee plenum:

What is needed . . . is persistence, selflessness and, if you like, courage. Here sometimes one has almost to learn things anew and to demand the same of others. He who is afraid of the new holds back development. It is from this position that one must proceed in evaluating cadres — both economic and party cadres.[11]

For such courage, new leaders would be required.

NOTES

1. Michel Tatu, *Power in the Kremlin from Khrushchev to Kosygin* (New York: Viking, 1970), pp. 399–428; George W. Breslauer, *Khrushchev and Brezhnev as Leaders: Building Authority in Soviet Politics* (London: George Allen and Unwin, 1982), pp. 61–114; and Edward Crankshaw, *Khrushchev: A Career* (New York: Viking, 1966).

2. Tatu, *Power,* pp. 399–428; and William Hyland and Richard W. Shryock, *The Fall of Khrushchev* (New York: Funk and Wagnalls, 1968), pp. 23–66.

3. Donald R. Kelley, "The Communist Party," in Donald R. Kelley, ed., *Soviet Politics in the Brezhnev Era* (New York: Praeger, 1980), pp. 27–54.

4. Donald R. Kelley, *The Politics of Developed Socialism: The Soviet Union as a Post-Industrial State* (New York: Greenwood, 1986), pp. 4–14.

5. Breslauer, *Khrushchev and Brezhnev,* pp. 137–68.

6. Kelley, "The Communist Party," pp. 29–35.

7. Jerry F. Hough, *Soviet Leadership in Transition* (Washington: Brookings, 1978), pp. 37–78; and Seweryn Bialer, *Stalin's Successors: Leadership, Stability, and Change in the Soviet Union* (New York: Cambridge University Press, 1980), pp. 69–126.

8. Breslauer, *Khrushchev and Brezhnev*, pp. 200–367.

9. Robert W. Campbell, "The economy," in Robert Byrnes, ed., *After Brezhnev* (Bloomington: Indiana University Press), pp. 68–124; and Alan H. Smith, "Soviet economic prospects: Can the Soviet economic system survive?" in Martin McCauley, *The Soviet Union after Brezhnev* (New York: Holmes and Meier, 1983), pp. 62–81

10. Adam B. Ulam, "The outside world," in Byrnes, *After Brezhnev*, pp. 345–422.

11. *Pravda*, November 28, 1978.

2

The Rise of Yuri Andropov

SETTING THE STAGE FOR SUCCESSION

While the malaise and immobilism of the last years of the Brezhnev era underscored the need for new and forceful leadership, they also compounded the difficulties already inherent in setting the stage for political succession. Having thwarted the attempts of earlier would-be rivals and claimants to the throne, Brezhnev was understandably reluctant until the very end to designate a visible heir apparent. Unlike Stalin, who had played potential successors off against one another, or Khrushchev, who had permitted the emergence of heirs apparent in Brezhnev and Kosygin, Brezhnev simply held all claimants at arm's length until almost the very end, when he tapped Chernenko to succeed him. Perhaps mindful that he did not possess the unchallenged power that permitted Stalin to manipulate his lieutenants and that Khrushchev's choice of successors made the attempt to unseat him all the easier, Brezhnev simply avoided the troublesome issue of succession.

The unlikelihood that Brezhnev would be removed from power before his death or willing resignation also made the question of succession arrangements difficult. There was only one precedent of a Soviet leader's falling to a de facto vote of no confidence within the Politburo and the Central Committee: Khrushchev's removal from power in 1964. In that instance, the erratic first secretary had fallen not so much because his policies had failed but rather because his attempts to reform the party had disquieting implications for an aging party elite that resisted such changes. Brezhnev's cautious leadership that stressed the stability of party cadres even at the expense of blatant policy failures and a growing sense of malaise and immobilism protected him against any preemptive strike from his colleagues, although it unquestionably engendered considerable resentment among the ranks of lesser party figures whose upward mobility was blocked by the secure tenure of their superiors and whose hopes for reforms were set aside in the interest of intraparty stability.

Brezhnev's seeming immunity from attack compounded the problems facing would-be heirs. The continuity of and seeming agreement among the members of the inner circle of top party leaders (composed of Brezhnev as general secretary, Andrei Kirilenko as party secretary in charge of cadres and heavy industry, Alexei Kosygin as chairman of the Council of Ministers, and Mikhail Suslov as chief ideologist) made it difficult for lesser figures even from within the Politburo to break ranks. Policy differences that might have provided ambitious candidates with the issues they needed to articulate implicit platforms and to appeal to various constituencies were muted, leaving the arcane and encripted dialogue of Soviet politics even less expressive of internal divisions than had been true in more volatile times. And while the General Secretary permitted and perhaps even wisely encouraged the representation of important functional and geographic interests within the Politburo and the creation of institutionalized patron/client ties that linked high-level party officials to politically important constituencies, he maintained party dominance over key areas such as the military and the KGB and removed from power or neutralized any challengers to his personal rule.

The relatively large field of would-be successors complicated the maneuvering for position and advantage. Only at rare moments did an obvious frontrunner emerge whose preeminence clearly divided important political forces into those who jumped on the bandwagon and those who joined a coalition to thwart it. For the most part the field of battle was more complicated, not only pitting numerous claimants against one another but also raising the generational issue that divided Brezhnev's contemporaries from the relatively younger cadre of party leaders who had risen rapidly in the late 1970s.

By the late 1970s, when Brezhnev's declining health and the growing immobilism of the regime were apparent to all, there were approximately a half dozen potential successors on the scene. Conventional wisdom labeled Andrei Kirilenko the likely heir apparent. A member of the Brezhnev entourage, he functioned as de facto second secretary, combining the portfolios of heavy industry and party cadres, although he was unable to use the latter as had his predecessors to build grassroots support within the party. Konstantin Chernenko was also counted among the possible successors. An even closer Brezhnev associate who had been elevated to full membership in the Politburo in 1978, he served as a personal aide to the General Secretary and headed the critically important General Department within the Secretariat. Yuri Andropov, head of the KGB, was also considered a candidate for General Secretary. Although he lacked significant administrative experience within the party apparatus itself and led an agency whose previous chiefs had been viewed with suspicion by other would-be successors, his strong record as an efficient and no-nonsense administrator, as well as his knowledge and experience in foreign affairs, placed him among the contenders. The Leningrad party first secretary, Grigorii Romanov, also had aspirations to higher office, although his reputation as a strict administrator who nonetheless advocated economic and managerial reforms was balanced against the political liabilities associated with the city of Leningrad as a power base. Romanov's Moscow counterpart, Viktor Grishin, also viewed himself as a possible successor, although his generally lackluster performance and heavyhanded attempts to press his own candidacy compromised his prospects.

There was also no lack of reputed kingmakers whose support would make or break aspirants to the top office. Most significant among them was Mikhail Suslov, who until his death in 1982 served as the party secretary in charge of ideology and who had played a critical role in the removal of Nikita Khrushchev in 1964. While he possessed no independently powerful constituency such as the military or the party apparatus, he nonetheless was regarded both as the most important member of the inner core of the Politburo who himself did not hope to succeed the aging leader and as a roadblock to the advancement of more ambitious figures such as Andropov. Of lesser significance was the foreign minister, Andrei Gromyko. Although he also lacked an important domestic constituency, he had served in his post since 1957, a longevity that clearly made him the Politburo's ranking expert on foreign affairs. Dmitrii Ustinov, the minister of defense whose civilian background in the defense industries gave him powerful allies in both quarters, was also thought of as an important force behind the scenes. Both the growing importance of the military and the political influence of the defense industries implied that these combined constituencies would play a role in selecting Brezhnev's successor.

STRATEGIES OF SUCCESSION

Although Brezhnev's tenacious grasp on the reins of power placed limitations on the ability of would-be successors to establish independent political identities and to court support from important power blocs, the frontrunners nevertheless developed clear strategies, rooted in career experiences and positions within the hierarchy.

For Andrei Kirilenko, who functioned as de facto second secretary for most of the Brezhnev era, the obvious two-fold strategy was to stress the logical succession of the experienced understudy and to build upon his ties to heavy industry and the party apparatus. Clearly Kirilenko was a member in good standing of the Brezhnev entourage. His career had been linked with Brezhnev's since World War II, when both were political officers in the 18th Army of the southern front. They remained associated in party posts after the war, with Kirilenko serving under Brezhnev in Zaporozhye and then succeeding him as party secretary in Dnepropetrovsk when the future General Secretary was sent to Moldavia in 1950. From 1955 to 1961, their careers diverged. Kirilenko served as party secretary in Sverdlovsk during this period and then rose to the post of deputy chairman of the Bureau for the RSFSR (Russian Soviet Federated Socialist Republic). When the Bureau was abolished in 1966, Kirilenko became, along with Suslov, one of the two senior party secretaries.[1]

Kirilenko's position as senior party secretary with overall responsibility for the functioning of the state apparatus and the economy placed him at a critically important control point within the intertwined party and state hierarchies, although it is questionable how far his authority descended down the administrative chain of command. But at the least, conventional wisdom would suggest that he would doubly benefit from this role. On the one hand, his wide-ranging responsibilities gave him needed experience in these two important domestic areas. His close ties to heavy industry further strengthened his position in any succession struggle. And on the other hand, he presumably was well positioned to develop a network of supporters and allies throughout both party and state hierarchies.

Kirilenko also presumably had overall responsibility for senior appointments to both party and state posts through his supervision of the *nomenklatura* system. At least until the late 1970s, there is clear evidence that I. V. Kapitonov, who headed the Organizational Party Work Department of the Central Committee that undertakes the day-to-day operation of the party-controlled appointments system, reported to Kirilenko, although in the last years of Brezhnev's rule, his subordination may have been shifted to the rapidly rising Chernenko. In any event, Kirilenko's influence over the cadres system, which historically had been the key to building a strong following, did not permit him to stack the deck against challengers. During the whole of Brezhnev's tenure, no subordinate was able to manipulate the cadres selection process to create a personalized political machine, much less to develop sufficient strength to challenge the General Secretary, and even under the best of circumstances, Kirilenko's ability to influence cadres selection never extended down to the middle and grassroots level.[2]

In addition, Kirilenko's candidacy promised both a continuity of Brezhnev's policies and a continued dominance of a loyal scion of the party machinery risen through the ranks to the top post. To those members of the aging elite who saw the regime's achievements at home and abroad as a confirmation of the Soviet Union's emergence as a major industrial nation and an international superpower, Kirilenko offered the promise of more of the same, untainted by any hint that their generation would be swept aside or blamed for the nation's shortcomings. Moreover, Kirilenko's eventual rise to general secretary would affirm that the conventional ladder of success that brought Soviet leaders from regional posts to national prominence remained unchanged, no small concern in a situation in which the other two frontrunners, Chernenko and Andropov, had far different career experiences.

But if being de facto second secretary implied a logical succession strategy, it also carried with it a number of liabilities. Not the least of these was association with the blatant policy failures of the Brezhnev administration and the growing sense of drift and malaise within the nation. No amount of self-congratulation within top party circles could diminish the fact that others in equally important posts or at lesser levels of the party and state judged the current regime more harshly. Kirilenko suffered the inevitable problem of establishing an independent political identity. Moreover, his own career experiences and current responsibilities had been deficient in two areas: he possessed no credible credentials in foreign policy and, despite his identification with heavy industry per se, he had no ties to the military-industrial complex, which fell under the supervision of Dimitrii Ustinov. In tactical terms as well, Kirilenko's posture as the presumed heir apparent established him as a target for other aspirants to the office of General Secretary. Whatever their differences, other high-ranking claimants and dark horses alike could agree that their first task was to stop Kirilenko.

Konstantin Chernenko's strategic options in the pursuit of the top office were also dictated by his earlier career experiences and by his close association with Leonid Brezhnev. From his less-than-auspicious beginnings as a minor party ideologist in the province, Chernenko rose rapidly once he hitched his star to Brezhnev's rising fortunes. The initial contact came in 1950, when Brezhnev was named first secretary of the Moldavian party organization. The two worked in tandem in Kishinev for only two years, but Chernenko subsequently followed Brezhnev to the all-union party organization, becoming head of the mass political work section of the Central Committee Propaganda and Agitation Department in 1956. When Brezhnev became chairman of the Presidium of the Supreme Soviet (i.e., president of the Soviet state), Chernenko was named chief of the Presidium of the Secretariat of that body, making him de facto chief aide to the future general secretary. The pattern was repeated when Brezhnev rose to power in 1964, with Chernenko advancing to the post of chief of the General Department of the Central Committee. Further confirmation of his continued rise came with his appointment as a member of the party Secretariat in 1976 and his rapid promotion to candidate member of the Politburo in 1977 and full member the following year.[3]

Chernenko's role as chief of the General Department placed him at a critically important position within the party apparatus. This department handles the flow of all classified information within the party, and as its chief, Chernenko controlled access to objective data about party and state affairs. Because of his close association with the General Secretary, he was thus able to function as a de facto secretary to the Politburo, in shaping the weekly agenda, one whose first loyalties clearly lay with his mentor. Evidence also suggests that he controlled the Administrative Organs Department, which oversees the police and the military, and came, at least from the late 1970s onward, to oversee the Organizational Party Work Department and at least some aspects of intraparty personnel selection, a function that he took from Kirilenko.[4]

Chernenko's successful pursuit to become general secretary depended both on the endorsement of Brezhnev and on his ability to allay the concerns that he was merely a colorless staff member with misplaced aspirations to top office. On the positive side, it became clear in the final months before the aging leader's death that Chernenko was being groomed as the heir apparent; while Brezhnev's endorsement had been long in coming, it presumably brought with it the support of the General Secretary's closest associates within higher party echelons and the symbolic mantle of continuity and stability. It was even rumored in the fall of 1982 that Brezhnev planned to step down voluntarily at the 60th anniversary of the formal creation of the Soviet state, which was scheduled for early 1983, although events soon overtook such intentions.[5]

On the negative side, however, Chernenko's status as an aide and staff director carried with it strong liabilities, not the least of which was his lack of a separate political identity or constituency outside the Brezhnev entourage. Even though he had served in top-level posts since Brezhnev's rise to power, Chernenko had never emerged as an independent figure. He had no natural constituency other than the general secretary himself, and he had been unable to use his high office to create either a regional or institutional following.

The strong, if belated endorsement by Brezhnev was in itself something of a mixed blessing. On the one hand, it was a boost to Chernenko's candidacy inasmuch as the incumbent's political weight now fell into place behind his designated successor. But on the other hand, the obvious frailty of the aging leader diminished his ability to line up support for his chosen heir. Perhaps more importantly, with such a clear endorsement, the failure of the current regime could now be visited upon the would-be successor. Chernenko's candidacy implied that the same sense of malaise and drift, to say nothing of blatant inefficiency and corruption, might well persist under the new leadership.

Even the Brezhnev endorsement could not lay to rest both the real concerns and the personal resentments of other members of the Politburo. Whatever his positive qualities as an aide to the General Secretary, Chernenko lacked high level executive experience as a decision maker; he had never been tested by the responsibilities of direct leadership. Moreover, he was alleged to be devoid of the qualities of firm leadership valued in the Soviet setting; he lacked both the force and discipline needed for the top post and the personal style and sophistication to deal with important leaders both at home and abroad. He was, as his detractors argued in the rumors that swept Moscow in the last months of the Brezhnev regime, merely a man of peasant stock brought to high office by his mentor.

Yuri Andropov's pursuit of the General Secretaryship was governed by far different strategic considerations. Neither a close personal confidant of Brezhnev nor a member of the inner circle of the Politburo, he faced formidable problems both in terms of establishing a separate political identity and of building a broader coalition beyond his personal power base in the KGB. His campaign for the top office was a combination of increasingly transparent attacks on the ineffectiveness and corruption of the Kremlin old guard in general and Brezhnev in particular and appeals to other important constituencies such as the military and industrial interests, based on his reputation for disciplined leadership within the KGB. Unlike Kirilenko and Chernenko, who were members of the inner circle and whose candidacies promised at least a measure of continuity and stability, Andropov ran as a relative outsider whose ascension to office would signal sweeping changes.

Andropov's career was also a departure from the usual ladder of success for aspirants to the General Secretaryship. His first party post was that of first secretary of the Yaroslav Komsomol, to which he was elected in 1938. Two years later he advanced to the more responsible post of first secretary of the Komsomol in the newly created Karelo-Finnish republic, a post that he held throughout the war. In 1944 he was named second secretary of the Petrozavodsk city party organization, and in 1947 he was promoted to the post of second secretary of the Karelo-Finnish republic, making him the de facto Russian overseer in this non-Russian region. Surviving the purge of the supporters of Andrei Zhdanov, with whom he had been indirectly linked through his own patron, G. N. Kupriianov, he remained second secretary until he was transferred to the Central Committee apparatus in Moscow in 1951, eventually becoming the chief of a subdepartment that dealt with trade union and Komsomol affairs.[6]

Andropov's transfer to diplomatic work in 1953 was a clear demotion, possibly associated with Malenkov's purge of real or imagined opponents. He initially served in the office within the Ministry of Foreign Affairs that dealt with Poland and Czechoslovakia and was then posted to Budapest as counselor to the Soviet embassy. He was promoted to ambassador in 1954 and remained at that post until 1957, through both the Soviet invasion that crushed the Nagy regime and the restoration of party authority under Janos Kadar. Andropov's cool performance under pressure during the crisis earned him a transfer back to Moscow, where he was named to head the newly created Central Committee Department for Liaison with Socialist Nations, a post that he held for ten years. Further indication of his growing status came with his appointment to the Secretariat in 1962.[7]

Andropov's appointment as head of the KGB in 1967 came at a time when the Brezhnev administration was anxious to restore strong leadership to an agency that had faltered in the mid-1960s. Although Andropov's personal association with intelligence and security affairs had been limited to his experiences with Eastern Europe, he was regarded as an effective administrator who would place the KGB's badly disorganized house in order and maintain party control and the agency's political neutrality in Kremlin politics. While he clearly benefitted from Brezhnev's backing in obtaining this post, Andropov was not regarded as a part of the growing entourage that surrounded the general secretary. It is probably far more likely that his selection came about as a compromise among Politburo factions, with no single top leader able to secure the appointment of his own man to the post. Brezhnev was able, however, to name two close associates, S. K. Tsvigun and G. K. Tsenev, to the posts of first deputy chairman and deputy chairman directly under Andropov.

Under Andropov's tutelage, the KGB grew both in stature and professionalism as an intelligence and internal security agency. To be a "Chekist" became once again an honorable calling, lauded by political leaders and the popular media alike. More importantly, the agency's scope of activities increased both at home and abroad. Whatever else may be said, it quickly became evident that its ability to crush the dissident movement within the USSR and to engage in widespread military and commercial intelligence gathering and other clandestine activities beyond Soviet borders made it a force with which to be reckoned.

His diplomatic and intelligence background aside, Andropov still found himself in an awkward position in terms of launching a bid to become general secretary. On the positive side, his record of strong leadership at the helm of the KGB stood out in sharp contrast to the lackluster performance of others. Moreover, the wide-ranging activities of that organization at least implied that he had acquired expertise in both foreign and domestic affairs, a mixed portfolio of responsibilities that no other would-be aspirant could claim.

The significance of the KGB itself as a power base offered both positive and negative aspects. Clearly its growing reputation as a disciplined and effective organization boded well for its director. And the agency's detailed personnel files on all important party and state personnel must be counted an important asset, especially when it became apparent that one key element of the strategy was the selective exposure of corruption in high office. But on the negative side, the KGB undoubtedly evoked the collective fears of other players, as Beria's removal from office and execution in 1953 demonstrated. Top party leaders had gone to great lengths to neutralize its overt political role even before Andropov's tenure as its director, and it is likely that a bid for power by anyone associated with it would be viewed with suspicion.

Andropov also faced the problem that his bid for power had to be based on overt criticism of the status quo and the aging leaders who had tenaciously clung to power, a risky strategy for someone with no institutional allies beyond the KGB and who had not climbed the usual ladder of success to top office. Such a strategy was viable only to the extent that other would-be successors such as Kirilenko and Chernenko consumed their energies in battle with one another and to the extent that the Brezhnev entourage itself had grown too weak and senile to protect its flanks.

ANDROPOV'S RISE TO POWER

While the rivalries among the contenders were veiled by the secretive nature of Soviet politics and the need to pay public homage to the aging Brezhnev, the muted competition could be seen by those with discerning eyes. Least visible among the presumed frontrunners was Andrei Kirilenko. Perhaps because of his status as de facto second secretary and his alleged close ties to the party apparatus and heavy industry, he thought it best to pursue the quiet strategy of an insider whose candidacy required no special activism beyond his preeminence within inner party circles. Whatever his views, he made no visible effort in the year before Brezhnev's death to establish a separate political identity or to speak out on domestic and foreign policy issues. His only public visibility beyond expected routine ceremonial activities was limited to a few noncontroversial speeches about economic affairs that departed in no way from the conventional wisdom of the last years of the Brezhnev era.

In contrast, both Chernenko and Andropov were far more visible and went to greater lengths to establish their own political identities, although their efforts had to be framed within acceptable boundaries. Chernenko pressed hard for the endorsement as the heir apparent that his mentor had long withheld, and was eventually rewarded by Brezhnev's visible backing in the months before his death. Andropov, on the other hand, pursued the more risky strategy of holding the present leadership's ineptness, immobilism, and personal vulnerability to charges of corruption and favoritism up for public view (cautiously, to be sure), through the indictment of the General Secretary's cronies and thinly veiled innuendo concerning his family and health.

While it is impossible to establish a firm date when the campaign for the succession began — rumors of Brezhnev's ill health or impending retirement had occurred periodically since the mid-1970s, and each provoked a round of speculation and maneuvering — the emergence of Kirilenko, Chernenko, and Andropov as the frontrunners and their choices of strategies can be dated roughly from the 26th Party Congress in 1981. Both at the congress itself and in the 20 months that followed until Brezhnev's death in November, 1982, increasingly visible signals appeared to confirm that a struggle was in progress.

The congress itself, held in February 1981, was a mixed blessing for both Kirilenko and Chernenko. While he maintained his position as de facto second secretary, Kirilenko was unable to signal any increase in his stature within the inner circle. Chernenko benefitted principally from the fact that he was known to have been the organizer of the meeting, although he was unable to obtain any open endorsement from Brezhnev, who showed no signs of tapping a potential heir or of stepping down from office. Andropov slipped completely from public view. During the proceedings of the congress itself, he was the only Politburo member who was denied the privilege of chairing one of the sessions.[8]

With the congress over, the contenders settled into a shadow war of innuendo and indirection. The General Secretary's ill health and unwillingness to step down were underscored in an indirect attack in the Leningrad literary journal *Aurora,* in December 1981. In an issue otherwise dedicated to Brezhnev's 75th birthday, a satirical story by Viktor Goliavkin entitled "Jubilee Speech" spoke of an aging writer, now long past his prime, who "does not plan to die." Making it clear that the writer had outlived his usefulness and lost touch with reality, Goliavkin lamented that the rumors of his death had been "premature."[9] Not surprisingly, the issue quickly sold out, as members of the Soviet intelligentsia read the story as a veiled attack on Brezhnev himself.

Rumors about scandals that reached directly into Brezhnev's family and the death of Mikhail Suslov in January, 1982, set the stage for the next round of confrontation. In the former case, the growing campaign to link Brezhnev's daughter, Galina, to high-level misdeeds bore the mark of Andropov's earlier use of the KGB to conduct politically significant anti-corruption efforts in Azerbaidzhan, Georgia, and the Baltic republics. By implication, the sins of the daughter, whose "disorderly" lifestyle, as the Russians would say, had long been a topic of Moscow gossip, would be visited on the father, who would be double injured not only because of his obvious approval of efforts to cover up her activities but also because his growing weakness now permitted his opponents to shed light on her associations with known or suspected criminals.

The cause celebre that linked Galina to the shadowy underworld of corruption occurred in December 1981, when her close associate and rumored paramour Boris Buriatia was involved in an elaborate jewel theft and extensive corruption within the Soviet circus. Galina had long been a camp follower of the circus and its flamboyant performers, and the scandal further portrayed her as an uncontrollable enfant terrible whose actions had been concealed by the authorities. Despite her resignation from a minor post in the Foreign Ministry, the rumors continued, and it was alleged that she was a part of other corrupt activities, including efforts, undertaken along with Brezhnev's son Yuri, to sequester large sums of money abroad. Even her second husband's position as first deputy minister of internal affairs — thus de facto second in command of the national police force — could not protect her from interrogation by the KGB.[10]

The actual investigation into Galina's involvement was conducted by General Semyon Tsvigun, first deputy chairman of the KGB, although it is not possible that he would have initiated these actions without his chief's approval. From the beginning, his position was extremely sensitive. On the one hand, the responsibilities of office required that he press forward with the investigation. But on the other hand, his awkward status as Brezhnev's brother-in-law, initially placed in the KGB to monitor the agency's activities, suggested that he participate in yet another cover-up. His hesitation permitted Andropov to bring the entire matter before Mikhail Suslov, who had functioned informally as the guardian of the inner elite's reputation. While the stories leaked to Western sources vary on whether Suslov sought once again to conceal high level corruption or opted to pursue the case to its inevitable conclusion, it is clear that there was a heated confrontation between Tsvigun and Suslov. Within a matter of days, Tsvigun died, reputedly by his own hand, and his official obituary was published without the customary signature of the general secretary.[11]

On January 21, less than a week after his confrontation with Tsvigun, Suslov suffered a severe stroke and remained completely incapacitated until his death several days later. While it is impossible to know whether the stress of his intervention into the Galina affair hastened his demise, it is certain that his departure had a major impact on the succession struggle. Not only did it remove one of the Kremlin's kingmakers who would have influenced the choice of Brezhnev's successor but also it opened up the post of chief ideologist, a position in the hierarchy that ranked third in the nominal pecking order just below Kirilenko's status as de facto second secretary. Suslov's passing triggered an intense competition between Chernenko and Andropov to assume these duties, for each had much to benefit from the move. For Chernenko, the assumption of Suslov's post would give him political status beyond his role as Brezhnev's aide and facilitate his efforts to establish a separate political identity. Andropov also stood to gain from such a move in terms of formally dissociating himself from the KGB, although there was little doubt that he would retain strong support from that quarter, and from the promotion to the Secretariat that would automatically follow.

Chernenko quickly moved to try to fill the void left by Suslov's death. At ceremonial occasions, he assumed the position in the protocol ranking between Brezhnev and

Tikhonov formerly occupied by Suslov, an action that signaled the General Secretary's willingness to acknowledge Chernenko's increased stature and strengthened the assumption that Brezhnev had tapped him as his heir. In April, he published an important article in the theoretical journal *Kommunist* on pluralism and democracy under socialism, and he stood in for the absent Brezhnev on a number of occasions.

Andropov also pressed his bid in the weeks that followed Suslov's death. Late in April, he delivered the speech to mark the 112th anniversary of the birth of Lenin, an important ceremonial occasion at which Chernenko had spoken the year before. His selection was doubly significant. It not only gave him a highly visible ceremonial occasion on which to speak out on issues normally removed from his narrow responsibilities at the KGB but it also indicated that he enjoyed considerable backing within the Politburo, which chooses who is to make this annual address.

Rumors about Brezhnev's ill health were heard frequently throughout the early months of 1982. In an effort to prove himself still in charge, Brezhnev travelled to Tashkent in March to present the Order of Lenin to the Uzbek republic for its economic advances under socialism. What was to have been a carefully staged demonstration of his continued leadership turned into a debacle. Although the presentation of the order went forward without difficulty, and the general secretary even managed to portray his comments on Sino-Soviet relations as a new step to restore better relations, he suffered a stroke on the flight from Tashkent to Moscow and had to be whisked past the official greeting party into seclusion in the Kremlin's elite hospital.[12]

The General Secretary's absence from public view further fueled the rumors of his incapacity or imminent demise, as did the postponement of the Central Committee plenum scheduled for April. Further indication of his diminished powers came through a multitude of rumors that circulated throughout Moscow in the late spring and summer. One held that there had actually been an attempt on Brezhnev's life while he was in Tashkent, and others argued that, although physically recovered, he remained mentally impaired.[13]

The rumors aside, the Soviet public witnessed solid evidence not only that the General Secretary was gravely ill and possibly unable to discharge the duties of office but also that neither he nor his protégés could shield him from public scrutiny. In the next few months, his public appearances were handled in a way that placed him in an unfavorable light. At the Moscow Art Theater he was seen as confused and disoriented or unable to control his emotions. He wept openly at the funeral of a former associate, General Grishevoi, a less than flattering performance that was carried unedited on Soviet television, and he appeared disoriented at a meeting of the Congress of Trade Unions.

On the eve of the May Central Committee plenum, which was to select Suslov's successor and hopefully scotch rumors that Brezhnev had lost control of events, Andrei Kirilenko suffered a major heart attack. With the de facto second secretary now effectively removed as a viable candidate, although he remained on the Politburo, the battle between Chernenko and Andropov grew even more heated, reputedly dividing the Politburo between the Brezhnev-led pro-Chernenko faction and another faction that backed Andropov, in part in an effort to stop Chernenko and in part because of Andropov's perceived leadership abilities and experience in foreign and defense matters. Emigré sources report that at the Politburo session immediately before the May plenum, only 11 of the 13 members were present, with the final vote on the Suslov succession set at five for Chernenko and six for Andropov.[14] Whatever the actual count, the session marked a clear loss not only for Chernenko, who remained within his mentor's shadow, but also for Brezhnev, who had been unable to provide his protégé with a suitable institutional position to strengthen his bid to become General Secretary.

Andropov's election to Suslov's post on the Secretariat meant that a new director of the KGB would be chosen. The two front runners were G. K. Tsvinev, a member of Brezhnev's Dnepropetrovsk mafia, who had initially been appointed first deputy chairman of the KGB to replace

Tsvigun, and V. M. Chebrikov, a former Brezhnev associate who had shifted loyalties to Andropov, under whom he had worked for 15 years. Evidence that Brezhnev and Andropov were locked in combat over the control of the secret police came even before the latter's promotion to the Secretariat. Although Tsvinev had quickly been named to replace Tsvigun (and presumably to continue to monitor the KGB's activities), Chebrikov was soon promoted to the same rank within the agency, creating two First Deputy Chairmen with presumably different political loyalties. It is probable that each faction vigorously pressed its candidate, leaving the Politburo with the unfortunate choice of further politicizing the KGB or finding another solution. The dilemma was resolved through the appointment of V. V. Fedorchuk, who had headed the KGB in the Ukraine. A professional police officer whose career with the KGB long predated Andropov's association with the agency, he was viewed as not having close ties to either camp and insufficient political stature in his own right to influence the succession struggle. Not yet even a member of the Central Committee, he was denied promotion to high party rank in connection with his new duties.[15]

Although he had been promoted to the Secretariat, Andropov did not assume all of Suslov's responsibilities, which included cultural affairs, ideology, and foreign affairs, especially with other socialist nations. In foreign affairs, Andropov was given responsibility for dealing with non-governing communist parties, while Chernenko inherited the task of dealing with bloc nations, a responsibility that permitted him to obtain considerable visibility in dealing with East European leaders. In cultural affairs, the two divided the responsibilities, although there is some evidence that Chernenko acquired control over the media. The division of labor on ideology was far less clear, although the publication of the second edition of Chernenko's book on the role of the party was touted as an event of major theoretical significance.

Although Chernenko's growing visibility signaled both his own increased stature and a greater commitment on Brezhnev's part to press his candidacy for General

Secretary, he was clearly not alone in the field. Kirilenko still remained a full member of the Politburo and a potential enemy if not counter claimant to the top post, and Andropov was once again pressing his attack, by demonstrating the General Secretary's diminishing powers. As with the case brought against Brezhnev's daughter, the attacks came indirectly, the first aimed at S. F. Medunov, party first secretary in Krasnodar. A close associate of Brezhnev, Medunov had been rumored to be involved in many scandals within his territory, which includes the Black Sea coastal areas where the top members of the Soviet elite have summer dachas. Attempts by the local KGB to look into his misdeeds had been barred by higher authorities, rendering him immune from prosecution. Yet in August, 1982, the investigation was reopened, and Medunov was removed from his party post and placed under house arrest. The event was read as far more than a regional tempest; Medunov's fall indicated both the growing power of the KGB and the diminishing ability of Brezhnev to protect his allies.[16] A similar fate befell K. V. Rusakov, first secretary of the Kuibyshev region, who was allegedly involved in the illegal sale of Zhiguli and Lada cars built in the Soviet Fiat plant in his region.[17]

Despite the growing signals that Brezhnev had consciously tapped Chernenko as his eventual successor, the General Secretary showed no indications that he intended to step down from office. In September, another trip away from the Soviet capital was scheduled to demonstrate the leader's recovery and return to active service. The location was Baku, the Azerbaidzhan capital on the Caspian Sea, where a major television address and a series of public meetings were planned. As before, both Brezhnev's failing capabilities and the seeming connivance of the media to present him in a poor light were evident. A. M. Aleksandrov-Agentov, a Brezhnev aide, allegedly gave him the incorrect text of his speech, an error that was discovered some seven minutes into the public address. Without comment, Aleksandrov-Agentov stopped the General Secretary and placed another text before him. When he realized what had occurred, Brezhnev insisted that the error was not his fault and began to read from the new document, although the balance of the speech was read by an announcer. The next day it was rumored that Brezhnev was ill once again, and the remainder of his engagements were cancelled.[18]

By October, however, the General Secretary had recovered sufficiently to make public appearances once again. On most such ceremonial occasions, Chernenko was inevitably at his side, meeting foreign delegations, welcoming cosmonauts, and otherwise strengthening the perception that he was Brezhnev's anointed heir. Emigré sources report that it was rumored in Moscow that at the November Central Committee plenum, Chernenko would officially be designated de facto second secretary, succeeding the still ailing Kirilenko, and that Brezhnev himself would step down from office in his protégé's favor only weeks later at the celebration of the 60th anniversary of the formation of the USSR. Whether accurate or not, the tales further enhanced Chernenko's standing and seemingly placed whatever weight remained of the Brezhnev entourage behind him.[19]

One roadblock to Chernenko's advancement was removed early in October. Kirilenko, whose own hopes for the top office were scotched by his illness, was dropped from the Politburo and the Secretariat at the Politburo session held on October 4, although no public announcement was made until after Brezhnev's death. However, the informal signs of status in the Kremlin pecking order clearly indicate when the fall occurred. On October 3, Kirilenko remained in sufficiently good standing to be permitted to sign an obituary of an important party member published on that day, but his signature was absent from another obituary that appeared two days later on October 5. In addition, his portrait was removed from the official displays of Politburo members during the first week of October, a clear sign that he had been dropped from his party posts.

Chernenko's candidacy received additional impetus late in October when he and Brezhnev played prominent roles at a specially convened meeting with top military officials. Although Andropov was a part of the select group of Politburo members who attended the session, along with Gromyko, Tikhonov, Ustinov, and Chernenko, the latter was given preferential treatment in an altered photograph published by *Pravda* and *Izvestiia* the following day. The armed services newspaper, *Krasnaia Zvezda,* however, ran the undoctored photograph, which did not seemingly position Chernenko ahead of all others in the protocol listing.[20] Brezhnev's comments clearly were designed to win the military to the side of his protégé; although he repeated the usual commitment to detente and lambasted the Reagan administration, he assured the military leaders that the party would "meet all your needs" and promised greater attention to "the further strengthening of the armed forces' material base," especially in high technology weapons systems.[21] Two days later, Chernenko made a major foreign policy statement of his own in connection with the presentation of the Order of Lenin to the Georgian capital of Tbilisi, an act in which he was presented as Brezhnev's personal emissary.[22]

A week later, the ailing General Secretary made his last public appearance in connection with the November 7 celebration of the Revolution. Reputedly against the advice of his doctors, he assumed the traditional position atop the Lenin mausoleum to review the parade, remaining there for three hours on a cold and windy day. Three days later, on the morning of November 10, he collapsed in his apartment on Kutuzovskii Prospect and died of a "sudden heart failure."

The death was not made public for 26 hours, during which time the nation was gradually prepared for the official mourning and, more importantly, the Politburo met to elect Brezhnev's successor. The first public hint of his demise came on the evening before the official announcement when Soviet television cancelled a live concert of popular music and substituted a film about Lenin. Later broadcasts were similarly changed to reflect the somber mood, and the announcers on the evening news show "Vremia" wore dark jackets. The following morning, at eleven o'clock, the official announcement was read by a weeping senior newscaster. The Soviet public and the world now knew that the Brezhnev era was ended; they did not know that the short-lived Andropov era had already begun.

THE ISSUES

Within the ebb and flow of Kremlin politics lay deeply rooted issues that transcended the personalities and strategies of the individual candidates. As is true elsewhere, jockeying for position and dominance involves more than the network of personal alliances or protocol ranking. The substantive issues of economic policy, internal party affairs, and foreign relations emerge a important reference points in defining the political identity of would-be successors and in communicating policy positions to broader political constituencies within the elite. To varying degrees of public visibility, candidates develop their own "platforms," crafted with tactical and substantive goals in mind.

Not surprisingly, none of the major candidates — Kirilenko, Chernenko, Andropov — completely rejected the Brezhnev heritage or suggested radical departures. Rather, their platforms and the positions they took on public issues carefully combined substantial adherence to conventional wisdom with the hint of changes that would come should they rise to power.

Andrei Kirilenko is the most difficult of the major contenders to characterize in political terms. He was the least publicly visible of the three, perhaps because of his preoccupation with day-to-day economic concerns and the self-assurance of the presumed frontrunner. His public comments departed little from the conventional wisdom of the Brezhnev years. Even his commentary on the economy reiterated the oft-heard assertions that improved technology and better trained managers were the key to revitalizing Soviet industry.[23] He was conspicuously silent on internal party affairs, suggesting that important concerns of party internal management had increasingly slipped from his control, most likely into the hands of his rival, Chernenko.

In contrast, Konstantin Chernenko was the most publicly visible and prolific of the heirs apparent. In part because of his wide-ranging activities in party, economic, and foreign affairs, and in part because he regarded such visibility as the best counterweight to the argument that he was merely Brezhnev's alter ego, he spoke out on the widest possible

range of issues in ways that signaled an emerging
independent identity and outlined the changes that might be
expected under his tutelage. Contrary to his image as a
Brezhnev crony elevated to high rank because of his loyalty,
Chernenko offered a moderately reformist platform that
suggested more aggressive experimentation with economic
reform, greater democracy within the party, increased
public involvement in policymaking, including more candid
discussion of the nation's problems, and a measured
decentralization of political power, especially to the union
republic level at the expense of central authority in
Moscow.24 He specifically lauded the Azerbaidzhan and
Georgian republics for their loosening of controls over intraparty and public discussion and called for the leadership's
greater attention to sociological research and public opinion
surveys. While he went further than his colleagues in
lamenting the negative consequences of Stalin's repressive
rule, he also tacitly reassured the party that his own brand of
reform did not entail a return to the undisciplined populism
of the Khrushchev era. On the most critical issue of all, the
security in office of the aging Soviet elite, Chernenko
reassured his contemporaries that his proposals would not
end their careers.

While generally close to the conventional party line in
foreign policy, he expressed a more sophisticated
understanding of relations with the United States than his
mentor — although he joined wholeheartedly in blaming the
Reagan administration for the deterioration of superpower
ties — and less of a commitment to give the military a blank
check to match the U.S. arms build-up. Although the
general secretary had called for increased allocations for
weapons development in his comments to military leaders
on October 28, 1982, two days later, speaking at an awards
ceremony ostensibly having nothing to do with Soviet-U.S.
ties, Chernenko asserted that the military was already
"strong enough" to deter U.S. adventurism.25

Yuri Andropov's platform was the product of his
reputation as an efficient and incorruptible administrator,
his more limited public pronouncements on matters beyond
narrow security affairs, and an undeniable campaign on the

part of his associates and supporters to paint him as a would-be reformer and closet liberal. Of the former, it can certainly be said that his reputation as an effective administrator of both the domestic and foreign activities of the secret police was well deserved. Not only did he receive high marks from conservatives for his suppression of dissent, he earned the grudging respect of more liberal elements for his sophisticated handling of the complex issue and his avoidance of a bloodbath. It was also undeniable that successful KGB efforts abroad had increased during his tenure and that confrontation with other security related and defense forces had been avoided. The KGB's reputation as a professional security and intelligence agency had grown over the same years, and the exploits of Chekists were lauded for public consumption in ways that raised the stature of the security forces to a new high.

Andropov's public pronouncements were far less numerous. To the extent he spoke out at all in the late 1970s and early 1980s, he utilized relatively insignificant occasions such as pro forma speeches to his constituents before Supreme Soviet elections, and he limited his comments to security-related or foreign policy issues, on which he took entirely predictable positions of warning against laxity and subversion while simultaneously endorsing detente with the West.[26]

His first significant opportunity to speak on a wide range of issues came with his selection in 1982 to deliver the Lenin anniversary speech. While he suggested that economic problems were the most important concern facing the nation, he failed to offer any concrete suggestions for reform, nor did he mention the problem of worker indiscipline and inefficiency. On the issue of investment priorities, he endorsed greater efforts for the production of food and consumer goods. His comments on the military and foreign policy had economic as well as political significance. Arguing that "the Soviet Union has never proceeded from the assumption that only military force and a policy built upon it can ensure lasting peace," Andropov offered the cautious formula that the nation should maintain its military capacity "at the proper level." Instead he lauded Soviet efforts to limit the arms race and prevent the deployment of American weapons in Western Europe.[27]

Andropov also tread lightly on the issue of corruption in Soviet society, although it is not likely that his remarks could have been missed amid the rumors of misdeeds that touched the very top of the hierarchy. He argued that "embezzlement, bribery, bureaucratic rigidity, and a disrespectful attitude toward people" justly deserved the "legitimate indignation of the Soviet people."[28]

Moscow's always-active rumor mills were a third source of the public persona put forward by Andropov. Because of his past association with reform-minded officials such as Otto Kuusinen and his ties to liberal scholars and think tanks such as the American and Canadian Studies Institute of the Soviet Academy of Sciences, he was viewed as something of a closet liberal whose own immediate circle of advisors would usher in a more flexible and experimental era of economic and political reforms. His continuing interest in reforms in Eastern Europe, and especially in Hungary, which had undergone the most successful radical departure from centralized planning, prompted rumors that he would draw from that experience. While it is difficult to tell how much of this image was built for foreign consumption — the assertions that he was a man steeped in Western culture and with Western tastes in literature and music were undoubtedly a part of the attempt to build a verbal Potemkin village — its domestic impact was to suggest that he was a man cut from a very different cloth from his less sophisticated contemporaries.

NOTES

1. Jerry F. Hough, "Soviet succession: Issues and personalities," *Problems of Communism,* 31 (September/October 1982):28–29.
2. Ibid.
3. Alexander G. Rahr, *A Biographic Directory of 100 Leading Soviet Officials* (Munich: Radio Liberty, 1984), pp. 37–39.
4. Hough, "Soviet succession," pp. 30–31.
5. Ilya Zemtsov, *Andropov: Policy Dilemmas and the Struggle for Power* (Jerusalem: Israel Research Institute of Contemporary Society, 1983), p. 92.

6. Amy W. Knight, "Andropov: Myths and realities," *Survey,* 28 (Spring 1984):23–29.

7. Ibid., pp. 35–36.

8. *Stenograficheskii otchet, XXVI sezd Kommunisticheskoi Partii Sovetskogo Soiuza, 23 fevralia-3 marta 1981 goda* (Moscow: Izdatelstvo politicheskoi literatury, 1981).

9. Viktor Goliavkin, "Iubileynaia rech," *Avrora* (December, 1981).

10. Zemtsov, *Andropov,* p. 77; and Jonathan Steele and Eric Abraham, *Andropov in Power: From Komsomol to Kremlin* (Garden City: Anchor/Doubleday, 1984), pp. 140–41.

11. Zemtsov, *Andropov,* p. 78; and Steele and Abraham, *Andropov,* p. 142.

12. Zhores A. Medvedev, *Andropov* (New York: W. W. Norton, 1983), pp. 9–10; and Zemtsov, *Andropov,* pp. 81–82.

13. Zemtsov, *Andropov,* p. 81.

14. Ibid., p. 86.

15. Knight, "Andropov"; and Zemtsov, *Andropov,* p. 86.

16. Steele and Abraham, *Andropov,* p. 148; and Medvedev, *Andropov,* p. 96.

17. Medvedev, *Andropov,* p. 16.

18. Ibid.

19. Zemtsov, *Andropov,* pp. 89–90.

20. *Pravda, Izvestiia,* and *Krasnaia zvezda,* October 28, 1982.

21. *Pravda,* October 28, 1982.

22. *Pravda,* October 30, 1982.

23. *Pravda,* June 21, 1980.

24. Mark D. Zlotnik, "Chernenko's platform," *Problems of Communism,* 31 (November/December 1982):70–75.

25. *Pravda,* October 28 and 30, 1982.

26. Iu. V. Andropov, *Izbrannye rechi i state* (Moscow: Politizdat, 1983).

27. *Pravda,* April 23, 1982.

28. Ibid.

3   Andropov in Power

THE BREZHNEV SUCCESSION

Brezhnev's death on November 10, 1982, ended the long period of waiting. With the long-suffering leader now removed both as a stumbling block and as a partisan participant in the selection of his own successor, the focus shifted to the Politburo, reduced to 11 full members by the General Secretary's departure.

Given the nature of Soviet politics, it is not remarkable that we do not know with certainty what transpired in the first days after Brezhnev's death. While we can see the final result — the election of Andropov to be General Secretary and his less-than-complete attempts to consolidate power in the early months of his rule — we cannot see the pulling and tugging of the partisan and institutional forces that resulted in that outcome. Yet we can reconstruct much of what probably occurred, in part from a careful reading of the public record, which reflects if not totally mirrors events, and in part from the underlying reality of Soviet politics in which the personal fortunes of individual leaders are intertwined with the fate of important institutional interests.

It is clear that Brezhnev's death provoked a vigorous struggle within the Politburo in which the final remnants of his personal entourage clashed with a more heterogeneous coalition that backed Andropov. Yet it would be inaccurate to portray the division of forces wholly in terms of the personal and institutional loyalties of those involved. At issue were not only the mutual networks of allegiance and support that had closely bound together this aging generation of leaders but also their conflicting images, hopes, and fears of what any new leadership would bring. At stake was not only the immediate question of who would be named General Secretary of the Communist Party but also the nature of the coalition — and its assumptions and demands about the course of national policy — that would back him in his bid for office.

The relatively long delay separating Brezhnev's death and the public announcement of his demise suggests that the Politburo found it difficult to come to any consensus on the difficult choice of a successor. Two days passed between the death between eight and nine in the morning on November 10th and the formal announcement on November 12th. The sketchy accounts available suggest that the Politburo was in virtually constant session on November 11th, with the first bid for power initiated by the Chernenko faction. The original scenario provided for a carefully staged show of unity among the closest of Brezhnev's former associates and an attempt to bridge any potential gap between party and state. Chernenko first proposed Premier Nikolai Tikhonov for the top party post. Citing his advanced age — then 77 — he declined and nominated Chernenko in his stead.

It is likely that Chernenko's losing coalition numbered no more than three or four full members of the Politburo, united as much by their desire to block Andropov's rise as by any direct loyalty to Brezhnev's chosen heir. Other than Chernenko himself, the coalition probably included Tikhonov, a Brezhnev loyalist whose own hold on the Chairmanship of the Council of Ministers would be endangered by widespread reforms, and D. A. Kunaev, the first secretary of the Kazakh party organization.

It is also possible that Viktor Grishin, first secretary of the Moscow party organization, backed Chernenko. While some emigré sources place him in the Andropov camp, it is also known that he clearly sided with the old guard to block Gorbachev's rise after Chernenko's death in 1984.[1] Given his own reputed desire for higher office, it is quite possible that his association with either faction in the fall of 1982 was designed simply to buy time for his own candidacy to mature as more forceful rivals among the senior members of the Politburo neutralized one another. Because of their advanced age and ill health, neither Chernenko nor Andropov was likely to serve in office for more than a relatively brief transition period. In the event Chernenko succeeded his mentor, Grishin would remain a senior member of the inner circle whose long association with the party apparatus would make him a focal point for those who continued to resent the new General Secretary's lack of experience beyond Brezhnev's shadow. And in the event Andropov rose to power and thereby discredited Chernenko's bid to represent the forces of stability, Grishin remained a member of the old guard who would prove difficult to dislodge from power, especially to the extent that a backlash against widespread reform would make party and state leaders long for more "respectful" leadership at the top. And as a relatively younger member of the inner circle — he was 68 at the time of Brezhnev's death — he could perhaps hope for a last bid for power as the other senior leaders were pushed from the scene and before the next generation had resolved the conflicts that would inevitably arise among the younger would-be heirs.

Andropov's own winning coalition was far more diverse, reflecting both his efforts to court backing from heavy industry and the military and the impact of the campaign to portray himself as a forceful leader. At the center of this group of backers were Dmitrii Ustinov, the minister of defense, and Andrei Gromyko, the foreign minister. Although senior members of the Politburo, they had risen to prominence because of their recognized expertise in defense and foreign affairs rather than because of any close association with Brezhnev's personal entourage. Their presence on that high body confirmed, as did Andropov's, that de facto representation of important institutional power bases had emerged during the Brezhnev era.

Several factors motivated their support of Andropov. It is likely that their personal resistance to the elevation of

Chernenko played an important role; whatever their thoughts concerning his suitability for office, they probably had long resented his sycophantic relationship with the General Secretary and his status as the designated heir who had risen to within grasping range of power solely through the patronage of his mentor. Chernenko's questionable qualities as a potential leader must also have played a role. With virtually no independent leadership experience in either party or state to his credit, Chernenko was at best a weak prospect to take firm control of an increasingly disorderly system. Moreover, Chernenko's attempts to establish himself as a proponent of a pro-consumer line in the economy and a vaguely populist and anti-bureaucratic posture in terms of administrative style would hardly endear him to the military and the more conservative elements of the foreign policy establishment.[2]

On the positive side, there was much to attract Ustinov and Gromyko to Andropov's side. Given the demise of Kirilenko, who was removed from the Politburo at the November 22 regular session of the Central Committee that quickly followed Andropov's rise to power, the former KGB chief was the only logical candidate around whom a stop-Chernenko coalition could form. Other senior figures such as Ustinov and Gromyko themselves had failed to broaden their narrow institutional constituencies, and Romanov and Grishin had at best limited bases in Leningrad and Moscow. Andropov's long experience in foreign policy and defense as head of the KGB also undoubtedly weighed in his favor, as did his reputation as an effective administrator who had brought the sprawling domestic and foreign activities of the agency under control.

It is also likely that Grigorii Romanov backed Andropov's bid for power, motivated both by his resentment of his relative isolation in Leningrad at the hands of the former leadership and by his own desire to see an interim leader emerge to permit time for his own aspirations for higher office to bear fruit. Although he had risen to Politburo status in 1976, six years after his appointment as first secretary of the Leningrad party committee, he suffered the same fate as many of his predecessors in being kept at arm's length by the central leadership in Moscow. His record as a tough-minded administrator and a pragmatist in terms of economic reform also placed him close to the Andropov camp in these matters.

It is also highly likely that Vladimir Shcherbitskii, the first secretary of the Ukrainian party organization, backed Andropov. While his ties to the deceased leader reached back to the very origins of the Dnepropetrovsk mafia, he was never a member of the inner circle of Brezhnev cronies within the Politburo. Increasingly isolated and under thickly veiled attack during the last years of Brezhnev's rule, he probably would have backed any leader representing a substantial departure from the past.[3]

It also seems certain that Mikhail Gorbachev supported Andropov, who was soon to take the ambitious expert on agricultural affairs under his wing. Yet it is difficult to ascertain whether their initial alliance was motivated by programmatic concerns or by partisan advantage. Both men had developed reputations as pragmatic reformers, with Gorbachev advocating the use of a controversial brigade labor system in agriculture that went far beyond the more cautious food program initiated by the Brezhnev administration. But on the other hand, his interest in agriculture would have placed him at odds with the seeming tilt of the new administration toward heavy industry. As the youngest member of the next generation of potential successors, Gorbachev may simply have decided to position himself on the winning side, hoping that the new General Secretary's penchant for pragmatic reforms and proffered patronage would position him for the next stage of the succession.[4]

It is far more difficult to assess the impact of Andrei Kirilenko and Avrid Pelshe. The former most likely played no role in the formal selection of Brezhnev's successor; events preceding the November 22nd plenum suggest that he had already been marked for dismissal. Pelshe's role is harder to ascertain. Emigré sources report that he too was absent from the critical Politburo session on November 12th, although his backing of any of the two final contenders would not have tipped the balance.[5]

Despite the initial conflict that delayed the announcement of Brezhnev's death, the eventual public disclosure of the selection of Andropov was handled so as to produce the appearance of unanimity. Chernenko formally nominated him at the November 12th session of the Central Committee, acting "on instructions from the Politburo" to demonstrate his endorsement of Andropov's selection. Yet the organization of the plenum itself suggested that Andropov went to extraordinary lengths to control events and that Chernenko carried at least the last vestiges of his battle before the larger body. Departing from protocol, Andropov himself opened the meeting and initially addressed the group, instead of maintaining a modest silence until his selection as General Secretary.[6] Chernenko's comments gave short shrift to the former KGB director's qualifications for office in comparison with his lengthy eulogy of the fallen leader and the accomplishments of his era, pointedly stressing the new General Secretary's "excellent grasp of Brezhnev's style of leadership [and] his attitude toward cadres" as well as his "passion for collective work," all code words suggesting pressures on Andropov to proceed cautiously in imposing his will on the Politburo and in shaking up the existing leadership.[7] Emigré sources suggest that Chernenko at least considered carrying the battle to the floor of the Central Committee session itself and was dissuaded by the offer of appointment to the largely ceremonial post of the chairman of the Presidium of the Supreme Soviet.[8]

Whatever the hidden agenda underlying the session, it was clear that Andropov's victory had been less than complete. While Kirilenko's neutralization was confirmed less than two weeks later at the November 22nd plenum and Geidar Aliev, the party secretary from Azerbaidzhan and a likely Andropov ally, was added to the Politburo, there were sure signs that Andropov's hold on power was less than secure. First, he had been unable to vanquish his obvious rival, Chernenko, or to pack the Politburo with a number of new appointees drawn from his own supporters. Chernenko remained an important member of the Politburo, emerging eventually as the acknowledged second secretary in charge of ideology. His continuing role in Kremlin affairs was confirmed a month later when he delivered the opening address at a special session of the Central Committee commemorating the 60th anniversary of the formation of the Soviet Union.[9] Second, until well into the summer, Andropov was unable to secure his own appointment to the other two posts formerly held by Brezhnev, chairman of the Defense Council and the chairman of the Presidium of the Supreme Soviet.

ANDROPOV IN POWER:
THE UNCERTAIN INTERREGNUM

For the 15 months he remained in power, Andropov sought to place his stamp on the nation. Yet even in retrospect, it is hard to assess the extent of his real impact. Much of what transpired during his rule — especially during the first few months when his health permitted him to exercise greater control — had at least its intellectual antecedents in the admittedly unsuccessful reform efforts of the Brezhnev administration. Proposals for economic reform, for the improvement of management, and for studying the East European experience had already been on the agenda, even if they had not occupied center stage. The limited experimental programs that were begun did little to break new ground or to suggest that the new regime had weighed the political costs of more extensive changes.

Like any leader new to office, Andropov faced political as well as economic and social realities that impelled him to action on certain fronts and stayed his hand on others. He faced three immediate tasks, each made more compelling by what must have been his own awareness of the incomplete nature of his victory and the frail condition of his health. First, he had to deal with the Brezhnev legacy, both to lay to rest the specter of the General Secretary who had ruled for the last 18 years and to cope with the remnants of the Brezhnev entourage who remained in office. Second, he had to establish the tone and style of his own leadership, to build upon what had been a mere promise of strong executive direction, and to find ways of institutionalizing and consolidating his own hold. And third, he had to develop his own policy initiatives and programs, hoping not only to confront the seemingly intractable problems that would face any successor but also to forge a program of action that would bring the support of pro-reform elements to his side and spark the imagination of the elite and the general population.

Not surprisingly, Andropov chose to proceed cautiously on virtually all fronts. Despite the great visibility accorded to the new leader during the first months in office, the substance of his actions clearly reflected a gradualist approach to the problems of party and state. In part because of the difficulties inherent in attempting to change any ossified bureaucracy, and undoubtedly in part because of opposition to his proposed reforms, the new General Secretary tempered his attempts to demonstrate strong leadership with a careful regard for the political realities that surrounded him.

In terms of leadership style, Andropov moved quickly to present himself as a vigorous leader who candidly dealt with issues. His first speech as General Secretary was characterized both by its directness and honesty as well as by its surprising absence of cant. In the weeks that followed, the persona of the new General Secretary became one of a direct, nondogmatic, and dynamic leader who sought to impose new life and direction on the nation.

Much of the initial image of the new administration also came about through its handling of the old. While he launched no direct attacks on the memory of Brezhnev and accepted a continuing role for members of the former General Secretary's entourage, including Chernenko, Andropov moved quickly against the worst excesses of corruption and malfeasance in office. The anti-corruption campaign that swept across party and state was designed not only to remove officials who had engaged in illegal practices under the former regime — and to permit Andropov to promote his own supporters to a growing

number of posts — but also to create the public image of a
vigorous leader who moved against violators even at the
highest level.

In addition to his attempts to build the image of a forceful
new leader and to picture himself in stark contrast with the
corrupt and ineffectual leadership of the past, Andropov
moved as rapidly as political realities would permit to build a
new constituency that would both consolidate his hold on
power and prove more receptive to the reform agenda that
would take form in the coming months. In the short run, the
new coalition was designed to circumvent the party old
guard, who would have increasingly good reason to fear
Andropov's efforts to revitalize the bureaucracy and to press
forward with economic and social reforms. But in the long
run, the political impact of the coalition would be even more
extensive, for it sought to bridge the gap between the
generation of aged leaders now in office and the next
generation of leaders who had been kept from power. Like
any political coalition, it had its own logic born of the political
expediencies of the moment and the bona fide interests of its
diverse participants; but it also had its own built-in strains
and contradictions.

Central in the new coalition was the new General
Secretary's former power base in the KGB. While it is
inaccurate to argue that the KGB became the principal base
of support for the new regime, it is certain that Andropov's
association with that agency conveyed important advantages
in the first months of his rule. He moved quickly to appoint
former associates to high positions within the Ministry of
Internal Affairs, consolidating his hold over the national
police force and furthering his ability to launch an effective
anti-corruption campaign. Less tangibly, his continuing ties
to the secret police struck justifiable fear in the hearts of
would-be opponents and potential victims, who assumed that
the agency's extensive files contained incriminating
evidence against them.

Also important in the new alignment was the military
establishment, whose perceptions of the drift and malaise in
the final years of the Brezhnev administration had brought it
to Andropov's side. The historical competition and jealousy

that had separated the secret police and the military had been laid to rest during the Brezhnev years by the growing professionalization of both, and the alliance formed between Andropov and Ustinov represented more than a rejection of Chernenko's candidacy. Both shared the perception that forceful leadership was needed in both domestic and foreign affairs. Andropov's expertise in foreign and security affairs made him a natural ally of a military establishment concerned with the growing confrontation with the West, as did his reputation for discipline and his record in crushing the dissident movement in the 1970s.

The new General Secretary and the military also shared a common concern about the poor performance of the Soviet economy and the likely costs of meeting the U.S. challenge, and both seemed to share the same conviction that greater discipline and economic reforms stressing the rapid development of high technology would solve the problem. Soviet military leaders such as Marshall Ogarkov spoke openly of the military's dependence on highly sophisticated weapons systems and lamented the economy's inability to master high technology. No less important was the looming question of paying for the development of sophisticated weapons systems. Already saddled with difficult choices in the civilian economy, the growing frustration of Soviet consumers, and the previous leadership's massive commitments to develop Siberian resources, the new leadership found itself facing thinly veiled demands from the military to provide the resources needed to meet the challenge from the United States.

Andropov faced a very different task in building support within the party apparatus. While he had clearly subordinated the secret police to the party's will and had extensive experience in interparty diplomacy within the socialist bloc, he had little direct experience within the domestic party apparatus, especially at the provincial or republic level. His brief tenure as chief ideologist after Suslov's death did little to fill the void. He thus had little in common with the most important constituency within the party itself, the regional party secretaries whose support had made — and broken — General Secretaries in the past.

Andropov moved on two fronts to deal with this dilemma. On the one hand, he quickly sought the backing of those elements of the party apparatus who had viewed the now-deposed Kirilenko as their candidate in the succession battle. This both gave him a growing source of support within senior elements of the party old guard and brought to his side specialists concerned with the management of the economy. On the other hand, he moved with deliberate caution to bring his own protégés to high office and to begin to rid the national and regional party apparatus of holdovers from the Brezhnev era. Throughout the spring and summer of 1983 a significant number of Central Committee department heads and regional party secretaries were removed from office, and Andropov added a limited number of his supporters to the Politburo and Secretariat. Even as his own physical condition deteriorated, the new General Secretary's supporters grew in number in the highest party bodies.

But if Andropov's new coalition offered the hope of dislodging the old guard and bringing a new generation of younger party and state officials to power, it suffered from palpable risks in the first months of its existence. In spite of his ability to add a limited number of new figures to the Politburo and Secretariat, Andropov proved incapable of removing the coterie of Brezhnev holdovers from both bodies. Like other General Secretaries before him, he found it easier to effect changes at the lower levels of the bureaucracy or in the provinces than to reshape the party's highest reaches of power. Moreover, his efforts to use the anti-corruption issue as the cutting edge and his propensity to picture his regime as initiating the long-awaited generational shift in Soviet politics did as much to engender resistance among entrenched political figures as it did to inspire hope among younger officials. While his own personal dynamism could sustain such leadership in the early months of his rule, it proved difficult to maintain such forward momentum when the initial hopes for rapid change yielded to no new vision of economic reform and the leader himself stumbled because of ill health.

FACTIONAL POLITICS:
KTO KOGO IN THE KREMLIN

Much of the political agenda of the Andropov administration, like that of its predecessors, can be traced in the personnel policies of the top leadership. In a status and protocol conscious world in which position and alliance determine power and influence, any new regime's ability to bring its own supporters to the fore — or its failure to remove opponents from office — signals both its political skill and the policies it wishes to pursue. And in a political milieu best described by the Russian phrase *kto kogo* — who dominates whom, in loose translation — much of conflict associated with any new leader's ability to consolidate his position and the attempts of his real or imagined foes to circumscribe his power will be fought over the real and symbolic meaning of appointments to high office.

Even in connection with the burial of Brezhnev, the symbolic dimensions of such selections were soon apparent. The first hint of Andropov's status as heir apparent came when he was named chairman of the funeral commission. Moreover, two members of the ruling elite were conspicuously omitted from that body. Absent were Grigorii Romanov, the Leningrad party secretary (whose own reputed aspirations to higher office may have accounted for the arm's length treatment accorded him by the other members of the Politburo) and Vladimir Dolgikh, who had served since 1972 as the party secretary in charge of heavy industry and as a candidate member of the Politburo since 1982. Closely associated with the Chernenko faction, Dolgikh had been given the largely unfulfilled task of solving the Soviet Union's growing energy problem, a shortcoming that, along with his association with Brezhnev's protégé, may have accounted for what was only the first of many signals of his declining political fortunes.[10]

Additional symbolic importance clearly attached to the new regime's choice of the individuals who delivered public eulogies at the funeral. Conspicuously silent was the deceased leader's most prominent protégé, Chernenko, whose undoubtedly honest sorrow at the passing of his mentor was spoken as a part of his nomination of Andropov. Mounting the top of Lenin's tomb to deliver the formal eulogies were a diverse lot of the powerful and the symbolic: Defense Minister Ustinov, whose presence signaled the military's backing of the new regime; the president of the Soviet Academy of Sciences, whose participation could be read as symbolic of Andropov's interest in building ties to the scientific and technical intelligentsia; a party functionary from the Ukraine, present perhaps to signal the regime's interest in promoting young blood from the provinces; and the obligatory common worker, whose presence added proletarian legitimacy to the proceedings.

The first significant personnel changes that signaled the new regime's policies and hinted at Andropov's strategy came at the November 22nd Central Committee plenum. Geidar Aliev, party first secretary in Azerbaidzhan, was promoted from candidate to full membership in the Politburo.[11] A career law enforcement officer, he had risen to the chairmanship of the secret police in that province in 1967. In 1969 he was elevated to party first secretary in Azerbaidzhan, and in 1976 he was named a candidate member of the all-union Politburo. He was responsible for a well-publicized anti-corruption campaign in a province known for the creative dishonesty of its public officials, and he was reputed to be a firm disciplinarian in terms of party internal affairs. While it seems virtually certain that both his career experiences and his own disposition inclined him to the Andropov camp, there is evidence that he may have flirted briefly with the Chernenko faction just before Brezhnev's death.

Whatever his attempts to ingratiate himself with both of the viable candidates for succession, Aliev was singled out by Andropov for a number of reasons and was held in particular esteem by the new administration. If emigré accounts are accurate, Andropov first proposed that Aliev be appointed both to full membership in the Politburo and to the Secretariat, a double honor that was undoubtedly opposed by those who resisted vesting such power in the hands of an associate of the new General Secretary. Shortly after the November 22nd plenum, Aliev was named first deputy chairman of the USSR Council of Ministers, giving him important posts in both party and state.[12]

While it is impossible to know with certainty what motivated Andropov to tap Aliev for high office, several factors seem likely to have entered into the calculation, each designed to make a point about the aims of the new administration or to pass a subtle political message to those who watched such events for their hidden meanings. Most obvious was the implication that the new regime intended to use the anti-corruption issue to its own partisan advantage. Aliev's appointment as first deputy chairman of the Council of Ministers further suggested that the state bureaucracy as well as the party would be the target of such scrutiny and conspicuously placed him in a position from which he might succeed the aging premier, Nikolai Tikhonov, who had backed Chernenko in the leadership struggle. Aliev's appointment also conveyed other more subtle messages. It signaled the new regime's intent to promote regional party leaders to positions of authority and visibly elevated a non-Russian to an important national post. It also quite possibly indicated the new leadership's willingness to take under its wing individuals and factions who might have supported, however briefly, other candidates for General Secretary, an important message to convey in the coming months as Andropov courted support form upper- and middle-level officials formerly associated with the Kirilenko faction.

The November plenum also saw the appointment of Nikolai Ryzhkov, first deputy chairman of Gosplan, to the Secretariat, where he assumed responsibility for heavy industry. A technocrat who had served as director of the Uralmash production association in the early 1970s, he had risen to the posts of First Deputy Minister of Heavy and Transport Machinery in 1975 and then to the Gosplan post in 1979. He was linked indirectly to the Kirilenko faction through his association with Ia. P. Riabov. His appointment bore two political messages, the first that the new General Secretary sought to build bridges to the remnants of the Kirilenko faction, and the second that a new economic team was being created, sidestepping Brezhnev appointees such as Vladimir Dolgikh.

The November 22nd plenum also confirmed the fall of Kirilenko, who had apparently played no active role in Politburo deliberations at the time of Brezhnev's death. His retirement was alleged to have taken place at his own request "for reasons of health," but it is certain that the Politburo action merely confirmed an earlier decision to strip him of his high party rank after the failure of his bid for top office.

The November 22nd plenum was also significant for what did not occur. Other than the removal of Kirilenko, which was an anticipated fait accompli, the session did nothing to affect the political fortunes of the senior Politburo figures who had been locked in political combat only weeks before. While the elevation of Aliev and Ryzhkov suggested that Andropov enjoyed limited success in promoting presumed supporters to high posts, the apparent lack of any attempt by the new general secretary to push for additional dismissals argues that he felt it necessary to move with caution against those who had opposed him. As had other newly selected Soviet leaders before him, Andropov faced the likelihood of a prolonged period of consolidation of his own powers, complicated on the one hand by the desire of friend and foe alike to remind him of the proper limits of "collective leadership" — Chernenko's warning on the matter delivered pointedly in his nominating speech cannot be forgotten or dismissed as the parting shot of the losing faction — and on the other by Andropov's own advanced years and ill health.

The personnel changes within top party and government posts that followed the November plenum reflected the political realities that attended the birth of the new regime and foreshadowed its strategy to consolidate power. Defense Minister Ustinov assumed de facto chairmanship of the Defense Council, a move that confirmed the military's key role in the earlier succession struggle and at least temporarily denied Andropov the second most powerful of the troika of formal posts held by his predecessor. In March 1983 Foreign Minister Gromyko was named a first deputy chairman of the Council of Ministers, a post that in itself did little to enhance his already considerable power and influence. Given the relative insignificance of the new title in comparison with his post in the Foreign Ministry, it can hardly be argued that the new promotion was offered as a reward for his support of Andropov's candidacy. Two other possible explanations are feasible, one consistent with the interpretation that Andropov was increasingly in control of events and maneuvering to consolidate his power, and the other in line with the argument that other senior members of the Politburo were acting to constrain his growing powers. In the first interpretation, Gromyko's new post could be seen as the first sign of a lateral move, perhaps preparing him to replace the aging Tikhonov as chairman of the Council of Ministers or perhaps placing him in line to assume the largely ceremonial presidency. Given his eventual move into the latter post shortly after Gorbachev's rise in March 1984, it seems easy to assume that this had been the design from the outset, but at the time another equally feasible interpretation was possible. Gromyko's appointment as deputy premier could also have been intended as a clearly visible counterploy set against the rising fortunes of Aliev, who was rumored to be Andropov's own choice to replace Tikhonov. If the latter interpretation is correct, Andropov was not the moving force behind the appointment but rather its intended indirect victim.

Whatever the nature of the deadlock within the Politburo itself, Andropov moved quickly along three fronts to consolidate his hold and to map out his strategy of attack. First, he brought the Ministry of Internal Affairs directly under his control through the appointment of Vitalai Fedorchuk to replace Nikolai Shchelokov, a Brezhnev crony who had tolerated and concealed widespread corruption at all levels. Fedorchuk, who had headed the Ukrainian KGB, was a close associate of the new General Secretary whose reputation as a stern disciplinarian foreshadowed Andropov's use of the anti-corruption issue as a political weapon. Second, Andropov assembled a new economic team whose own youth and association with reform efforts in industry and agriculture suggested that his administration intended to move boldly in this direction. And third, he began the gradual process of replacing aging and frequently inept party officials, beginning with highly visible initial appointments that foretold the shape of things to come.

As he had done to discredit Brezhnev even before his death, Andropov turned to the corruption issue both to forge a weapon he could use against party and state officials and to win widespread popular support for his willingness to deal with misconduct at the top. It was a double-edged sword. On the one hand, it cut deeply against all segments of the generation of Soviet leaders who had clung to office through the Brezhnev years. Virtually all were guilty of some degree of petty corruption or influence peddling, and all feared the new General Secretary's access to KGB records that might detail their wrongdoings. On the other hand, the corruption issue easily became a more generalized attack on the widespread lack of discipline within society as a whole and an indictment of the malaise that had come to characterize the whole of society in the latter years of Brezhnev's rule. It became a focal point of criticism — and perhaps a convenient scapegoat — for those who resented the power and status of their superiors, the shoddy performance of the economy, and the absence of a sense of public morality.

The anti-corruption campaign felled highly visible figures such as the chief of the Ministry of Internal Affairs, Nikolai Shchelokov, and ministers whose agencies had been singled out for poor performance such as Ivan Pavlovskii, Minister of Railways, Stepan Khitrov, Minister for Agricultural Construction, Alexander Struev, Minister of Trade, Mikhail Mikhailov, Deputy Minister of the Aviation Industry, Anatoly Yershov, Deputy Minister of Light Industry, and Ignaty Novikov, Chairman of the State Committee for Construction. In each case, the victim had been associated with a problem in the economy such as consumer goods or transportation or had been known to run a particularly corrupt agency.[13]

In the broader perspective, these well publicized dismissals were intended to accomplish a dual purpose. They clearly signaled that the new regime had little "respect for cadres," the code phrase of the Brezhnev years that had promised political longevity for senior- and middle-level party and state officials whose support sustained 18 years in office. To be sure, even the somnambular Brezhnev had chafed at the poor performance of his cohorts and cajoled them to higher accomplishments in the name of economic reform and the scientific and technological revolution. But what Brezhnev had lacked in political will to force reforms and honest performance on the establishment, his successor more than made up for in terms of his willingness to make proper examples of high level officials.

The anti-corruption campaign was also used as a highly visible way of mobilizing general pubic support for the new leader, at least until it became apparent that petty corruption and poor discipline were so widespread that too exacting a program would prove politically counterproductive. During the winter and spring, all forms of corruption and indiscipline became the topic of public scrutiny and condemnation; from chronic alcoholism and pilfering to more profitable and imaginative forms of corruption, the media reported widespread scandals and arrests. Special police units patrolled stores and other public facilities to identify those who were absent from work without authorization, and the general public was urged to turn in shirkers and others whose activities fell short of legal and moral norms. By the late spring, the most vigorous phase of the public campaign had ended, undoubtedly the victim of a law of diminishing returns and a limited public attention span. But it had served its purpose. The new administration had made its point about its willingness to move against heretofore protected figures in authority, and it had established its intent to make discipline in the workplace one of the central features of its economic reforms.

Andropov also assembled a new economic team, a move that both opened the door for him to seek the backing of Kirilenko's extensive network of supporters and to advance his most visible protégé, Mikhail Gorbachev. The move also established an obvious counterweight to the remnants of the Brezhnev economic team, which included Tikhonov and Dolgikh, and closed the door for Chernenko to assume a powerful portfolio in economic affairs.

In many ways, Gorbachev was an unlikely candidate to assume responsibility for the economy. A graduate of Moscow State University's law faculty in the closing years of the Stalin era, he had almost exclusively been identified with agricultural concerns during his rapid rise through the apparatus. He began his career as a Komsomol organizer first at the university and then as the first secretary of the Stavropol city youth organization, rising in the late 1950s to second and then first secretary of the Stavropol Komsomol organization. In 1962, he became the party official responsible for the region's collective and state farms. Then in rapid succession, he rose to the posts of first secretary of the Stavropol city party organization in 1966, to second secretary of the *oblast* organization two years later, and to first secretary in 1970, a post that he held for eight years until his appointment to the Secretariat. In 1979, he became a candidate member of the Politburo, and a year later rose to full voting membership in that body.

In political terms, he rose as the protégé of Fyodor Kulakov, then the ranking party official in charge of agricultural affairs, and Mikhail Suslov, whose regional base was in Stavropol. Both associations proved to be particularly helpful: the former because it brought him to the attention of the top leadership at a time when they, for political reasons of their own, were willing to pour massive resources into agriculture and to discuss, if not fully implement, modest reforms in the organization of production; and the latter because it brought him under the protection of a member of the inner circle of the Politburo. The initial tie to Andropov is more difficult to discern. While it is certainly possible that a senior figure like Suslov lauded the accomplishments of his young protégé to other members of the Politburo and that Andropov, who occasionally vacationed in Stavropol, may have met this ambitious young party official in that setting, there is little to indicate any direct tie until after Brezhnev's death. Gorbachev's ascension to the Politburo in 1979 clearly occurred before the ailing General Secretary began to lose control of events, making it unlikely that he was viewed as any immediate threat to the Brezhnev faction. Rather it is likely that his rise simply occurred at a time when the Brezhnev administration itself wished to infuse new leadership into agriculture and to make at least a token attempt to bring a relatively unthreatening figure to the fore.

Andropov's choice of Gorbachev to exercise general oversight over the economy probably had less to do with his admittedly questionable expertise in industry than with the symbolic importance of advancing a younger and more dynamic figure who had been associated with reform efforts in agriculture. In purely technical terms, Gorbachev's long association with agriculture was compensated for by the industrial expertise of Nikolai Ryzhkov, whose earlier appointment to the Secretariat placed him in a position to deal with day-to-day problems in industry but not yet in a position to have the political and institutional influence to challenge more conservative senior members of the Politburo. In contrast, Gorbachev was a member of both bodies and could be presumed to be better able to draw upon the support of his new mentor to press for reforms. In political terms, Gorbachev was also an ideal choice. He had no discernible ties to either the Chernenko or Kirilenko factions, making it unlikely that his support of Andropov would be colored by past associations. Given his relative youth — 52 at the time of Brezhnev's death — and his own background, it was also likely that he would emerge as a rallying point for the impatient young technocrats whom the Andropov administration wished to attract to its camp.

Andropov's own political fortunes took a turn for the better in the spring. Sometime before the end of May, he assumed the post of chairman of the Defense Council, an important body consisting of the Minister of Defense, the Foreign Minister, the head of the KGB, the party secretary in charge of defense industries, and other high level party and state officials dealing with military questions. This added the second jewel to the crown that Brezhnev had worn, although the matter-of-fact way in which the public disclosure was made by Defense Minister Ustinov suggested that a decision had been made to avoid fanfare about the appointment.

The June 1983 Central Committee plenum witnessed an apparent deadlock on appointments of new members to fill the depleted ranks of the Politburo and confirmed Chernenko's continued role as a member of the inner circle. Despite the absence of further personnel changes, Andropov scored an important political victory through his assumption of the title of chairman of the Presidium of the Supreme Soviet, the ceremonial presidency that had been held by Brezhnev. While the addition of this post to Andropov's formal responsibilities conveyed no real political power, it did complete the symbolic transition, leaving the new General Secretary now in possession of the three major party and state offices held by his predecessor.[14]

The June plenum also confirmed a continuing role for Chernenko, indicating that he maintained sufficient support within the Politburo to block any efforts to remove him from power. For his part, Chernenko seemingly accepted Andropov's enhanced status; he was chosen to make the public nomination of Andropov for the presidency, and his comments contained none of the thinly veiled criticisms and warnings about collective leadership reflected in his November speech nominating him for General Secretary. Instead, he referred to the Politburo as "led by Yuri Vladimirovich Andropov," a deferential reference not seen since the fawning tribute paid to Brezhnev and not yet echoed by any other member of the Politburo. Chernenko's own continued role was underscored by his selection to make the keynote address to the plenum dealing with ideological affairs, a choice that confirmed that he had assumed the responsibilities in that key area once held by Suslov and then Andropov.[15]

The June plenum also saw the appointment of Grigorii Romanov, the Leningrad party secretary, to the Secretariat. A hard-line regional secretary who had built a reputation for effective economic management and stern discipline, Romanov had made his entire career within Leningrad, rising to first secretary of the *oblast* party committee in 1970, to candidate membership in the Politburo in 1973, and then to full membership in 1976. Devoid of evident patrons within the senior party leadership before Brezhnev's death, he had been denied hope of further promotion and transfer to Moscow. His appointment to the Secretariat both ended his isolation and brought him at least within reach of future succession to the top post.

Two interpretations may be offered to explain his transfer to Moscow. One simple explanation would hold that he was merely being rewarded for his support of Andropov at the time of the succession. Another possible interpretation suggests more complex motivations were at work, even if the new General Secretary was the source of Romanov's advancement. Given the timing of the Romanov appointment and the signals that the plenum itself reflected a relative deadlock between the Andropov and Chernenko factions, it is possible that his transfer to the Secretariat represented an attempt to create a counterweight to Gorbachev's and Ryzhkov's rising stars. Romanov's appointment to the Secretariat cleared the way for his own eventual bid for the General Secretaryship, counterpoising him to the younger Gorbachev, who was emerging as Andropov 's likely choice for the role. The former Leningrad party secretary also was given important responsibilities for defense related industries, the only remaining economic portfolio that had not come under the direction of Andropov's new economic team.

Other changes at the June plenum reflected the seeming balance of political forces and the propensity of the new General Secretary to seek support among those who had grievances with his predecessor. Mikhail Solomentsev, who had served since 1971 as the Chairman of the RSFSR (Russian Soviet Federated Socialist Republic) Council of Ministers and a candidate member of the Politburo, was named head of the Party Control Committee, replacing the deceased Avrid Pelshe. Reputedly bitter about the denial of promotion to full membership in the Politburo, which should have accompanied his long service in the RSFSR post, Solomentsev was unlikely to have been close to the Chernenko faction. While the nature of this transfer was hard to read at the time of the June plenum, the subsequent elevation of Solomentsev to full membership in the Politburo suggests that it was intended to draw him firmly into the Andropov camp and to strengthen this key watchdog agency, which plays an important role in disciplinary affairs within the party. Vitalii Vorotnikov, who had been sent by Brezhnev into virtual political exile as Soviet ambassador to Cuba, was also named to candidate membership in the Politburo and to the chairmanship of the RSFSR Council of Ministers. A specialist in industrial management who had served in important party positions in Kuibyshev and Voronezh before he was posted to Cuba in 1979, he returned to the USSR in July 1982 to replace Sergei Medunov as party secretary in the corruption ridden Krasnodar province. Medunov's fall had been orchestrated by Andropov as a part of his use of the anti-corruption campaign to discredit Brezhnev's closest associates, and Vorotnikov was clearly indebted to the former for his political rebirth.

The resolution of other personnel issues within the party during the summer and autumn of 1983 also indicated that Andropov enjoyed less than complete success in his attempts to consolidate power. On the positive side, Chernenko's removal as head of the General Department, from which he had functioned as de facto secretary to the Politburo under Brezhnev, moved him one step away from the actual levers of power. It also became evident that he had failed to inherit Suslov's full range of responsibilities even in the field of ideology. His age and poor health also affected his political fortunes. He dropped from public view for several months in the late summer, fueling rumors that his alleged "extended holiday" was a cover for serious illness.[16]

The summer and autumn also witnessed a strengthening of Andropov's hold over the central and regional party apparatus. Within the central party apparatus in Moscow, nearly a third of the department heads had been replaced by early autumn, the pattern suggesting that the axe had fallen with particular speed on department heads who were closely associated with Brezhnev such as Georgii Pavlov, who headed the Administrative Affairs department, Evgenii Tiazhelnikov, who led the Propaganda Department, and Sergei Trapeznikov, who ran the Department of Science and Education. In addition, certain reorganizations occurred that placed the new Andropov appointees in a better position to effect reforms. The Planning and Finance Department was reorganized as the Economic Department under Nikolai Ryzhkov, and responsibility for food processing was transferred to the Agriculture Department, which was renamed the Agriculture and Food Industry Department.[17]

The new General Secretary had undertaken the more complex and politically more dangerous task of renewing party cadres at the *oblast* level. By the end of 1983, over 20 percent of the regional party secretaries had been replaced. The choice of their successors fell to the newly appointed Egor Ligachev, the head of the Department of Organizational Party Work, and his deputy, Evgenii Razumovskii, both of whom had functioned under the general supervision of Gorbachev. Clear patterns emerged in the selection of new appointees that signaled the intent of the new leadership to abandon the practice of the Brezhnev administration of appointing reliable cadres from within the local party organization. Rather, the new regional secretaries came overwhelmingly from secondary positions within the state apparatus or from the ranks of second secretaries in other regions. The Leningrad pattern was illustrative. Romanov was replaced by Lev Zaikov, formerly chairman of the Leningrad City Executive Committee, instead of by the second secretary then in office, who was in fact demoted to fill the position vacated by the new party chief.[18]

Yet in other areas, it was difficult to see the new General Secretary's hand at work. The summer and autumn saw no significant personnel changes within Gosplan, the central planning agency, the Central Statistical Administration, or other central staff agencies that were concerned with economic planning. Rather, the highly visible dismissals and charges of malfeasance were limited to the branch ministries, which dealt with the day-to-day operation of the economy, instead of the planning agencies, where extensive changes would also be necessary if the new regime were to pursue the sort of thorough economic reforms hinted in its earlier pronouncements.[19]

Even within the party's inner circles, there were indications that Andropov's efforts to consolidate power were meeting opposition. While Chernenko had relinquished his control over the General Department in connection with his assumption of Suslov's duties in the area of ideology, the new appointee was not tied to the Andropov faction. He was

Klavdii Bogoliubov, who had served for years as the first deputy head of the department under Chernenko's direction. At age 74, he could hardly be considered to be anything more than a temporary appointment. His selection most probably signaled an attempt to prevent the General Department from falling under the control of the new General Secretary.[20]

THE ANDROPOV SUCCESSION

By the late summer of 1983, it was apparent that Andropov's days were numbered. In admittedly frail health even when he took office, he quickly declined to a point where he was reputedly placed on dialysis as early as April. His last public appearance occurred on August 18, 1983, and his prolonged public absence during the fall and winter — coupled with the unbelievable official story that he merely suffered from a headcold — fueled rumors that he was seriously ill.

Any stocktaking of his political fortunes at the end of the summer would indicate that, at least to date, his victories within the party had been less than complete and that the stage was being set for the next round of the succession. Within the Politburo itself, it was likely that he commanded at best only a bare plurality. Only Aliev and Gorbachev could be counted on as firm supporters. The continued backing of Ustinov and Gromyko was dependent on the General Secretary's willingness to maintain a firm hand at home and to pursue a hardline policy abroad, a posture that clashed with certain elements of his own reform efforts. Moreover, Andropov's ability to provide vigorous leadership, which had attracted Ustinov and Gromyko in the latter months of the Brezhnev administration, had clearly eroded as his medical problems became more acute.

It is also likely that Chernenko faced a similar political reality at the end of the summer. While the political deadlock that had emerged within the Politburo permitted him to maintain an important position as de facto second secretary for ideology, he had not been able to inherit all of Suslov's powers in other areas. He could probably count on the support of Tikhonov, Kunaev, and possibly Grishin, although their continuing resentment of his aide-de-camp role to Brezhnev and, in the latter case, personal ambition for the top post, would have qualified their support. Rather it is likely that Chernenko emerged as a focal point for two differing and, in many ways, conflicting tendencies within the Politburo and the party at large. On the one hand, he was the logical rallying point for members of the old guard who both resented Andropov's reform efforts and resisted his attempts to promote younger party and state officials. Whether they personally feared the anti-corruption campaign or merely saw it as the rationalization to shake up the senior ranks of party and state officials, these aging members of the generation of leaders who rose to power as a consequence of Stalin's purges and assumed top posts in the 1960s saw in Chernenko what appeared to be a protector and kindred spirit. But on the other hand, Chernenko also probably emerged as a convenient short-term, interim candidate in the eyes of younger figures who had not yet built their power base for the more important choice of a younger, and therefore presumably long-term, successor who would preside over the passing of the older generation.

The logic of the situation dictated that a virtual deadlock existed within the Politburo. Neither Andropov nor Chernenko had the strength to move against the other; they would remain locked in an uneasy truce until one or the other could significantly alter the composition of the Politburo or the Central Committee or until unforeseen events changed the balance. Similarly, an uneasy balance also existed among the younger would-be successors. Gorbachev and Romanov vied not only for support from more senior figures but also for the backing of younger officials whose interests lay in an as-yet undefined program of reform and renewal of party and state leadership.

Romanov's increasing visibility after his transfer to Moscow lent credence to the argument that he was emerging as a potential counterweight to Gorbachev. He was chosen to deliver the speech commemorating the November 7th celebration of the revolution, an honor bestowed the previous year on Andropov himself. While the speech paid the necessary ritual homage to Andropov, referring to him as the "head" of the Politburo, the General Secretary's conspicuous absence from the ceremony held in the Palace of Congresses on November 5th underscored the frailty of his leadership and the fact that Gorbachev had not been tapped to speak in his place.[21]

The significance of Andropov's absence and Romanov's growing visibility aside, the speech itself was a study in careful moderation. Quoting Andropov, Romanov cautioned against "running ahead and setting impossible tasks" and against "resting on our laurels . . . failing to utilize our full potential." He avoided signaling any clear choice in terms of economic priorities and instead lauded the successes of construction in the Far East, the food program, and improvements in the standard of living. On the issue of managerial reform, he endorsed an "improvement in centralized planning" instead of the experimental programs to expand enterprise autonomy.[22]

Andropov's increasingly grave illness lent added urgency to the need to sort out the deadlock within the Politburo. His cancellation of a planned trip to Bulgaria and his highly visible absence from events as important as the November 7th celebration in Red Square underscored his human as well as his political weaknesses. While he continued to attempt to hold the reins of power and to direct the affairs of party and state from his special hospital suite and through the use of aides, who shuttled daily between the hospital and their offices, he was unable to take the bold action needed to leave his mark on Soviet society and to set the stage for the choice of his protégé, Mikhail Gorbachev, as his successor.

The December Central Committee plenum, held, remarkably, in the absence of Andropov himself, provided the last opportunity for him to create a firm working majority within the Politburo. Two new members were named, confirming the ability of the ailing General Secretary to win advancement for his protégés even when his own personal fortunes were declining. These were Mikhail Solomentsev, who had been shifted from his post as chairman of the Council of Ministers of the RSFSR to the head of the Party Control Commission at the May plenum, and Vitalii Vorotnikov, who had advanced from political exile to the chairmanship vacated by Solomentsev. Neither had been closely associated with Andropov before the May plenum, and neither could be regarded as the cutting edge of the new generation of Soviet leaders who would push aside the Brezhnev entourage: Solomentsev was 70 and Vorotnikov was 57 at the time of their advancement.

Other changes at the December plenum were more auspicious for the General Secretary. Viktor Chebrikov, an Andropov protégé who had assumed control of the KGB after Fedorchuk's transfer to the Ministry of Internal Affairs, was elevated to candidate membership in the Politburo, and Egor Ligachev, who had assumed control of the politically sensitive Department of Organizational Party Work (which supervised the selection of lower-level cadres), was appointed to the Secretariat. While the first appointment reflected the continuing importance of the secret police, the fact that Chebrikov won only candidate, non-voting membership in the party's highest body probably indicated the reluctance of at least a majority of Politburo members to see that organization play a critical role in the next succession.[23]

The new year brought difficult choices for the Politburo. No clear majority had emerged despite the changes made at the December plenum. While the addition of Vorotnikov and Solomentsev hardly lent any comfort to the Chernenko faction, because of the presumed grievances that they held against Brezhnev for damaging their careers, it hardly solidifed Andropov's control of that body, especially if the confrontations occurring in the next round of the succession struggle were cast along generational lines. Only two options lay open. On the one hand, the Politburo could choose to endorse another interim candidate drawn from among its own senior members. Such a course of action would be the least controversial option if it were assumed that the Politburo elders could reach agreement among themselves on who would be tapped for the post and if it were likely that the younger members who hoped for a chance to become General Secretary in the future either agreed to the tacit compromise to live with another interim leader or were so badly divided among themselves that they neutralized one another. On the other hand, the Politburo could cut the Gordian knot and elevate a younger figure to General Secretary. Such an action would have two consequences. First, it would force all elements to take sides on a far more serious question than merely choosing another interim successor; any choice of a younger figure such as Romanov (age 61 at the beginning of 1984) or Gorbachev (age 53) would have created the likelihood that the new General Secretary would remain in power for an extended period of time. Second, the selection of a younger leader would have opened the floodgate for the removal of the old guard itself as the new General Secretary brought his own protégés into positions of power.

The Politburo's dilemma was compounded by the fact that only three of its members fit the traditional qualifications of joint membership in the Secretariat as well as the top party body itself: Chernenko, Gorbachev, and Romanov. It was from among this limited field of three that the next likely successor would be chosen, and it was from the interplay of the strategies of these figures that the final months of the Andropov administration took shape.

In one important way, these final months were similar to the period that preceded Brezhnev's death just a year before. Once again there was an ill leader whose days in office were numbered and whose control of events was less than complete. And once again, there were at least three major contenders waiting in the wings, each with a strategy that touted either close identification with the regime in power or promised a welcome respite from things as they were.

Mikhail Gorbachev was now cast in the role of heir apparent, tapped by Andropov to continue his reform efforts. As before, the support of the ailing leader proved to be both an asset and a liability. On the one hand, it presumably placed the support of the Andropov faction behind his candidacy and lent such public support for reform as existed in broader sectors of the Soviet elite behind his cause. The replacement of nearly 20 percent of the regional party secretaries and extensive changes within the central party apparatus strengthened his hand, as did his obvious control of the sensitive *nomenklatura* process, which handles appointments to important posts in party and state. But on the other hand, Andropov's endorsement was also something of a liability. The new appointees to the Politburo and the Secretariat were indebted to Andropov for their rise to power; they had no direct loyalties to the designated heir and no past ties to his own political fortunes. In such a setting, the direct transfer of support from Andropov to Gorbachev was at best problematical, at least to the extent that the latter had developed no personal constituency within the party and state other than the narrow base in the agricultural apparatus. In this regard, his dilemma was remarkably like that of Chernenko only a year before. The endorsement of Andropov was the strongest card in his hand, and yet the General Secretary's declining health made it at least possible that the next round of succession would occur before he could complete the arrangements for the transfer of power.

Gorbachev's status as the heir apparent also made him the natural target of a coalition to stop the frontrunner and the scapegoat for all of the resentments that had surfaced as a result of Andropov's attempted reforms. The new regime's attacks on corruption and privilege within the elite had produced the predictable backlash of resentment and opposition, just as the limited success of attempted reforms in the economy and the sense of malaise and leaderlessness at the top caused others to look for a strong hand to take control. Gorbachev naturally bore the brunt of the former and was largely untested in his own right as a potentially strong leader, especially in contrast to the firm leadership that had been associated with Romanov's long years as party secretary in Leningrad.

Romanov's position was not unlike that of Andropov a year earlier. A new member of the Secretariat with no personal base of support in the apparatus, he had been denied access to the inner circles of power in Moscow during Brezhnev's years in power. His move to the Secretariat only months before had not been of his own making; whether it came as a reward from the new General Secretary for his backing at the November 12th plenum or as a result of a consensus within the Politburo to establish a counterweight to the rise of Andropov's protégés, it did not establish a broad base of support for Romanov. He was given a mandate only in the area of defense-related industries, a significantly smaller bailiwick than Gorbachev's overall responsibility for economic affairs and Ryzhkov's charge to implement economic and managerial reforms.

Romanov's principal strength lay in his availability as a less threatening alternative to Gorbachev. Known as a disciplined party executive who had run a tight ship in Leningrad, he had nonetheless avoided the excesses associated with Andropov's indiscriminate campaign against corruption at the highest levels. And while his zeal to suppress the dissident movement within that northern city had earned him high marks among conservatives, his successful experimentation with economic reforms in Leningrad enterprises had labeled him a pragmatic manager concerned with modernizing industry.

Chernenko's candidacy now stood on a very different foundation. He was no longer merely Brezhnev's chosen heir and the candidate most likely to continue the policies of elite stability associated with the Brezhnev years. He now stood as the most viable candidate of a whole generation of party leaders whom Andropov had begun to sweep from the scene. On the positive side, he represented not only stability in terms of internal party affairs — and this meant more than just an end to the anti-corruption campaign, which in fact continued under his rule — but also the known and familiar conventional wisdom about the role of the party in Soviet society and the style of its leadership. While his brief experience as de facto secretary in charge of ideology presumably had given him a broader base in terms of party activities, he still lacked experience in the economy or independent service in managing any significant enterprise beyond his years as Brezhnev's chief aide.

On the negative side, Chernenko's advanced age — he was 73 at the time of Andropov's death — and admitted ill health, which had kept him from his duties for several months during the summer of 1983, made him a questionable candidate for a long-term succession. Although he probably won some marks for his ability to survive the initial loss to Andropov and to turn the ideology post into a platform for his continued viability, he nonetheless was a man who had once been rejected for the top post. His greatest chance at inheriting Brezhnev's mantle lay in the hope that the next round of the succession would be shaped by obvious generational considerations or that Gorbachev and Romanov would divide what otherwise might have been a majority of the Politburo, perhaps convincing one or both to bide their time and wait for yet a third round of the succession.

Chernenko's political fortunes improved markedly after the deterioration of Andropov's health in August. He once again emerged from the relative obscurity that had been imposed by his role as chief ideologist and his own prolonged illness and published a major article in *Kommunist,* the party's theoretical journal, and other pieces on issues as diverse as foreign policy and human rights.[24] When Andropov failed to appear at the November 7th celebration of the revolution, he took the ailing General Secretary's place as senior member of the leadership.

From August until December 1984 the General Secretary's increasingly lengthy absence was acutely felt in the Kremlin. Veiled comments in the press criticized the excessive secrecy that surrounded Andropov's "cold," and the slow response of civilian leaders to the shooting down of a Korean civilian airplane probably signaled uncertainty not only on how to explain an embarrassing international incident but also on how to deal with the military, whose prominent role had prompted allegations from civilian commentators such as Fyodor Burlatskii that they had mishandled the affair.[25]

The late summer and autumn of 1984 were also marked by a slowing of the pace of personnel changes at both the central and regional levels, suggesting a deadlock among senior officials on the sensitive question of appointments. The leadership was also indecisive about the scheduling of the next session of the Supreme Soviet, which by law was required to meet before the end of the year. When the decision was finally made to hold the session late in December, the announcement came after the required month's advance notice.

The immobilism at the top only thinly veiled a growing conflict over the coming succession. As it became apparent that Soviet leaders soon would be forced to choose one of their number for the top post, attention focused on the vagaries of elite politics. But as always, there was more to the political battle than the question of *kto kogo* in the Kremlin. However brief its tenure in office, the new regime had also launched new initiatives in the economy and foreign policy whose success or failure would play a role in the selection of a new leader.

THE ECONOMY: DISCIPLINE AND CAUTIOUS REFORM

Yuri Andropov's ascension to power in November 1982 was marked by contradictory signals in terms of the new regime's hopes for the economy. Consistent with its inability to take firm hold of the institutions of party and state and the evident presence of conservative opposition, it moved with great caution in calling for a series of experimental managerial reforms. While it spoke with considerably greater candor about the seriousness of the nation's economic ills and the need for extensive changes, its actions were circumscribed by the political realities it faced not only within the highest party bodies but also stretching throughout the cumbersome bureaucracy that had tenaciously — and successfully — resisted change in the past.

In other areas, the new regime acted more boldly. It launched a vigorous campaign to root out corruption and improve labor discipline. While the former was aimed principally at misconduct among party and state officials and at conveying the message that the new regime would not tolerate corruption, the latter was targeted more directly at the rank and file worker, whose propensity for shirking responsibility at the workplace cost the Soviet economy enormous loses in terms of wasted manpower and low quality production. Despite the public fanfare, the issue of greater efficiency was hardly new. Even before Brezhnev's death, it had become a central theme in the regime's hopes for greater production. In an economy in which scarce capital and diminishing human and material resources limited the ability of central planners to pour greater investment and more raw materials and workers into industry, the only recourse lay in the more efficient utilization of existing resources. The keys to further economic growth and the modernization of Soviet industry became the dual themes of the scientific/technological revolution, which was to provide industry with more efficient and technologically sophisticated production processes, and improved labor productivity, which was to increase the output of each individual worker. Yet attempts to improve worker productivity ran headlong into the prodigious lethargy of Soviet workers, whose inattention to exacting productivity standards and even the most basic workplace regulations was motivated both by the absence of any workable system of incentives and sanctions and by the seeming unconcern of their superiors.

In the broader perspective, even the most cautious reform efforts on the part of the new regime raised the specter of reopening old and very basic issues about national economic priorities. A seemingly inescapable dilemma of choice faced the new leadership: any serious attempt at structural reforms to modernize the increasingly technologically backward sectors of industry or to revamp the managerial structure to introduce more efficient ways of utilizing material and human resources would encounter widespread opposition from the entrenched bureaucracy and reopen old questions about investment priorities. It took little political insight to see that the tacit bargains about the priority of certain sectors of the economy or the development of selected regions were now open to reassessment, and it took little time for competing claimants to make their wishes known.

Even before his elevation to General Secretary, Andropov had made the themes of improved discipline and cautious reform important elements of his platform. Given the less than complete nature of his victory, however, it is hardly surprising that he moved with relative caution.

In his address to the November 22nd Central Committee plenum, he differed little from the priorities enumerated by the resolution on the 1983 draft plan that had been approved shortly before he spoke. Like similar documents of the Brezhnev era, the resolution placed priority on the food and fuel programs and on improvements in the standard of living, although the theme of improved labor discipline was added as a fourth topic. The General Secretary's opening comments also placed priority on the continued growth of the consumer goods sector and the agro-industrial complexes, although in the following paragraph he echoed Chernenko's promise "to provide the Army and Navy with everything they need." Only late in the text was the theme of labor discipline added much as an afterthought.

Turning to the more basic theme of economic reform, Andropov confessed that he had "no ready recipes" to guide his actions and then cautiously ventured an observation:

A good deal has been said recently about the need to expand the independence of associations, enterprises, collective farms, and state farms. It would seem that the time has come to take up the practical resolution of this question. . . . We must act circumspectly here, conduct experiments if necessary, weigh matters carefully, and take the fraternal countries' experience into account.[26]

Andropov then added, perhaps to reassure those in his audience who feared Chernenko's populist leaning or merely were concerned that reforms would be implemented without proper consultation, that "party organizations, economic managers, and engineering and technical personnel" would take the lead in considering such changes.

The first hint of the campaign for improved discipline came with the beginning of the new year. The transfer of Vitalii Fedorchuk, who had replaced Andropov as head of the KGB, to the Ministry of Internal Affairs signaled the beginnings of the campaign against corruption and poor labor discipline. In the former case, the arrest or dismissal of selected middle- and high-level officials was intended both to end the most blatant instances of corruption and to serve as public notice that party and government officials were no longer immune from examination and punishment. In the latter case, the campaign for increased labor discipline took on the tone of a crusade, with Andropov himself telling factory workers that "although everything cannot be reduced to discipline, that's where we must begin, comrades."[27] The campaign took an ever sharper tone as co-workers were urged to turn in shirkers and absentees and police and other security forces conducted surprise raids in Moscow stores and other public facilities during business hours to catch workers absent from their duties without authorization. By late spring, the highly visible police sweeps had ended, although the press continued to report high-level indictments throughout the bureaucracy and in traditionally corrupt areas such as Georgia and Armenia. Far more exacting regulations concerning labor discipline were also enacted to permit supervisors to withhold bonuses, to cut pay or other benefits, or to demote careless workers, with further guarantees that their questionable records would follow them to future posts.

Andropov's next major pronouncement on the economy came in a lengthy article in the February 1983 edition of *Kommunist,* the party's theoretical journal. Speaking at a more abstract level, he placed the primary blame for the nation's economic woes on the fact that "our efforts to improve and restructure the economic mechanism and the forms and methods of management have been lagging behind the demands posed by the present level of Soviet society's development." Although he cited the impact of agricultural problems, the rising cost of fuel and other raw materials, and the high costs of priority projects in the North and East as contributing causes, Andropov made it clear that the present managerial structure and the style of management were under serious review. Once again he recommended the thorough study of the experience of fraternal socialist countries, calling on an interdepartmental commission created by the previous regime to examine East European reforms to complete its studies. He warned, however, that Soviet planners must "eschew any attempts to manage the economy by methods that are alien to its nature." In an equally cautious observation, he took note of potentially disruptive political and institutional implications of reform measures and warned that any such efforts must "give precise consideration to individual and local interests and to the specific requirements of . . . social groups."[28]

Speaking at a special meeting of republic and territorial party leaders held in Moscow in April, Andropov discussed the state of Soviet agriculture.[29] Without the customary laudatory reference to the Brezhnev food program, he offered a strong endorsement of the agro-industrial associations that were intended to create a greater degree of vertical integration of food producing and processing enterprises. In the face of earlier commentary in the press that in some regions the associations had not taken charge of affairs or that their component ministries and other agencies were resisting integration into the larger administrative whole, Andropov demanded that the local party committees take stronger action to facilitate changes.

In political terms, the April endorsement of the agro-industrial associations signaled an important change in the regime's approach to agricultural problems and can be read as indicating the increasing influence of Mikhail Gorbachev, who had advocated structural reforms in agricultures since his days in the Secretariat. Under the Brezhnev administration, overall investment in agriculture had risen dramatically; clearly one of the highest national priorities, it had been the willing beneficiary of massive investments to mechanize farms, improve production facilities, provide needed commodities such as fertilizer, and create greater financial incentives for collective and state farmers. Yet despite this favored position, agriculture had failed to meet the needs of the nation, in part because of occasionally disastrous weather and more frequently because of poor organization and management. By the end of the Brezhnev era, many economists had begun to argue that continued massive investments would soon or perhaps already had reached a point of diminishing returns. The solution lay not in throwing more money at the problem but rather in improving efficiency through the introduction of production brigades at the farm level — Gorbachev had been closely identified with the production brigade system, in which work teams are simply given overall production targets and permitted great autonomy in the planning of production — and the more efficient integration of production, processing, and distribution networks.

What made economic good sense was politically questionable in the eyes of collective farm officials who would surrender control over the work teams and of traditional enterprise and ministry officials who would see both the prerogatives and patterns of subordination of their agencies altered. Moreover, the long-range implications of Andropov's argument that the key to solving the nation's agricultural problem lay in more efficient organization at all levels were clear to all: if the problem were basically organizational rather than inadequate funding, then it would be possible to redirect investments away from that sector, which had received preferential treatment, toward other more pressing needs. What had begun as an argument seemingly over the efficiency of agriculture had become an argument over basic economic priorities and over agriculture's ability to command the lion's share of new investments.

The Andropov handling of the consumer goods issue suggested a similar approach. The first major pronouncement on the issue came in the form of a joint Central Committee and Council of Ministers resolution in May that deftly avoided any direct reference to whether higher priority would be attached to consumer goods production over other competing priorities and merely referred to the issue of consumer goods as being of "decisive importance."[30] While promises were made for a "substantial increase in the production of consumer goods," the resolution's strongest passages suggested that two of the major causes of the scarcity and poor quality of such goods lay in poor management and lax labor standards. Several individual ministers were singled out for criticism and instructed to put their ministries in order. In referring to steps that must be taken to improve production, the resolution placed the "better use of enterprises' internal reserves" ahead of the promised "additional allocations of raw and other materials and equipment." The message was clear: improvements in this sector would have to be squeezed out of existing material and human resources, and the regime would deal harshly with ministry officials who were unequal to the task.

Further indication of the new administration's thinking on the economy can be drawn from Gorbachev's speech at the 113th anniversary celebration of Lenin's birth. His first major pronouncement on the economy since assuming overall responsibility for economic affairs, the speech introduced two major themes that spelled out new economic priorities. The first established the priority of heavy industry, noting that the "development of heavy industry has been and remains an unconditional prerequisite for the accomplishment of all economic and social tasks." Gorbachev paid particular attention to the importance of the machine building industry, which was the cornerstone of improving the mechanization of Soviet industry. Second, he spoke of the prospects for the "technological reequipment" of the more backward sectors of industry, including machine building, suggesting that priority would now shift away from the development of new industrial capacity — and, implicitly, the new industrial centers in the East and Central Asia — to the refitting and modernization of industrial centers in the European sector and the Urals.

Gorbachev's comments also underscored the deemphasis on agriculture and consumer goods production. While he referred to the fulfillment of the food program as a "most urgent and most important task," he made it clear that improvements were to come through better use of "existing material and technical facilities. . . . " He chided agricultural officials that there "should be fewer references to the weather and so-called objective reasons and more order on the land. . . . " The message for the consumer goods sector was much the same: greater emphasis was to be placed on the more efficient utilization of "reserves," a shorthand way of saying that existing facilities must be employed more efficiently.[31]

Andropov's comments on the economy at the June plenum gave evidence of a further downgrading of the discipline and pro-consumer themes and set the stage for the experiments on greater enterprise autonomy that were to be announced the following month. His message was simple: "we must put what we have in good order" if the economy is to operate more efficiently. He lamented that "we were not vigorous enough, that not infrequently we resorted to half measures and could not overcome the accumulated inertia fast enough." "Now we must make up for what we have lost," he continued. "This will demand, among other things, changes in planning, management, and the economic mechanism, and we are obliged to make such changes in order to enter the new five year period . . . fully armed."[32]

The issue of discipline shifted from the central priority that it had occupied in his earlier comments and was mentioned merely as one of the "component parts" of the overall economic program. In what was almost a glancing reference, Andropov contented himself with the observation that

Mention was made in the report and in the discussion of the struggle to strengthen discipline and order and to increase the organization and responsibility that has gotten underway in the country at the party's initiative. . . .

Without launching a direct attack on the priority of the consumer goods, which he had supported at the November 22nd plenum, Andropov introduced an interesting qualification into the discussion consistent with the deemphasis on this sector:

The formula "raising the living standard" is often used in our country. But sometimes it is interpreted in an oversimplified manner, as meaning only an increase in the population's income and in the production of consumer goods. In reality, the concept of the living standard is much wider and richer.

According to the General Secretary, such "richness" was to include the "steady growth of the people's consciousness and standards, including . . . a standard of reasonable consumption" and "exemplary public order. . . ."[33]

The Brezhnev food program, which had been slighted in the earlier discussion of agricultural reforms, fell to even lower priority in Andropov's comments. It was mentioned in a brief two-sentence reference only late in the text and was given equal billing with the relatively insignificant issue of improved public health.

Three new themes entered into Andropov's economic discourse. The first dealt with the need for a "uniform scientific and technical policy" in industry. Speaking not only of the short-term technical needs of the economy but also of its long-term ability to translate the scientific and technological revolution into a Soviet version of the second industrial revolution, the General Secretary made such scientific advances the key to the future:

A uniform scientific and technical policy is of decisive importance at this point. An enormous amount of work awaits us in the creation of machinery, mechanisms and production processes, both for today and for tomorrow. We have to automate production, ensure the widest possible use of computers and robots and the introduction of flexible processes that make it possible to quickly and effectively retool production for the manufacture of new articles.... All of this will lead to a veritable revolution in our national economy.[34]

Second, Andropov argued that the introduction of new technology was being hampered by a system of rewards and incentives that led managers to avoid the risk of innovation. Factories that experimented with new equipment and processes or whose overall output suffered because of the time lost to retool old production technologies frequently were penalized by higher authorities concerned only with total output or profitability. The safer course of action lay in no action at all; there was little incentive to introduce more efficient production processes when the short-term penalties exceeded the long-term rewards. To correct this situation, Andropov called, as had other Soviet leaders before him, for the creation of "a system of organizational, economic, and moral measures that will give managers and workers ... a stake in the updating of equipment and that will make working in the old way unprofitable."

Third, Andropov stressed the importance of material incentives and warned that the distribution of wealth in a socialist society must be based on the level of a worker's productivity. Implicitly critical of the policy in the Brezhnev years of increasing the wages of industrial workers across the board, the General Secretary reminded his listeners that "every citizen in our society has a right only to that measure of material goods that corresponds to the quantity and quality of his socially useful labor, and only to that measure."

While the General Secretary's call for reforms did little more than to lend a more urgent tone to the need for structural transformations that had been discussed — and even attempted — since the early Kosygin reforms of the mid-1960s, the disclosure that a confidential memorandum prepared by the Institute for Economics and Organization of Industrial Production of the USSR Academy of Sciences urging more extensive changes had received favorable attention within the Andropov camp added to the expectation that serious changes were in the offing. Written by Tatiana Zaslavskaia, a noted reform economist, the memorandum dealt candidly with the declining growth rate of the Soviet economy over the last several decades and lay the blame squarely at the door of the "outdated nature of the system of industrial organization and management . . . [and] the inability of the system to insure complete and efficient utilization of the working and intellectual potential of society." Reflecting that the system had been designed five decades earlier for the tasks of industrial development, it recommended "a profound restructuring of state economic management by abandoning administrative methods, with their high degree of centralized economic decision making, in favor of a transition to truly economic methods of management."[35]

In administrative terms, such changes would require a reduction of the powers of "intermediate levels of management" at the ministry level, where both conservative leadership and parochialism had blocked past attempts to improve efficiency, and the enhancement of the powers and responsibilities of central planners and enterprise-level personnel. The report spoke candidly of the political difficulties of abolishing "many departments, administrations, trusts, corporations, and so forth that have been mushrooming in the past decade." "It stands to reason," it continued, "that executives who now occupy warm places with an ill-defined range of responsibilities but with quite respectable salaries are not happy at this prospect." Even at the enterprise level, where a new freedom of initiative was expected to broaden the opportunities to modernize production methods, only the "better qualified and more vigorous" administrators and workers would welcome such changes; the "less qualified and more inert group of older workers" would likely shrink from the added responsibilities that accompanied the reform.

A month after the June plenum, the Central Committee and the Council of Ministers issued a joint resolution on additional measures to expand the powers of enterprises and production associations.[36] Intended to simplify the indices and guidelines under which enterprises operate, to reward innovative activity, and to grant greater local control over investment for technological modernization and over the wage and bonus funds, the reforms were offered as a solution to the growing propensity of ministry-level officials to encroach on enterprise powers. The resolution reasserted the need for effective centralized planning at the highest levels and reflected the argument made in the Academy of Sciences report that the ministries were to blame for the failure of past reforms. Yet in concept the measures did not break any new ground to grant significantly greater prerogatives to enterprise personnel; the themes of local control of investment and wage funds, as well as the simplification of the factory's success indicators, had been a part of past reform efforts since 1979.

Perhaps in light of the implications of the proffered reforms — and perhaps in light of their political sensitivity — the administration chose to begin cautiously with the limited experimental application of the new measures in the Ministry of Heavy Transport Machinery, the Ministry of the Electrical Equipment Industry, the Ukrainian Ministry of the Food Industry, the Belorussian Ministry of Light Industry, and the Lithuanian Ministry of Local Industry.

Some indication that even this cautious approach may have frightened less adventurous central authorities may be found in the differing interpretations of the actual state of the economy offered by the General Secretary and high level planners. Speaking to party veterans on August 15th, Andropov again spoke of the urgent need "to make up for lost time" and offered the collective self-criticism that "we have not been energetic enough in seeking ways to accomplish new tasks, have frequently resorted to half-hearted measures, and have not been able to overcome built-up inertia quickly enough."[37] Yet at a press conference two days later in which N. K. Baibakov, Chairman of Gosplan, and other leading economic officials discussed the proposed reforms, the primary emphasis fell on the cautious and experimental nature of the new measures. Confirming the "circumspect approach" being taken toward the reforms, Baibakov spoke in a far more positive tone of the combined role of "proven forms and methods of management" and the new "additional measures to expand the rights of production associations. . . ."[38]

Chernenko's views on economic reforms were far more difficult to discern. While he avoided a frontal attack on Andropov's programs, there are subtle indications that he did not share the new General Secretary's penchant for harsh discipline and had serious misgivings about the consequences of stressing heavy industry over the satisfaction of consumer demand. Now principally concerned with ideological questions, he couched his observations in theoretical terms. Speaking at the June plenum, he gave only passing reference to "defects in the economic mechanism" and "unsatisfactory labor productivity." Rather his emphasis fell on the important role of ideology in "mold[ing] a new type of economic thinking that is oriented toward initiative, socialist enterprise, greater responsibility. . . ."[39]

Chernenko's commentary on the nature of developed socialism in the USSR also hinted at differing economic priorities. Whereas Andropov had consistently taken the line that the USSR was only at the beginning stages in the creation of a developed socialist society, implying that extensive reform measures were needed to build a modern industrial infrastructure and stern discipline was required to lead society through this potentially disruptive transition period, Chernenko argued that the nation was further advanced toward a fully mature developed socialist order and well on the road to communism. In economic terms, this would imply that emphasis would shift away from the expansion of modern industry toward the satisfaction of consumer demand, and in political terms, that a more contented and sophisticated populace would respond positively to efforts to lead society through democratic rather than authoritarian means. This was entirely consistent with Chernenko's long-standing argument that the leadership needed to be closely in touch with growing demands for a higher standard of living and greater involvement in government in order to avoid the emergence of a Soviet version of the Solidarity movement that had rocked Poland.[40]

FOREIGN POLICY

Unlike economic policy, the foreign policy initially pursued by the Andropov regime differed little from that of its predecessor. The general deterioration of Soviet–U.S. relations, which began in the latter years of the Carter administration because of the Soviet invasion of Afghanistan and accelerated with the military build-up of the Reagan administration, continued despite Soviet calls for a return to detente. The new leadership soon found itself facing a turning point in East–West relations because of the breakdown of the intermediate nuclear forces (INF) and strategic arms reductions (START) talks and the approaching deployment of U.S. Pershing II and cruise missiles in Western Europe. While it launched new initiatives in its dealings with the People's Republic of China and the Middle East and expressed a tentative hope for a political settlement in Afghanistan, the regime undertook no major revisions of existing policies until it had become apparent that efforts to block deployment of American missiles would prove unsuccessful.

Given the new regime's domestic agenda and the nature of the coalition that backed its rise to power, it is hardly surprising that foreign policy issues should occupy secondary priority or that the conventional wisdom of the

1970s should guide the new leadership. The new regime chose to direct its greatest energies at the problems of economic reform and inefficiency and corruption at home, issues that hopefully not only forged a new coalition on which Andropov could consolidate power but also that forced the USSR to turn inward. The priority given to economic reforms further underscored the leadership's interest in returning to the detente of the mid-1970s and preventing an acceleration of the arms race, especially at the level of intermediate range missile forces, where the Soviets had acquired tactical advantage through the deployment of SS-20 missiles in Western Europe. In the short run, any U.S. challenge to what the Soviets saw as a recently acquired nuclear parity would both force a reassessment of economic priorities between the civilian and defense sectors and risk upsetting the consensus among the senior members of the Politburo about the desirability of detente.

The important role in Andropov's ascension played by Foreign Minister Gromyko and Defense Minister Ustinov further increased the likelihood that the USSR would follow a cautious course aimed at preserving the political and military advantages that had flowed from detente. In political terms, both had been closely identified with a U.S.-centered foreign policy in the 1970s that had permitted the Soviet Union to win recognition as a diplomatic equal on the world stage and to achieve a substantial military build-up even within the framework of arms control efforts. While there had been the usual battles over the allocation of resources to civilian or military ends, a broad consensus existed within the highest party and military circles that detente was a wise policy from both strategic and tactical perspectives.

The most immediate problem facing the new Soviet leadership was the deadlock over arms control efforts. Having rejected a "fatally flawed" SALT II agreement, the Reagan administration shifted the terms of discussion to focus on a new round of talks about strategic weapons now known by the acronym START and a new set of discussions about medium-range missiles known as the INF (intermediate nuclear forces) talks. U.S. positions in both negotiations were hardly conducive to agreement: in the START talks, the Americans scrapped much of the framework of the successfully negotiated but never implemented SALT II agreement and argued instead for deep cuts that weighed disproportionately against the Soviet reliance on its strategic missile forces, and in the INF talks, they initially pursued a "zero option" position that was designed to provide time for the deployment of Pershing II and cruise missiles in Western Europe. While the Soviets ominously warned of counterdeployments and sought to influence potential host nations to reject the placement of U.S. intermediate range weapons on their territory, they continued to call for an improvement in Soviet–U.S. relations.

Andropov's first pronouncements on foreign policy stressed Soviet interest in returning to detente. In his first major address before the Central Committee on November 22nd — a speech that dealt with the nation's economic problems and clearly relegated foreign policy issues to secondary priority — he argued that "the policy of detente is by no means a stage that is over and done with. The future belongs to it."[41] He warned, however, that "we are not a naive people" and rejected "the viewpoint of those who are trying to impress people with the idea that force and weapons decide everything," an ambiguous formulation perhaps directed as much at domestic critics who urged new Soviet armament efforts in light of the U.S. build-up.

Speaking at a ceremony commemorating the 60th anniversary of the formation of the Soviet state a month later, Andropov reiterated proposals dealing with both strategic and intermediate range weapons, including a 25 percent reduction of strategic arms, to be matched by a similar U.S. cutback, and a freeze on the further expansion of strategic arsenals.[42] He also repeated the Soviet pledge to reduce the number of missiles aimed at West European targets to the total of the combined British and French missile forces, a move that would have considerably cut the number of SS-20s but also would have forestalled the deployment of U.S. Pershing II and cruise missiles. He warned, however, that the USSR would respond to further

American advances at both the strategic and intermediate levels with equal build-ups.

By March 1983, however, Andropov's tone had grown more strident. While he continued to urge mutual restraint and to suggest that Reagan's bellicose tone was primarily intended for a domestic audience, he accused the president of "deliberate untruth[s]" in describing Soviet actions and noted that it "does not become those who scuttled the SALT-II Treaty . . . to try to pose as peacemakers. . . . " He warned that the Reagan administration was on a "dangerous path" and lectured on the wisdom of such action:

Questions of war and peace must not be treated so lightly. All attempts to achieve military superiority over the USSR will be unavailing. The Soviet Union will never allow this; it will never be caught unarmed in the face of any threat. Let Washington learn this well. It is time that people there stopped thinking up more and more new ideas on the best way to unleash a nuclear war in the hope of winning it. Doing this is not just irresponsible, it is insane.[43]

Foreign Minister Gromyko and Defense Minister Ustinov soon added their own condemnations to the increasingly sharp attacks on the Reagan administration. At a press conference early in April, the former warned that the "strong words and insults" used by the Reagan administration "are no way to do business," while the latter warned that the deployment of missiles in Europe would not go "unpunished" and bring "retribution" directly against the United States in the event of war in Europe.[44]

In mid-April, Andropov acknowledged that the talks on intermediate range missiles were "deadlocked" and expressed the fear that a new arms race was "outdistancing the talks."[45] Just over a week later, he again lectured the Reagan administration on the implications of the deployment of Pershing II and cruise missiles, his comments conveying a growing fear about the destabilizing role of such weapons:

We are now at a very crucial point: One has only to pull the string, and the ball will start rolling. The deployment of American Pershing and cruise missiles in Western Europe is capable of playing such a role. If, after all arguments of reason notwithstanding, matters come to this, a chain reaction is inevitable. The USSR, the GDR, and the other Warsaw Treaty member countries will be compelled to take retaliatory measures.[46]

On August 18, in his last public appearance, Andropov took a more conciliatory tone in a meeting with nine visiting U.S. senators. While he characterized the current state of Soviet–U.S. relations as "tense in virtually all fields," he emphasized that success at the Geneva talks was still possible if the U.S. side would accept the Soviet proposal to limit the number of intermediate range missiles to a balance of forces between the combined British and French arsenals on the NATO side and an equivalent number of SS-20s.[47] Andropov also devoted greater attention to the militarization of outer space, offering to dismantle the primitive Soviet antisatellite weapon system in exchange for an American pledge not to develop similar weapons.

A week later, he offered another concession to forestall the deployment of American missiles. In his answers to questions posed by *Pravda,* Andropov promised to dismantle all Soviet intermediate range missiles as a part of an overall reduction to cut the number of SS-20s to the combined British and French levels. Previous positions had merely spoken of their removal from the European theater, posing the threat that they would be redeployed in Asia or held in reserve closer to potential Western targets.[48]

The worsening tone of Soviet–U.S. relations received another sharp setback on the night of August 31st/September 1st when Korean airlines flight 007 was shot down while in Soviet airspace. While it seems likely that the decision to bring down the aircraft was made by the regional commander, the response of higher Soviet authorities in the first week after the crisis revealed both confusion on how to deal with such an embarrassingly aggressive act at a time when the Kremlin was attempting to blunt U.S. rearmament efforts and an apparent lack of leadership that may have resulted from Andropov's declining health. The initial official response came from low-level figures within the Foreign Ministry and Ministry of Defense, and it was not until September 7th that Soviet officials acknowledged publicly that they had intercepted the plane. Even when the Kremlin responded with greater candor more than a week after the crisis, the burden of explanation fell to Marshall Ogarkov, Chief of the General Staff and First Deputy Minister of Defense.[49]

Perhaps more important was the impact of the KAL 007 crisis on the tone of Soviet–U.S. relations. Predictably the Reagan administration condemned Soviet action in the sharpest possible tones, and the Kremlin responded in kind, accusing the U.S. leader of "pathological anticommunism" and charging that the destruction of the plane was being used as a cause celebre to destroy all hope of agreement in Geneva.[50] Holding to its line that the USSR had acted properly to defend its airspace against a blatant espionage mission, Soviet commentators sharpened their attacks on U.S. motives and on the president himself.[51]

Accusing the United States of pursuing a "militaristic course," Andropov soon offered the sharpest personal attack on Reagan yet heard. Rejecting the moral outrage of the West over the KAL 007 incident as blatant hypocrisy, the statement charged Reagan with

heaping mountains of slander on the Soviet Union and on socialism as a social system, and the tone is being set by the U.S. President himself. It must be said straight out that it's a sorry sight when, setting themselves the goal of denigrating the Soviet people, the leaders of such a country as the U.S. resort to what amounts to foul language, alternating this with hypocritical preaching about morality and humaneness.[52]

Despite the escalation of the verbal confrontation, a month later Soviet authorities linked a final concession on overall intermediate weapons levels with an ominous warning. In a statement issued in the name of the ailing Andropov, the USSR reiterated its willingness to limit the number of SS-20s to that of the combined British and French forces and then added the concession that it was willing to deal with the issue of strategic aircraft capable of reaching Soviet targets by "establish[ing] for the USSR and for NATO equal aggregate levels of medium-range delivery planes in a mutually acceptable quantitative range, even if these levels differ substantially from our earlier proposal."[53] Observing optimistically that if U.S. negotiators "were to display a genuine desire to reach a mutually acceptable accord, not much time would be required to work out an agreement," the Soviet statement offered an ominous warning:

Everything should be perfectly clear on this point: The appearance of new American missiles in Western Europe will make the continuation of the talks now underway in Geneva impossible. On the other hand, the Geneva talks can be continued if the U.S. does not begin the actual deployment of the missiles.[54]

After a brief flurry of hope that the two sides might reach agreement based on informal exchanges between the heads of the two delegations, Soviet officials rejected such overtures as American ploys to "create an illusion of progress" and withdrew from the Geneva talks on intermediate nuclear forces and subsequently from the START talks on strategic weapons and the Vienna-based talks on Mutual and Balanced Force Reductions, both of which had also deadlocked.[55] In his statement concerning the withdrawal, Andropov abrogated Soviet commitments to observe a moratorium on the deployment of new SS-20s in Eastern Europe and announced plans to accelerate the placement of such weapons in Czechoslovakia and the German Democratic Republic. He also announced the deployment of Soviet submarine launched missiles to create a situation in which the threat to the American homeland "would be equal to the threat the American missiles that are being deployed in Europe will create for us. . . . "[56]

Soviet withdrawal from the talks froze Soviet–U.S. relations at a level of hostility and recrimination that remained unchanged until after Andropov's death. Speaking at the Stockholm Conference on Confidence and Security Building Measures and Disarmament in Europe, Foreign Minister Gromyko lamented the "dangerous slide toward the abyss" and accused the United States of "flagrant violations . . . of its commitments under international treaties and accords."[57] In his last statement on foreign policy, Andropov demanded that the United States "show a readiness to return to the situation that existed before the deployment of the Pershing II and cruise missiles began." Accusing Washington of lacking serious intent in the arms talks, he lamented that

From all indications, the American leadership has not renounced its intention to conduct talks with us from a position of strength, from a position of threats and pressure. We resolutely reject such an approach. In general, moreover, attempts to conduct "power diplomacy" with us are futile.[58]

Soviet policy toward other nations showed greater flexibility under the brief Andropov regime, although new initiatives sometimes proved incapable of solving old dilemmas. Such was the case with Soviet involvement in Afghanistan, where efforts to pursue a military disengagement and a diplomatic neutralization of that nation produced no results. Speaking with Pakistani President Zia-ul-Haq shortly after Brezhnev's funeral, Andropov reiterated Soviet interest in indirect peace talks sponsored by the United Nations, and a *Pravda* editorial soon pointed out that "from the beginning, it was officially announced that the military assistance was limited and temporary in nature" and called for a "political settlement" that provided for an end to "foreign intervention" and the creation of a "neutral and nonaligned state. . . . "[59] Andropov expressed his own hopes for such talks in April 1983, although he charged that they were "proceeding with difficulty" because of American inspired Pakistani intransigence.[60] Two rounds of these negotiations were held in April and June, and it was rumored that the outlines of a tentative agreement had been reached. Yet despite such hopeful soundings from Moscow and Kabul, Soviet forces continued to strengthen their military presence and extend their control over virtually all aspects of Afghani internal affairs.[61]

The new leadership continued a policy begun in the last years of the Brezhnev administration of seeking improved relations with the People's Republic of China, whose foreign minister, Huang Hua, was singled out for attention in the meetings that followed Brezhnev's funeral.[62] Weeks later, in his comments to the November Central Committee plenum,

Andropov spoke of the need for "common sense" and noted that his administration was "paying great attention to every positive response from the Chinese side."[63] Both sides toned down their rhetorical attacks on each other, and a second round of normalization talks was held in March 1983, in Moscow. While the talks produced no results on important issues such as the Soviet presence in Afghanistan and Mongolia and Soviet-backed Vietnamese action in Kampuchea, they did discuss force reductions and confidence building measures along the Sino–Soviet border. Reportedly a Soviet offer to sign a nonaggression treaty with Beijing was turned aside by the Chinese because of lack of progress in other areas. Despite the lack of positive action on the central issues, both sides agreed to a third round of talks, and parallel negotiations on commercial relations provided for an increase in trade.[64] Cultural relations also improved in the year after Brezhnev's death, and friendship delegations and research teams began once again to exchange visits.[65]

Andropov further sought to underscore his interest in improved ties with Beijing in his answers to questions from *Pravda,* published on August 27th. Noting some "positive tendencies" in Sino–Soviet ties, he called for an even greater volume of trade and for economic, scientific, and technical cooperation and closer ties in cultural affairs, sports, and other areas.[66] The positive tone was carried forward through the visit to Beijing of Deputy Foreign Minister Mikhail Kapitsa in September. A Sinologist with extensive experience in the People's Republic before the break, Kapitsa reassured his hosts that the Soviet Union was interested in improved economic ties and would not transfer SS-20 missiles withdrawn from the European theater to Asia.[67] Despite these overtures, a third round of direct talks held in Beijing in October produced no results on the central issues of borders, Afghanistan, or Kampuchea, although the earlier trend toward improved economic and cultural ties continued.[68]

Although overshadowed by the U.S. deployment of Pershing II and cruise missiles, Soviet relations with Western Europe provided some hints that the Kremlin sought new openings. Despite blatant meddling in the West German campaign in the spring of 1983 and their preference for a Social Democratic government that would oppose deployment, the Soviet government attempted to recoup at least a part of its losses by mending fences with the reelected Kohl government over the summer, and the German chancellor visited the USSR in July.[69] Moscow's relations with the equally conservative Thatcher government in Great Britain remained at a low ebb, however, with the only official diplomatic exchange of emissaries occurring in the visit of a junior Foreign Office official to Moscow in April 1983.[70]

The new administration also sought improved relations with France, which under Mitterrand had held the Soviets at arm's length because of Afghanistan and Poland and declared its support for the deployment of U.S. missiles. Despite this chill, the two reached an agreement on improved economic ties in January 1983. The following month Foreign Minister Claude Cheysson visited Moscow, only to return to Paris with strongly negative impressions of the new Soviet leader, who was "lacking in human warmth."[71]

Both sides remained unyielding on the status of the independent French nuclear force, with the Soviets insisting that it fall under any accord reached with the Americans on intermediate missiles and the French demanding that it retain its separate character. A further blow to Franco–Soviet ties fell in April when Paris expelled 47 Soviet officials for espionage.[72]

A new Soviet effort to break the deadlock came in September, when Gromyko stopped in Paris on his way to the Helsinki follow-up conference in Madrid. A mission already postponed at French request because of the KAL 007 incident, Gromyko's visit had little impact, due both to Moscow's preoccupation with the missile-deployment issue and Mitterrand's continuing reluctance to edge closer to the Soviet Union.[73] While First Deputy Premier Ivan Arkhipov's visit to Paris produced an economic agreement in the last month of Andropov's rule, Franco–Soviet relations remained at one of their coolest levels throughout the brief tenure of the new General Secretary.[74]

In the Middle East, the new regime moved quickly to improve relations with the Arab world. In December 1982 Andropov met with an Arab League delegation headed by King Hussein and endorsed its plan for peace in the region. Particular attention was given to the Saudi delegate, Foreign Minister Saud al-Faisal, who was granted a private meeting with Gromyko, marking the first high-level exchange between Saudi and Soviet officials. Moscow also edged away from its strict neutrality in the Iran–Iraq war, and arms shipments to Baghdad were increased. Overtures were also made toward Egypt, with which no formal ties had existed since the expulsion of the Soviet ambassador in September 1981. Anatolii Gromyko, the foreign minister's son and a noted expert on African affairs, was sent on an exploratory mission to Cairo, and an economic mission soon followed.[75]

Moscow also quickly sought to improve its relations with the PLO, which had been strained since the mild Soviet reaction to the Israeli invasion of Lebanon. Yasser Arafat visited Moscow in January 1983 to meet the new leader. The Soviet Union also strengthened its ties with Syria, its closest Middle East ally, by providing SAM-5 anti-aircraft missiles to Damascus to replace less sophisticated weaponry that had been destroyed during the war in Lebanon; previously such advanced weapons had not been positioned outside the Soviet Union.[76]

Despite its heightened interest in the region, Moscow was not able to secure a role in the peace process, although informal consultations between Soviet and U.S. officials occurred in September 1983, in spite of the general chill in relations that resulted from the KAL 007 incident. On the eve of Andropov's death, Geidar Aliev, a Politburo member and first deputy premier, was scheduled to visit Syria and possibly other locations, but the trip was cancelled because of the General Secretary's death.[77]

In Africa, the Soviet commitment to Angola deepened, and in January 1983 Moscow announced that it would increase military aid to the Cuban-trained army, which had fared poorly in recent clashes with South African forces. Despite these efforts, Angola reached a separate agreement with South Africa for military disengagement along the

Namibian–Angolan frontier in February, 1984, and Mozambique, another close Soviet ally, signed a similar nonaggression agreement with Pretoria shortly thereafter.[78] Relations with the government of Mengistu Haile Mariam in Ethiopia also deteriorated throughout 1983, in part because of preoccupation with the nation's domestic problems and in part because of pressure from Moscow to create a Soviet-style regime in Addis Ababa. A low point was reached in February 1984 with the expulsion of two Soviet diplomats, reputedly including the KGB station chief.[79]

A BIPARTISAN FOREIGN POLICY?

Despite the incomplete nature of Andropov's victory in November and the obvious jockeying for position that occurred as his health worsened, there is little indication that such differences affected the basic line of Soviet foreign policy. Preoccupied with the deployment of U.S. missiles, the new leadership found even its best intentioned efforts to build better ties to Western Europe subsumed under its concern over worsening Soviet–U.S. ties. On the critical issue of superpower relations, the new general secretary, Foreign Minister Andrei Gromyko, and Defense Minister Dmitrii Ustinov were of virtually identical minds. Gromyko's comments unfailingly reflected the general deterioration of the relationship. At a press conference on April 2, 1983, he noted the harsh tone of the Reagan administration's condemnation of the USSR as a "center of evil" but then called upon Washington to

take a more objective approach to questions of Soviet–American relations and to understand that normal or, even better, good relations between the U.S. and the Soviet Union are not only in the interests of the international situation as a whole but also in the interests of the American people.[80]

By mid-summer, his tone had grown sharper. Speaking to the Supreme Soviet shortly after the June Central Committee plenum, he offered a more strident indictment of U.S. intentions, accusing Washington of preaching a "cult of force in international relations and aspiring to remake the world to their own standards. . . . "[81] While he repeated the Soviet intention to maintain military parity with the United States even in the face of the deployment of Pershing II and cruise missiles in Europe, he expressed the hope that relations would return to an "even keel" and regretted that "differences in the social systems of states and ideological divergences are being turned into a foundation on which foreign policy is built and questions of war and peace are resolved."

By January 1984, shortly after the deployment of U.S. missiles had begun, Gromyko's tone had hardened even further to reflect Moscow's extreme displeasure. At the Conference on Confidence and Security Building Measures in Stockholm, he spoke of the current "dangerous slide toward the abyss" and the "fatal nature of a course based on the replacement of cooperation with confrontation. . . . " Seeking to justify Soviet withdrawal from all arms control talks, he qualified Soviet interest in future exchanges with the U.S. side:

We have always favored a political dialogue between the East and the West, and we have no intention of renouncing this position in the future. But, needless to say, our stand assumes that such a dialogue, not in words but in deeds, will be directed toward the easing of tension in the world and the elimination of the danger of war.[82]

Defense Minister Ustinov also reflected the seeming consensus on foreign policy, although his comments throughout the summer and autumn of 1983 predictably made the military's case for greater resources to meet the challenge of the U.S. arms build-up. Perhaps understandably, he stressed the ability of Soviet forces to counterbalance the U.S. initiatives in Europe and promised that "retribution" would follow "against the United States itself" if U.S. intermediate-range missiles struck Soviet territory.[83] But on at least two occasions, he publicly linked the promise of adequate defense with barely concealed demands for increased funds for the military. Speaking at an awards ceremony in Sevastopol early in September, he averred that "the communist party and the Soviet state cannot fail to strengthen the combat might of the armed forces," and in November, he argued that the "sharp exacerbation of the international situation is making ever higher demands on the level of the preparedness of the Soviet armed forces, on the improvement of their management and their technical equipment."[84]

Given his domestic responsibilities for party affairs and the economy, Gorbachev only rarely addressed foreign policy issues. In one such rare reference, in his comments on the anniversary of Lenin's birth, he reiterated the common line that a "war party" had come to power in Washington. Yet he also deviated slightly from the overriding fixation on Soviet–U.S. ties evidenced by some of his colleagues in recommending that the USSR cultivate its relations with "many Western countries" in light of the deteriorating relationship with the United States.[85]

Grigorii Romanov's few comments on foreign affairs reflected a more strident tone, but on the whole, they departed in no significant way from the apparent consensus within the Kremlin. Speaking at the November 7th celebration of the revolution, he mirrored the harsher tone that had emerged from the Kremlin by the late autumn and warned that the deployment of U.S. missiles would result in Soviet countermeasures and an end to the disarmament talks. But he then added that "our armed forces are equipped with everything they need to discourage anyone from staging a test of strength," suggesting that he had little sympathy with Ustinov's request for greater resources. His reluctance to back the military on this issue was surprising in light of his recent appointment as party secretary in charge of the military-industrial complex and his general reputation as a hardliner on foreign policy, and perhaps reflected his efforts to build bridges to more liberal elements who favored economic reforms.[86]

While Chernenko was equally reticent on foreign policy questions, his few public comments suggested that he favored a return to detente. Speaking before the June plenum, where he dealt primarily with ideological issues, he nonetheless criticized the "nuclear madness" of the arms race and argued that the Soviet Union should "uphold the principles of peaceful coexistence and detente."[87] Consistent with his well-known preferences for consumer priorities at home, the emphasis placed on attempting to return to the improved relations of the early 1970s implied a resumption of successful arms control efforts and a reduction of tensions between the superpowers.

NOTES

1. Ilya Zemtsov, *Andropov* (Jerusalem: IRICS Publishers, 1983), p. 94.

2. Mark D. Zlotnik, "Chernenko's platform," *Problems of Communism* 31 (November/December 1982).

3. Yaroslav Bilinsky, "Shcherbytskyi, Ukraine, and Kremlin politics," *Problems of Communism* 32 (July/August 1983):1–20.

4. According to some accounts, Gorbachev may have abstained; see Zemtsov, *Andropov,* p. 94.

5. Ibid.

6. *Pravda,* November 13, 1982.

7. *Pravda,* November 12, 1982.

8. Zemtsov, *Andropov,* pp. 96–98.

9. *Pravda,* December 22, 1982.

10. Zemtsov, *Andropov,* p. 104.

11. *Pravda,* November 23, 1982.

12. Zhores A. Medvedev, *Andropov* (New York: Norton, 1983), p. 115; and Zemtsov, *Andropov,* p. 125.

13. Jonathan Steele and Eric Abraham, *Andropov in Power* (Garden City: Anchor, 1983), p. 161.

14. *Pravda,* June 16, 1983.

15. Ibid.

16. Radio Liberty Research Bulletin (hereafter "Radio Liberty"), 330/83, August 31, 1983.

17. Radio Liberty, 339/83, September 9, 1983.

18. Radio Liberty, 64/84, February 10, 1984.

19. Radio Liberty, 283/83, July 27, 1983.

20. Radio Liberty, 330/83, August 31, 1983.

21. *Pravda,* November 6, 1983.

22. Ibid.

23. Radio Liberty, 481/83, December 26, 1983.

24. *Kommunist* (no. 15, 1983); and Mark Zlotnik, "Chernenko succeeds," *Problems of Communism* 33 (March/April 1984):17–31.

25. Zlotnik, "Chernenko succeeds."

26. *Pravda,* November 23, 1982.

27. *Pravda,* February 1, 1983.

28. *Kommunist* (no. 3, 1983).
29. *Pravda,* April 19, 1983.
30. *Pravda,* May 7, 1983.
31. *Pravda,* April 23, 1983.
32. *Pravda,* June 16, 1983.
33. Ibid.
34. Ibid.
35. *New York Times,* August 5, 1983.
36. *Pravda,* July 26, 1983.
37. *Pravda,* August 16, 1983.
38. *Izvestiia,* August 18, 1983.
39. *Pravda,* June 16, 1983.
40. Radio Liberty, 206/83, May 25, 1983.
41. *Pravda,* November 23, 1982.
42. *Pravda,* December 22, 1982.
43. *Pravda,* March 27, 1983.
44. *Pravda,* April 3 and 7, 1983.
45. *Pravda,* April 25, 1983.
46. *Pravda,* May 4, 1983.
47. *Pravda,* August 19, 1983.
48. *Pravda,* August 27, 1983.
49. *Pravda,* September 10, 1983.
50. *Pravda,* September 7, 1983.
51. *Pravda,* September 4, 5, and 6, 1983.
52. *Pravda,* September 29, 1983.
53. *Pravda,* October 27, 1983.
54. Ibid.
55. *Pravda,* November 22, 1983.
56. *Pravda,* November 25, 1983.
57. *Pravda,* January 19, 1984.
58. *Pravda,* January 25, 1984.
59. *Pravda,* December 16, 1983.
60. *Pravda,* April 25, 1983.
61. Radio Liberty, 418/83, November 8, 1983.
62. Radio Liberty, 88/83, February 22, 1983.
63. *Pravda,* November 23, 1983.
64. Radio Liberty, 127/83, March 22, 1983.
65. Radio Liberty, 265/83, July 12, 1983.
66. *Pravda,* August 27, 1983.
67. Radio Liberty, 340/83, September 9, 1983.
68. Radio Liberty, 414/83, November 3, 1983.
69. Radio Liberty, 254/83, July 1, 1983.
70. Radio Liberty, 131/94, March 27, 1984.
71. Radio Liberty, 142/83, April 6, 1983.
72. Ibid.
73. Radio Liberty, 333/83, September 2, 1983.

74. Radio Liberty, 45/84, January 27, 1984.
75. Radio Liberty, 31/83, January 13, 1983.
76. Ibid.
77. Radio Liberty, 92/84, February 23, 1984.
78. Radio Liberty, 33/84, January 18, 1984, and 133/84, March 29, 1984.
79. Radio Liberty, 133/84, March 29, 1984.
80. *Pravda,* April 3, 1983.
81. *Pravda,* June 17, 1983.
82. *Pravda,* January 19, 1984.
83. *Pravda,* April 7 and July 31, 1983.
84. *Pravda,* September 10 and November 19, 1983.
85. *Pravda,* April 23, 1983.
86. *Pravda,* November 6, 1983.
87. *Pravda,* June 15, 1983.

4   Chernenko in Power

CHERNENKO'S ASCENSION TO POWER

The death of Yuri Andropov on February 9, 1984, marked the end of the long deathwatch that had preoccupied Kremlin leaders for virtually the last half of his brief tenure in office. Although his medical condition had been cloaked in secrecy and disinformation during the long months of absence from public view, the medical bulletin that accompanied the announcement of his death was explicit and revealing. It disclosed that the General Secretary had succumbed to a host of maladies and that kidney failure had caused him to be placed on dialysis as early as February 1983.[1]

Although the approaching succession had been obvious to all, Andropov's death caught Kremlin leaders in a deep internal division about the choice of a new leader. It is unlikely that Chernenko's supporters constituted a majority within the Politburo at the time of Andropov's death and highly probable that the former General Secretary's reformist coalition split apart in the absence of his firm leadership. The naming of a successor was delayed for several days, suggesting that considerable time was required both to confirm the choice of a new General Secretary and to work out the political arrangements that would characterize his leadership.

The months that preceded Andropov's death had been marked by signs of increasing infighting among Soviet leaders. From September onward, when Andropov could not take part in the regular weekly meetings of the Politburo, a careful political balance was reached in which the sessions were chaired in turn by Chernenko, Romanov, and Gorbachev.[2] Yet despite his absence, the ailing leader was still able to secure the appointment of his allies to the Politburo at the December plenum. The advancement of Vitaly Vorotnikov to full Politburo membership, of Viktor Chebrikov to candidate membership, and of Egor Ligachev to the Secretariat signaled the political strength of the Andropov coalition, as did the replacement of 16 *oblast* first secretaries in December and January. Two of Gorbachev's protégés who had served with him in the agriculture department won appointment to important regional offices during the same period. A sharp attack on corruption within the Moldavian party organization in December was a thinly veiled attack on Chernenko and the Brezhnev legacy, because of their close association with that republic.[3]

Chernenko's rising political fortunes were evident shortly before Andropov's death. Late in January, he and Tikhonov signed obituaries of two high ranking officials ahead of the normal alphabetical listing, and he was second only to Andropov in the number of districts in which he was nominated as a candidate in the approaching Supreme Soviet elections. In the subsequent list of names of candidates, which was published out of alphabetical order, Chernenko came immediately after Andropov and Tikhonov.[4] A new and expanded edition of Chernenko's collected articles and speeches was published early in the year and reviewed in glowing terms in a *Pravda* editorial only one day before Andropov's demise.[5]

Whatever the political machinations that preceded Andropov's death, the events of the first few days of the post-Andropov interregnum suggested that the choice of a new leader was proving to be difficult. Although Andropov's long anticipated death occurred on February 9, the Politburo did not name Chernenko to head of the funeral commission until the following day, and the public announcement was delayed until the 11th. Although this strongly hinted that Chernenko was the likely successor — Andropov had headed

Brezhnev's funeral commission, just as Khrushchev had been chosen for the honor after Stalin's death — the final choice was not made public until the Central Committee plenum on February 13th, resulting in the longest formal transition in party history.

During the brief interregnum there were clear signs of conflict. The postponement itself suggests either that there was dissension on the selection of Chernenko or, more likely, that there was intense bargaining between the old guard and the younger figures who had risen under Andropov over the division of responsibilities within the new leadership. Evidence suggests that the Politburo was in virtually constant session from the 9th onward and possibly that key members of the leadership were excluded from important sessions.[6] Further evidence of division comes from the inconsistent treatment accorded Gorbachev, whose prominent role at the Central Committee plenum on the 13th was obscured in the initial press coverage.[7]

The most likely divisions during those critical days lay only partially along generational lines. Rather the initial line-up probably saw differences of opinion both among the older members of the Politburo and also among the newer and presumably ambitious members added during Andropov's brief rule. For one thing, the Politburo had undergone important changes over the 16 months since Brezhnev's death. The old guard's control had diminished as a consequence of attrition and the appointment of new members. Since Brezhnev's death, two senior members had departed, Kirilenko through forced resignation at the time of Andropov's rise and Pelshe, who died in office. Three new members had joined the body: Aliev, whose career likely linked him to the Andropov faction; Vorotnikov, whose slipping career prospects at Brezhnev's hands were rescued by Andropov; and Solomentsev, who also likely resented that Brezhnev had left him languishing as a candidate member of the Politburo.

A counting of heads suggests that the old guard alone would have found it difficult to elect Chernenko. As best we can calculate, he could have counted on only five votes from this group, which constituted less than a majority of the 12 surviving members of the Politburo. In addition to his own vote, he is likely to have received support from Gromyko, Ustinov, Kunaev, and Tikhonov. Shcherbitskii, the Ukrainian party leader and another member of the old guard, would probably have opposed his rise because of the poor treatment accorded him by Chernenko's mentor, Brezhnev, and there is evidence that an effort was made to exclude him from the initial deliberations. The only other possible support from the old guard might have come from Grishin, the Moscow party secretary, whose own ambitions to be General Secretary make his position difficult to judge. Thus only a scenario in which Grishin backed Chernenko from the beginning and Shcherbitskii was absent from the key Politburo sessions would have given Chernenko a majority composed of his cohorts among the old guard.

There is a more likely scenario, however, linking the minority faction of senior figures who backed Chernenko with one or perhaps several of the younger members of the Politburo who saw themselves as viable candidates for General Secretary after a brief period in office by an admittedly ill new leader. The old guard would join in such a coalition to secure Chernenko's appointment and to divide the former Andropov group. The younger coalition partners' motivation is also easy to guess: none of the presumed heirs apparent — Gorbachev, Romanov, and possibly Aliev — would think it in his best interest to enter into an intense battle with the others or to split completely from the senior leadership unless he thought it likely he would win the General Secretary post at this time, and this was an unlikely scenario given the support for Chernenko and the likelihood that none of the younger members who hoped to ride out a brief Chernenko regime would have accepted a solution that placed any of the others into office for a decade or more of rule. Since it was likely that the former Andropov coalition that linked both older members of the Politburo with the new appointees split apart with the death of its leader, the more plausible strategy lay in both blocking the emergence of any other long-term successor and securing the most advantageous position within the new hierarchy.

This scenario is all the more likely if one assumes that Gorbachev was the presumed frontrunner among the younger candidates. By the summer of 1983, he was the fastest rising figure in top party circles; he had been closely associated with the deceased General Secretary, who had expanded his domestic and foreign policy responsibilities and, more importantly, placed him in a position to supervise appointments to party and state posts. But he also had weaknesses, chief among them his association with agriculture and his lack of ties to heavy industry and the military. Even if Gorbachev did not actively bid for the top post, his status as Andropov's protégé would have made him vulnerable to a stop-the-frontrunner coalition.

The long delay in announcing the new leader suggests that one of two scenarios was being played out within the top leadership. Either Gorbachev and possibly Romanov among the younger leaders had made a bid for power and was defeated after prolonged conflict, or there was early acceptance of Chernenko's rise and much time was consumed in striking various bargains with key figures in the Politburo in return for their endorsement of this arrangement. While we cannot be certain which occurred, the evidence supports the conclusion that the second scenario is closer to the mark. One thing that did not occur during Chernenko's tenure is significant: none of the senior figures such as Gromyko or Ustinov or younger leaders such as Gorbachev or Romanov were reduced in stature, and no new members were added to the Politburo to challenge their authority. Indeed, all seemingly emerged with enhanced powers. Gromyko and Ustinov were all the more active as spokesmen on questions of foreign and military policy, and Romanov received increased powers through his control of defense-related industries. But clearly the biggest winner was Gorbachev, who not only emerged as the key secretary in charge of ideology — the presumed stepping stone to General Secretary — but also was soon acknowledged as the third-ranking member of the hierarchy after Chernenko and Tikhonov and de facto second secretary within the party apparatus.

By the Central Committee plenum held on February 13, the arrangements had come into place, and Nikolai Tikhonov, a long-standing Brezhnev ally who was not himself a candidate for the top party post, was entrusted with the task of nominating Chernenko. His selection lends further support to the argument that there had been no serious challenger who attempted to take the nomination away from Chernenko; in such cases, the losing candidate would have offered the nomination as a gesture of unity, as had occurred when Chernenko nominated Andropov just over a year before.

Tikhonov's nominating speech was an exercise in careful balance. While he lauded Andropov's achievements and the significance of the November 1982 Central Committee plenum, reference to which had become the catchword for identification with reform efforts, he avoided effluent praise of the fallen leader and stressed the importance of the Brezhnev dominated 26th Party Congress rather than the November plenum in setting forth the party line. In similar fashion, his description of the incoming General Secretary was straightforward and without excessive praise. Chernenko was lauded as a person of broad experience, with a particular penchant for strengthening party ties with the masses and for "his ability to unite comrades for harmonious collective work."[8]

Chernenko's speech to the plenum did little to suggest that major changes were in the offing. Indeed, his comments promised loyalty to the reformist and anti-corruption programs of his predecessor, although he offered his own special twist on how such changes were to be accomplished. In assessing the impact of his predecessor, he took the position that the reformist November plenum had offered "further creative development" to the line established at the 26th congress, a subtle formulation that suggested that he took a position on the question of economic and social reforms closer to that of the Andropov faction than to the conservative Tikhonov, who had reversed the reference in his nomination.[9]

Chernenko was quick to stress the themes of the party's separate political identity and its unique role in mobilizing the masses. Arguing for a clear demarcation of the role of party bodies and state administrative agencies, he asserted that the party must remain an instrument of "political leadership" rather than day-to-day economic management. He reasserted a vaguely populist theme that had long been at the center of his approach to party leadership in maintaining that contact with the people had been "the most important source of the strength of the party" and further that "our economy owes every one of its major achievements" to the activism of the masses.

Both arguments were meant to serve a dual political purpose. On the one hand, insistence on preserving the party's uniquely political role was a transparent attempt to draw the support of the party apparatus to his side. Andropov's appointments had slighted the conventional apparatus and drawn instead from sources in the state bureaucracy and the KGB. Moreover, the proffered economic reforms ran the political risk of vesting increasing powers into the hands of professional economic managers, a prospect that undoubtedly concerned even the most forward looking *apparatchiki*. Chernenko's attention to the distinctly political role of the party was therefore a tacit argument to preserve not only that institution's special place within the system but also to suggest that its style of leadership would transcend the mundane functioning of even the most reformed agencies.

On the other hand, Chernenko's emphasis on the importance of the party's ties with the masses was meant both to assert his own brand of reformism and to underscore even further the party's role in mobilizing popular action. In terms of its reformist implications the argument held both that greater attention must be given to public opinion and that increased popular involvement in consultative and quasi-administrative activities through workers' collectives and public organizations would foster grassroots reformist sentiment and act as a check on and hopefully a prod to the conservative bureaucracy.

Chernenko's comments on the proposed economic reforms were no less forceful than his predecessor's. He repeated the formulation that the economy was in need of "serious restructuring" and promised that work in this area "has only just begun." And while he expressed understandable caution and a desire "to look before you leap," he chided managers who were merely marking time during the experimental phase of the reforms and who "have no wish whatsoever to reckon with changed conditions and life's new requirements."

Chernenko did not directly address the issue of investment priorities, although he offered a veiled reference to the significance of improved consumer goods production by pointing out that the further maturation of Soviet society required a "firm foundation of economic and social policy." The military fared less well in terms of economic concerns; although he pledged that the military would have sufficient armaments "to cool the hot heads of bellicose adventurists" in the Reagan administration, his treatment of the issue implied that the American arms build-up had not yet upset the existing equilibrium of strategic forces, a formulation that suggested that no reallocation of resources was presently necessary.

Chernenko's rhetoric on the anti-corruption and discipline campaigns was milder than the strident indictments offered by his predecessor. But while he limited himself to the observation that "disorderliness and irresponsibility" have been costly to society, he pledged that there would be "no slackening of effort" in the regime's attempts to deal with corruption and restore discipline in the economy.

THE NEW HIERARCHY

Evidence that the succession had produced a carefully arranged new hierarchy combining both the old guard and the newer appointees soon emerged. Gorbachev's posture as the third person in the leadership and the de facto second secretary within the party was confirmed by the eventual disclosure that he had offered the closing remarks at the February 13th plenum that elected Chernenko and from the preferential timing of his address to his constituents, when he spoke third in rank, followed only by Tikhonov and the new General Secretary himself. The timing of the comments of other key Politburo members suggested the new arrangement. Gorbachev's speech was published on March 1st, preceded by Defense Minister Ustinov's on February 29th, Foreign Minister Gromyko's on the 28th, and Romanov's and Grishin's on the 26th, with lesser figures speaking earlier.

The description of the new leadership by two Politburo members on diplomatic missions presented almost the same picture. During visits to Syria and India, Aliev and Ustinov separately presented the same official greetings to the host governments from Chernenko, Tikhonov, Gromyko, and unnamed "other leaders." Ustinov's omission from the list is less significant than Gorbachev's absence; the former could hardly be expected to include himself, and Aliev's reflection of the same hierarchy suggests that the formulation had been carefully prepared in advance. While Gorbachev's absence is technically correct since he held no formal post in government dealing with foreign affairs at the time, in political terms his omission suggests that the old guard maintained control over foreign policy.[10]

With the new hierarchy in place, Chernenko used the occasion of the April 10th Central Committee plenum to strike a balanced tone that combined reformist and conservative themes. While he argued for the reduction in the size of managerial agencies across the board, he offered hope that the search for "new forms and structures of economic activity" would not "divert us from the more efficient use of existing management institutions." He assured his listeners that "putting existing capacities fully into action will be enough."[11] He also forcefully reasserted his argument for greater involvement of the masses in quasi-administrative activities and called for a larger role for the local soviets, especially in monitoring economic and governmental agencies at the grassroots level.

While there were no significant personnel changes at the April plenum, the General Secretary pointed out that a new party congress would be held "soon" and that the leadership should begin to consider "questions of present-day policy concerning personnel." The remark underscored what top leaders already knew: the approaching election of delegates to the congress and the subsequent selection of a new Central Committee could well shape the future of the party beyond the present leadership.

The Supreme Soviet session that followed confirmed that the new leadership combined both old and new elements and completed Chernenko's formal consolidation of power. The General Secretary was elected Chairman of the Presidium of the Supreme Soviet (or "president" of the Soviet state), and it was disclosed after the session that he had also assumed the chairmanship of the Defense Council. In terms of positions within both party and state, he now equalled his two immediate predecessors.

The session also named Gorbachev chairman of the Foreign Affairs Commission of the Council of the Union, a post usually held by the de facto second secretary. In the past, this chairmanship has also been held by the party secretary in charge of ideology, a position that emerged as an important stepping stone in the Brezhnev and Andropov successions. Gorbachev's new assignment in foreign affairs and possibly ideology further expanded his responsibilities, leaving him the only secretary dealing with internal party, economic, and foreign policy concerns. Further indication of Gorbachev's new authority came from his selection to nominate Chernenko for the presidency, a contrast to the striking solidarity of the old guard when Tikhonov was chosen to nominate him for general secretary only two months earlier.[12]

Despite the fact that both the plenum and the Supreme Soviet session had occurred without unexpected personnel changes and that the new leadership had put forth a united front, the agreement was more apparent than real. A close reading of the pre-election speeches of top leaders indicated significant differences of tone and content. Perhaps understandably, the remaining members of the Brezhnev entourage stressed the themes of continuity, the "achievements" of the Brezhnev administration, and caution on economic reforms. Only Gromyko and Ustinov, whose positions in the new hierarchy suggested that they had come to terms with the Andropov faction, mixed praise of the Brezhnev years with positive comments about his successor. Other members of the old guard were less generous in their assessment of the events of the last 16 months. Ivan Kapitonov, who under Andropov lost his post in charge of party cadres and was shifted to the less significant task of managing light industry, stressed continuity with the policies of the 25th and 26th Party Congresses, suggesting loyalty to the Brezhnev legacy. The Kazakhstan party leader, Dinmukhamed Kunaev, reflecting the same priorities, praised Chernenko as a leader "of the type of L. I. Brezhnev and Yu. V. Andropov." Nikolai Tikhonov virtually ignored the Andropov interregnum in his comments, mentioning the fallen leader briefly only once, in contrast to his warm praise of Chernenko.[13]

The younger leaders who had risen to prominence under Andropov spoke instead of their impatience to get on with reforms and of the need to place Chernenko's selection as General Secretary into perspective. Gorbachev's comments were typical, lauding the "positive changes" that had occurred since the November 1982 plenum and slighting the Brezhnev legacy. He avoided personal praise of the new leader and instead took note of his dedication to "collective activity," a veiled reference to the evident distribution of authority among top leaders. Egor Ligachev's comments also demanded continued change, noting the "positive changes" and "new, creative situation" that had emerged under Andropov and the need to bring younger leaders into top-level posts. Similar comments came from Vorotnikov, who had risen to new prominence since November 1982, Nikolai Ryzhkov, a Brezhnev appointee to the Secretariat who had earlier advocated economic reforms, and Romanov, the former Leningrad party secretary who had shifted to the Secretariat under Andropov.[14]

In April the party's theoretical journal, *Kommunist*, carried further evidence of divisions. Two articles on the negative consequences of party factionalism appeared side by side, one written by Evgenii Bugaev, a conservative ideologist close to Chernenko, and the second by Valentine Chikin, a journalist who had written vigorously on reform themes during Andropov's rule. While both authors decried factionalism and pointed out its deleterious consequences in the past, each seemed to suggest that the other side had been responsible for the rift.[15]

Despite their obvious differences, the diverse elements of the new leadership avoided open skirmishes throughout the summer and early autumn of 1984. The tone of the new administration suggested that Kremlin leaders were delicately balancing the need for continued reform and the hope of more positive change in the future with the need for caution and consensus at the present. The period was marked by contradictory signals from many quarters. On the one hand, the regime declined to press ahead with vigorous economic reforms, although the experiments begun in the previous year were continued. Perhaps more importantly, it avoided raising the delicate political issue of further changes within the leadership itself. No new appointments were made either to the Politburo or Secretariat during Chernenko's brief rule, and there were no significant dismissals from high party circles.

Further evidence of relative stability came from Chernenko's willingness to continue to be served by key foreign policy and economic advisors who had previously worked under Brezhnev and Andropov. Of the six key advisors closest to the new General Secretary, four had served previous administrations, including Andrei Aleksandrov-Agentov, a foreign policy specialist who first joined Brezhnev's entourage in 1961 and shifted to Andropov with the transition, and Arkadii Volsky, who served as an economic advisor to Andropov. Of the remaining four, two had been closely linked to the Andropov camp, and only two had ties solely to Chernenko.[16]

But on the other hand, the anti-corruption campaign begun under Andropov continued, albeit with less public fanfare. Disclosures of corruption and malfeasance continued in the media, and indictments and dismissals of mid-level bureaucrats and party officials still occurred with regular frequency. Obvious differences of opinion between the party leadership and the military surfaced with the dismissal of Marshal Ogarkov in September. Chernenko's prolonged absence from public view, which began in August amid new rumors of his declining health, further fueled the growing competition between Gorbachev and Romanov, who had emerged as the seeming frontrunners among the younger leaders.

Chernenko's continuation of the anti-corruption campaign clearly indicated that his rise to power was not a signal for a return to business as usual. The media regularly reported wide-ranging investigations of party and state officials, and dismissals and indictments reached deeply into the central bureaucracy and the provinces. Particular attention was given to the results of an 18-month investigation in Uzbekistan, where corruption, bribe taking, and distortion of official reports to Moscow had involved the top-level party leadership of the republic.[17] In his comments to an October conference of people's controllers — civilian watchdogs who monitor state agencies — Chernenko called for more vigorous surveillance of public officials by these volunteer activists, and party commissions lodged within other organizations were also called upon to cast a watchful eye over their charges.[18] By early winter there were indications that the campaign against corruption had perhaps overstepped its bounds. Writing in *Literaturnaia gazeta,* one legal commentator related the tale of an overeager local prosecutor who had brought groundless charges against a local party official so his unnamed city would be seen as "keeping up with the times. . . . "[19]

The sudden dismissal of Marshal Ogarkov early in September underscored the frictions that had existed between civilian leaders and certain factions of the military since Chernenko's rise to power. It was no accident, as a Russian might say, that the military's role in the formal proceedings of the succession was substantially downgraded. While Defense Minister Ustinov was the only Politburo member other than Andropov to speak at Brezhnev's funeral, he was demoted to third in the speaking order at Andropov's ceremony, following Gromyko and a factory worker. Military displeasure with the new General Secretary became evident shortly after the February plenum; while most major Soviet newspapers carried detailed accounts of Chernenko's election, *Krasnaia zvezda* succinctly reported the event without the usual favorable commentary.[20]

Long an advocate of increased defense expenditures and a highly visible figure since the press conference explaining Soviet action in downing the Korean airliner, Ogarkov undoubtedly became both a major actor in the battle over economic priorities and a symbol of the military's role under the new leadership. In economic and strategic terms, he endorsed aggressive arms development and procurement programs intended to match U.S. efforts, especially in the creation of high technology weapons systems, and argued, counter to the prevailing view among civilian leaders, that a nuclear war would produce a clear winner rather than the mutual destruction of all participants. Such views stood in sharp contrast to the desire for arms control talks with the Americans and to the Chernenko administration's preference for greater investment in consumer goods production, even at the expense of the military. There is evidence suggesting that there had been strong pressure from the military to shift resources from an ambitious social program, including consumer production, into military expenditures, and that party leaders had reacted by firmly reasserting the pro-consumer stance and forcing the military to fall into line.[21] Ogarkov's dismissal at a time when his likely ally, Grigorii Romanov, party secretary in charge of defense industries, was out of the country and his reassignment to unnamed duties in the Western theater of operations further fueled speculation that his removal was motivated by conflict at the highest levels.[22]

Ogarkov's dismissal coincided with Chernenko's return to active political life following a prolonged "vacation" from public view. As with his two immediate predecessors, Chernenko's ill health had become a subject for speculation among both Soviet and Western audiences, and his lengthy absence from public view from mid-July until early September undoubtedly intensified the rivalry among would-be successors, especially in light of widely circulated rumors that he had been hurriedly returned to Moscow in August for medical treatment. His public reemergence came both in a carefully staged presentation ceremony for returning cosmonauts and in his widely reported participation in important high-level meetings, including the Politburo session that sacked Ogarkov.[23]

Despite the return of the General Secretary to political life, it was undoubtedly obvious to the members of the inner circle that his days were numbered by ill health and perhaps by the growing restiveness of younger leaders. Rumors were heard in the Soviet capital suggesting that the next Central Committee plenum would bring extensive personnel changes and perhaps the voluntary retirement of a general secretary too ill to discharge the responsibilities of office.[24] There also were visible signs of growing discord among the potential successors. The implicit designation of Gorbachev as de facto second secretary and heir apparent was cast into doubt by a series of substantive and symbolic acts that suggested that his preeminence had prompted the resentment of both the more senior members of the Politburo and his younger cohorts who had risen during Andropov's rule. At the same time, Grigorii Romanov and Viktor Grishin emerged as potential counter heirs.

THE RISE OF MIKHAIL GORBACHEV

For the whole of the brief period in which Chernenko, however infirmly, held the reins of power, the question of his successor could never have been far from the minds of his colleagues and would-be heirs. His own selection as General Secretary had come as a result of a political arrangement that served the interests of the aging old guard as well as the younger figures who had not yet sorted out their political fortunes, and it was unlikely that the temporary bonds that had led them to choose Chernenko as yet another interim leader would survive the strains inherent in choosing his successor. As it became apparent throughout the summer and autumn of 1984 that the General Secretary's days were numbered, the struggle either to affirm Gorbachev's credentials as presumptive heir apparent, or to challenge his lead as de facto frontrunner, began.

Gorbachev's status as the most prominent member of the young guard had been apparent from the very beginning. The initial suppression of his closing comments to the February 1983 plenum was quickly reversed through their publication in a commemorative pamphlet on the session and subsequently in *Kommunist,* the party theoretical journal, only weeks later.[25] In these comments, Gorbachev spoke "on behalf of the Politburo" to urge the assembled leadership to "act in the spirit of unity, solidarity, and lofty exactingness and responsibility," themes that suggested that he had been entrusted with the task of offering the traditional unity speech.

Gorbachev's ascendancy was soon confirmed by events both abroad and at home. In comments to reporters from the Japanese newspaper *Ashai Shimbun,* Viktor Afanasev, the chief editor of *Pravda* and a frequent source of reliable information about top leadership, confirmed that Gorbachev now functioned as de facto second secretary. Similar disclosures to the Swedish *Dagens Nyheter* revealed that Gorbachev supervised the work of the Secretariat, controlled cadres policy at all levels, and reviewed certain aspects of military and KGB activities. He also continued to supervise the economy, except for military-related industries, which were placed under Romanov's control. The tasks of supervising state administrative organs were divided between himself and Romanov.[26] In his comments to the Swedish paper in March 1984, Afanasev revealed that Gorbachev had not yet assumed control over ideology, which remained directly in Chernenko's hands. Yet there are other indications that Afanasev may have erred in suggesting that the ideological role still eluded Gorbachev; as early as late February, Gorbachev's signature appeared on the obituaries of cultural and scientific personnel, indicating that he held operational responsibility for these activities.

Further confirmation of his increasing stature came at the April Supreme Soviet session, at which he nominated Chernenko for the chairmanship of the Presidium, the so-called "presidency" held previously by Brezhnev and Andropov.[27] Less than a year before, Chernenko had offered a similarly worded nomination of Andropov at the June 1983

Supreme Soviet session at a time when his emergence as de facto second secretary had become evident. The April 1984 session also saw Gorbachev's election as chairman of the Foreign Affairs Commission of the Council of the Union, a post that had been held for almost 20 years by the chief ideologist, Mikhail Suslov, and then by Chernenko.[28]

Gorbachev further strengthened his hand by appointing past associates from Stavropol or the agricultural apparatus of the Secretariat to important posts. The post of administrator of day-to-day affairs of the Central Committee went to Nikolai Kurchina, the former first deputy head of the agriculture department, and A. K. Vedernikov, a former secretary of the Stavropol party committee, was appointed to an important post in the Department of Organizational Party Work. Lesser appointments also came from the Stavropol or agricultural organizations, in keeping with the tradition of building one's political machine from among the ranks of past subordinates.[29]

Despite this growing prominence, Gorbachev's ascendancy did not go unchallenged. Within the Politburo itself, a virtual deadlock on appointments to the highest levels of the party hierarchy remained in force, preventing Gorbachev or any other would-be successor from placing allies or protégés on the Politburo or Secretariat. In January 1985, as it once again became apparent that Chernenko's health had deteriorated and that substantial responsibilities had been delegated among other leaders, Afanasev reported that either Gorbachev or Romanov chaired meetings of the Secretariat, a position consistent with the argument that they divided the day-to-day supervision of party affairs.[30]

Gorbachev's agricultural policies also came under attack. Long an advocate of improving agricultural output through greater reliance on private plot production and more efficient organization, Gorbachev had been forced to soften his advocacy of both positions in the past, first moderating his support of private production in the early 1980s in light of conservative opposition and then downplaying the importance of the brigade system, which he had strongly touted during Andropov's reign. The latter experiments in the creation of so-called "normless work teams" had been particularly close to his program for agricultural reforms and had been successfully utilized in Stavropol under his tutelage.[31]

Further evidence of Gorbachev's problems in agriculture came at the October 1984 plenum, which opted for massive land reclamation as a solution to the nation's food production difficulties. Consistent with the time-honored Soviet position that greater production could be obtained through expensive programs to place more land under cultivation, such reclamation efforts ran contrary to Gorbachev's approach to obtain production increases through organizational reforms. Chernenko and Tikhonov were the two main speakers at the meeting, and each remained conspicuously silent about past achievements in agriculture that might be attributed to Gorbachev's six-year tenure as head of the agriculture department. For his part, Gorbachev offered no comments at all at the plenum, a remarkable lapse that probably signaled both his replacement as party spokesman for agricultural affairs and his opposition to the program.[32]

It had also been rumored in Moscow that the October plenum on agricultural affairs would make personnel changes in the highest party bodies and perhaps even witness the voluntary resignation of an ill General Secretary. Yet the Politburo session that preceded the meeting discussed what were pointedly labeled "Comrade Chernenko's proposals concerning some questions of contemporary cadres policy," and no changes occurred at the plenary session, indicating a continued deadlock over the delicate question of new appointments to the Politburo and Secretariat.[33]

The extraordinary handling of the coming year's production plan in industry and agriculture confirmed Gorbachev's political difficulties on other fronts as well. Normally a plenary session of the Central Committee would be called in November just prior to the scheduled Supreme Soviet session that approved the next year's economic targets, and Soviet authorities had gone to great lengths earlier in the year to indicate that the November session would take up the question of economic reforms. But the session never materialized. An expanded session of the Politburo was offered in its place. More remarkably, Gorbachev, who had primary responsibility for the economy, failed to attend the session. Both he and Vorotnikov, the Russian Republic premier, were reputedly "on vacation" at the time; Vladimir Dolgikh, the Central Committee secretary for heavy industry, also missed the meeting in connection with a diplomatic mission to Indochina.

Perhaps because he had been denied a platform within the Politburo and Central Committee from which to voice his economic policies, Gorbachev took the occasion of a conference on ideology early in December to outline his reform proposals. From among the other full members of the Politburo, only Grishin and Romanov were also present, perhaps indicating the unwillingness of others to be identified with a call for extensive reforms. While Gorbachev offered the ritual reference to Chernenko as the "head" of the Politburo and lauded its "spirit of collectivism," he was quick to turn the meeting to his own purposes. His tone was one of a moderate reformer, anxious both to assert his own agenda of economic and institutional change but also to reassure party leadership of his realism concerning the pace of reforms.

Gorbachev called for the party to "carry out profound transformations in the economy and in the entire system of social relations. . . . " He averred that the nation needed to take a critical look at the "interaction between present-day productive forces and socialist production relationships," the proper Marxist terminology to signal a reexamination of both the technological levels of industry and the broader questions of administrative control and popular incentives. He linked further improvements with the tasks of raising the economy "to a qualitatively new scientific-technical and organizational level" and of "combining the economic interests of society, labor collectives, and each worker." Pointing out that the next scheduled Central Committee plenum would deal with technical progress in the economy, he argued that priority "should be given to fundamentally new, truly revolutionary scientific and technical solutions capable of increasing labor productivity many times over."

Despite the call for seemingly sweeping reforms, Gorbachev cautioned against "putting the cart before the horse" in pressing for reforms. Yet he also warned against "sluggishness" in dealing with shortcomings and demanded "unswerving implementation . . . of the accountability of all executive agencies" in dealing with malfeasance and corruption.[34]

Gorbachev's comments also contained a thinly veiled criticism of increased arms expenditures, which had been demanded by the military in light of the U.S. build-up. Commenting that "unremitting attention to social questions" should be at the center of attention for state, economic, and public organizations, he rejected any reference to "objective circumstances . . . to justify inattention to people's needs." He also maintained that the Soviet Union "has exerted and continues to exert its main influence on world development through its economic policy," a formulation that seemingly deemphasized the importance of military factors.

Whatever his difficulties in acquiring a domestic audience for his economic program, Gorbachev increased his stature as a spokesman of Soviet interests abroad with his journey to Great Britain in December 1984. While his earlier trip to Canada had earned him little visibility within the Soviet Union itself — although Western audiences were impressed with his performance — the London visit was widely and positively reported in the Soviet media.[35] Although his comments on the renewal of arms talks and opposition to the Reagan administration's star wars proposals broke no new ground, he was seen as a vigorous and open proponent of the Soviet cause capable both of charming and of dealing forcefully with foreign leaders.

IN THE WINGS: ROMANOV AND GRISHIN

Despite Gorbachev's acknowledged preeminence as de facto second secretary, his automatic rise to power upon Chernenko's demise was hardly assured. Throughout party history, no second in command had ever emerged as the long-term successor. Both because of the inevitable tendency for other aspirants to join in an attempt to block the frontrunner and because of the fear that Gorbachev's rise would resuscitate vigorous and politically disruptive reform efforts, other would-be candidates were also waiting in the wings for the death of the ailing general secretary.

Grigorii Romanov, the former Leningrad party secretary who had been transferred to the Secretariat by Andropov to assume control over military-related industries, emerged as one possible counter heir as Chernenko's health further deteriorated throughout the winter. Like Gorbachev, he was a member of both the Secretariat and the Politburo, dual membership in which has been regarded as a sine qua non for the top post. He had served as Leningrad party secretary since 1970, having built his entire career in party work in that northern city after brief experience as an engineer and designer in a shipbuilding factory. In 1973 he was made a candidate member of the Politburo and advanced to full membership in 1976, four years before Gorbachev reached similar status.[36]

While Romanov's brief tenure as party secretary in charge of the military-industrial complex would ordinarily have conveyed considerable influence, both personnel changes in the military and the seeming disaffection of the Chernenko regime with the armed forces cast his fortunes into doubt. The death of Ustinov in November 1984 and the unexplained demotion only months earlier of Ogarkov removed the military's strongest party and professional advocates. The appointment of Marshal Sokolov as Minister of Defense and Marshal Akhromeev as Chief of Staff hardly brought the military's representation to equal levels; the former was already in his 70s and not yet even a candidate member of the Politburo at the time of his appointment, and the latter had been made a member of the Central Committee only in 1983.

Romanov's record as party steward in Leningrad also was a mixed blessing. On the one hand, he had acquired the reputation of a tough and capable administrator, and the city's technologically sophisticated industries were frequently put forth as a model for other more backward sectors of the economy. Intolerant of dissent and a proponent of order and discipline in the economy, he was philosophically in tune with many of the reforms of the Andropov administration.

But on the other hand, there were numerous political liabilities. Leningrad had offered Romanov a limited power base, and one that had never successfully been used by any past leader to climb to the apex of the Soviet hierarchy. Like most *Leningradtsi,* he had made his career exclusively within the city party organization, never having the opportunity to build support and create loyal political organizations in other parts of the country. There is also strong evidence to suggest that he did not choose his own successor in Leningrad itself; Lev Zaikov, head of the city government, was promoted over the heads of a number of more prominent local party figures and later rose rapidly within the Gorbachev administration, suggesting that his loyalties did not lie with his former superior.[37]

Romanov also lacked obvious patrons within the leadership. Although his effective management of the city had brought him to national attention and eventual Politburo status, he was always held at arm's length and denied service in the central party apparatus during Brezhnev's tenure. His promotion to the Secretariat under Andropov was difficult to interpret in partisan terms; while it may have been initiated by the new General Secretary to reward Romanov for his support during the critical November 1982 Politburo and Central Committee sessions, it may also have occurred at the behest of the embattled Brezhnev faction hoping to contain the rise of new leaders such as Gorbachev and Aliev.

Romanov's style of leadership and personal life also created difficulties. While he was admired for his effective management of party affairs in Leningrad, Romanov evidenced an authoritarian style that must have created doubts within a party hierarchy nurtured by long years of "respect for cadres" and collective leadership. He was a man who ostentatiously enjoyed power, from the visible perquisites of office to the creation of a leadership cult within his bailiwick. Although no hint of personal enrichment or corruption had emerged, he was known to have used his office to establish himself as a virtual "tsar" in the former capital, an action that could only have provoked the resentment of his immediate colleagues and the suspicions of others in the national leadership.

In the last months of Chernenko's brief rule, attention increasingly shifted to the Moscow party secretary, Viktor Grishin, as a second counter heir. Already age 70, he hardly fit the stereotype of the new leaders brought forward under Andropov. He had risen to full membership in the Central Committee a year before Stalin's death, to candidate membership in the Politburo (then Presidium) in 1961, and to first secretary of the Moscow city party committee in 1967; full membership in the Politburo came in 1971. A political survivor, he had aligned himself with a succession of party leaders from Stalin onward. He was widely travelled in both the West and in the Eastern bloc and had used his long tenure as Moscow party chief to speak out on virtually the full range of party, economic, cultural, and foreign policy issues, always taking safely orthodox, if not blatantly conservative, positions on the issues.

For his own part, Grishin was thought to be a man of considerable political ambition for the top post. Even before the first round of succession launched by Brezhnev's death in 1982, he had been identified with attempts to discredit then more prominent frontrunners in the hierarchy, and he was widely regarded as a viable compromise candidate in 1982 should a deadlock emerge. His prospects had been over-shadowed by the emergence of the Andropov coalition linking senior figures such as Gromyko and Ustinov with younger leaders and by the understandable tendency for the survivors of the Brezhnev group to coalesce around Chernenko. But with the imminent demise of Chernenko now close at hand, Grishin again emerged a a viable candi-date, as least in the eyes of members of the old guard who hoped yet again to stave off the rise of the next generation of Kremlin leaders and perhaps also in the minds of younger figures such as Romanov, whose own bid for top office had flagged in the last months of Chernenko's rule.

There is considerable evidence that Chernenko himself put Grishin forward as his chosen heir. From January 1985 onward, as it became apparent that the ill Chernenko could no longer publicly conduct the affairs of party and state, Grishin increasingly stepped forward as his replacement. According to Western reporters such as Max Frankland of the *London Observer,* rumors had already begun to circulate in the Soviet capital that Grishin was "the man to watch" as the succession arrangements emerged.[38] When Chernenko failed to make the obligatory appearance before his constituents in Moscow's Kuibyshev district before the republic soviet elections, his speech was read in his absence by Grishin, whose own placement in the hierarchy had risen dramatically to outstrip Gorbachev's, as measured by the timing of their own speeches to their constituents. Grishin also was visible as the only other member of the hierarchy present at the brief ceremony at the end of February at which Chernenko was officially presented his credentials as a member of the legislature. Rumors circulated in Moscow that Chernenko intended to announce his own resignation at the up-coming March 1985 session of the Central Committee and to endorse Grishin as his hand-picked successor, a plan that never materialized because of his own death shortly before the scheduled meeting.[39]

Whatever the machinations of Kremlin politics in the last months of Chernenko's reign, larger political, economic, and foreign policy realities underlay the coming succession struggle. However brief its tenure in office, the Andropov regime had launched a debate about the possibility of important changes in the economy and society, and the discussion and limited reform efforts continued throughout the more cautious leadership of his successor.

THE ECONOMY

The economic policies of the brief-lived Chernenko regime followed the major outlines of reform set forward by its predecessor, although the vigor with which such efforts were pursued varied with the ebbing fortunes of the General Secretary. Certain precepts remained virtually intact: the commitment to some form of economic restructuring was quickly reiterated by the new regime, and the experimental managerial reforms initiated under Andropov remained the model for an extension of reform efforts. The anti-corruption campaign also survived the transition, and the number of party and state officials who faced official sanctions for their misconduct increased visibly throughout 1984. What was different was the tone of Chernenko's leadership on economic issues. While the essential content of the Andropov program remained, the sense of dynamism and urgency was gone, suggesting that the new administration was offering at best mixed signals. On the one hand, the demands for improved performance and cautious experimentation continued. But on the other, it was clear that the regime wished to signal its intention to move even more cautiously, reassuring important segments of the bureaucracy that changes would be less disruptive than originally envisioned and reaffirming the leading role of the party in making economic policy.

Chernenko's first speech as General Secretary set forward the balanced tone characteristic of his administration. Promising, as did Andropov, a "serious restructuring" of "economic management and our whole economic mechanism," he called for a broadening of the experiments in increasing the rights and powers of individual enterprises. The General Secretary also offered a carefully balanced treatment of the themes of reform and corruption. On the former, he admitted that some economic managers had used the limited experiments as a rationalization to avoid change within their own operations:

Doesn't the anticipation of the results of the experiments serve some economic managers as a cover for their passiveness and desire to work in the old way? The updating of economic structures is an important matter, of course. Here it would be advisable to follow the wise old rule: Look before you leap. But this by no means justifies those who have no wish whatsoever to reckon with changed conditions and life's new requirements.[40]

The treatment of Andropov's efficiency and anti-corruption campaigns also showed evidence of compromise. While Chernenko referred to the problems at hand as merely manifestations of "disorderliness and irresponsibility," he nonetheless noted that earlier efforts had enjoyed a salutary effect on production and promised that there would be "no slackening of effort" in pursuing the campaign.

Chernenko also reassured the party that its special role in economic policy making would be preserved. Reviving the never-ending question of the relationship between the party and state, he argued that party bodies should maintain their unique "political" role and eschew the temptation to become involved in day-to-day management, a theme consistent with his own penchant for leading industry through proper personnel selection and ideological guidance rather than by means of constant party intervention:

One such question [of the party's role in the economy] is a clear delimitation between the functions of party committees and the tasks of state and economic agencies and the elimination of duplication in their work. This is a major question of political significance. Frankly, some things in this area have not been arranged properly. Sometimes officials of soviets, ministries, and enterprises do not display the necessary independence but shift to party agencies questions that they should resolve themselves. The practice of usurping the functions of economic managers dampens the zeal of cadres. Moreover, it is fraught with the danger of weakening the role of the party committee as a body of political leadership. For party committees handling economic matters means, above all, dealing with people who manage economic entities. This must always be kept in mind.[41]

Less than a month later, Chernenko reiterated his commitment to consumer priorities. Speaking to his constituents before the Supreme Soviet election, he confessed that "difficulties" in the international situation had forced the Soviet leadership to "divert" considerable resources to defense purposes. "But even under these conditions," he continued, "we regarded it as unthinkable to curtail social programs."[42] The food program and consumer goods production were cited as the highest priorities of the economy, although it was made clear that improvements in these areas were to be dependent on increasing the efficiency of the work force.

In the same speech, Chernenko once again argued for a "serious restructuring" of management. No clear blueprint appeared in his comments concerning the outlines of such reforms. Instead he called ambiguously for planners "to strengthen centralized management and planning and strive to make them more effective and flexible" while simultaneously extending the results of economic experiments to give individual enterprises greater autonomy. Consistent with his earlier writings, he also recommended greater reliance on the mobilization of worker input and commentary. Obliquely criticizing those who argued that the scientific and technological revolution contained the answers to the nation's economic problems, he pointed out that "in the final analysis, every job is conceived of by man and its results are judged by man. Scientific and technical progress will never invalidate this old truth."

Speaking to the April 1984 Central Committee plenum, the General Secretary simultaneously attempted to reassure and to warn the economic bureaucracy. On the one hand, he called for "the more efficient use of existing management institutions," especially the soviets. "Here," he continued, "there is no need to create new capacities. Putting existing capacities fully into action will be enough."[43] But on the other hand, he also warned of the need to reduce the size of the "swelling" administrative apparatus, not only at the lower and middle levels but at the top as well. Observing that this was "serious business" that called for real transfers from office work to the production line instead of the usual shuffling of agencies, he opted for a larger role for the soviets and for the public in general in monitoring the reduction of administrative entities.

Speaking at an April meeting of the commission drafting a new party program, Chernenko struck a tone of realism and caution that urged primary attention be focused on the immediate problems facing the economy and society rather than on the description of a visionary future society. Arguing that the future will be marked by a "gradual advance to communism," he recommended that the program eschew "excessive use of figures and all sorts of particulars" (a clear slap at the 1961 program, which offered a precise timetable for the attainment of communism) and deal instead with "the basic line of development. . . ."[44]

Chernenko's comments on the program also reinforced the conclusion that the new regime initially placed consumer production at the top of its priorities, although conflicting signals were soon to appear even in the General Secretary's comments. A call for a "steady rise in the people's well-being" headed the April list, ahead of the capital needs of industry and military expenditures. As before, particularly favorable reference was made to the "initiative . . . of the masses," especially in supervising the introduction of advanced technology and management reforms.[45]

By the late autumn 1984, Chernenko's tone concerning economic reform and the need for far-reaching changes had grown more urgent, perhaps reflecting the growing influence of reform-oriented elements and his declining control over events. In a long theoretical piece on the new program published in the December issue of *Kommunist*, he offered a more candid assessment of the problems facing the nation:

It is extremely important that we make a realistic assessment of our enormous achievements and of existing shortcomings, an assessment that neither exaggerates nor belittles one or the other. The reality of our society is a contradictory combination of major, truly historic successes, unaccomplished tasks of the present and problems inherited from the past — problems that, in principle, could have been solved at earlier stages of our development.[46]

Chernenko's December comments also softened the reference to the priority of consumer goods production, offering instead the observation that sectors such as agriculture, construction, transportation, and the service industries should be the subject of rapid modernization programs. A more strident tone appeared in the reference to corruption and mismanagement, which were attributed to the "attempts of some people to prosper at the expense of others. . . . " Lauding the expanded role for popular involvement through the reinvigoration of the soviets, he recommended closer direct ties between party leaders and rank-and-file party members and criticized the "oversimplified" approach taken by some administrative agencies to reduce the size of their burgeoning staffs.

Chernenko's speech to the expanded Politburo session that approved the guidelines for the draft plan for 1985 also reflected the shift in priorities.[47] While the General Secretary reiterated an old theme that the single most important development in the economy in recent years had been "the favorable effect on the Soviet people's standard of living," his comments on the priorities of the new plan revealed a shift toward a balance of industrial modernization and consumer goods production. The technological reequipment of key sectors such as energy production, metallurgy and machine building was listed ahead of other goals such as the implementation of the food program and consumer goods production, although the latter were promised "priority rates." As before, the military fell conspicuously at the bottom of the list and was promised only "due consideration" in the allocation of resources.

In his final public comments, the ailing Chernenko seemingly reverted to earlier priorities favoring consumer goods. The occasion was his February 22, 1985, speech to his constituents in the Kuibyshev district in Moscow just prior to the Russian Republic soviet election; because of the deterioration of his condition, he was unable to attend the meeting, and his seeming chosen heir, Viktor Grishin, read his comments to the audience.[48] The declining state of his health strongly suggests that the General Secretary was not the true author of the remarks offered in his name; more than likely they were prepared by his staff without extensive guidance.

The speech itself was brief and devoid of the usual references to the increasing role of the masses and the need for thoroughgoing economic and managerial reform. Instead it merely linked the need for increased labor productivity, a long-standing issue that predated the recent spate of experimental reforms, with the proffered increase in the standard of living. Particular attention was given to improving the quality of consumer goods, better housing and health care facilities, and more extensive day care facilities for working mothers. At least for the public record,

Chernenko closed his long career in party service and his short tenure as General Secretary by dealing with the issues that had always seemed closest to his heart; the vision of sweeping reforms that was first ushered in by Yuri Andropov would have to await the advent of new leadership.

It is not surprising that Chernenko's public commentary on the economy should have ended on such an indecisive and irresolute note. His brief tenure in office had been marked both by mixed signals on managerial reforms and the choice of new economic priorities and by the growing presence of conservative thinkers in the debate on economic reform that had begun in earnest with Brezhnev's death.

Such mixed signals are clearly seen in the discussion of the experimental managerial reforms begun with such fanfare during the last months of Andropov's rule. While they were intended to promote greater enterprise autonomy, create clearer and more compelling incentives to modernize production processes and cut inputs of raw materials and labor, and provide for stable short- and medium-range plans, the initial results were far from encouraging. A review of the first seven months of performance in one of the factories working under the experimental reforms published in *Pravda* revealed that few of the goals were being met. The report cited instances in which "relapses" had occurred in which ministry and other higher agencies had interfered in enterprise affairs, attempts to introduce advanced technology had been thwarted, and seemingly stable production plans had been altered as many as ten times.[49] As one analyst put it, "first impressions can only put us on alert," a hardly surprising conclusion in light of the lack of success of similar reform efforts during the Brezhnev years. Yet despite the palpable shortcomings of the experiments, the Chernenko regime promised in November that similar programs would be undertaken in 21 union and republic ministries and in many consumer service industries the following year.[50]

Similar conflicting signals emerged in the treatment of agriculture and the food program. While the food program reemerged as a central priority of the new leadership, consistent with its overall preference for consumer-oriented issues, it did not produce any clear decision on how greater production was to be obtained. Although advocates of structural changes and economic incentives continued to state their case, albeit now with greater caution, emphasis shifted to the more conventional approach of increasing production through massive capital investment to reclaim potentially arable lands for cultivation. During the Chernenko interregnum, reforms such as the brigade system or the creation of integrated agro-industrial complexes received less emphasis, and attention fell on a massive land reclamation program approved by the October Central Committee plenum (at which Gorbachev did not even speak).[51]

During Chernenko's brief rule, the open debate over economic reforms that had flowered in the academic journals and increasingly in the mass media during Andropov's tenure was joined by conservative critics, who imposed a more orthodox tone on the discussion. While academicians-cum-advisors such as Tatiana Zaslavskaia and Abel Abegenian continued to suggest various models of reform combining improved centralized planning with limited decentralization efforts, bolder thinkers who had ventured to advocate market-oriented reforms and to suggest that Lenin's NEP of the 1920s might present a viable model for the 1980s were publicly called to task, and one conservative writer went so far as to laud the centralized wartime command economy of the Stalin years as superior to today's sprawling and uncoordinated bureaucracy.[52]

The conflicting signals coming from political leaders and academicians alike were accompanied by a disturbing reality: the production levels and growth rates that had begun to improve as a result of recent discipline campaigns and other efforts to improve economic performance once again began to dip, indicating that neither of the General Secretaries who had followed in Brezhnev's footsteps had found solutions to the nation's economic problems. For the economy as a whole, the positive results seen in 1983 were not duplicated in the following year. While the overall growth rate for 1983 was 3.5 percent, it dropped to 2.6 percent for 1984, largely because of a likely four to five percent decrease in the output of the agricultural sector. Although the growth rate for the industrial sector held constant at 4.2 percent for both years, the decline evidenced by agriculture was politically disturbing, both for a current administration that placed great emphasis on improving the lot of the Soviet consumer and for a would-be successor whose six-year tenure as party secretary in charge of agriculture had ended on such an ominous note.[53]

FOREIGN POLICY

Chernenko's foreign policy was shaped both by his overriding concern with domestic problems and by the impasse in East–West relations that he inherited from his predecessor. Although less bold in its approach to domestic issues, the new regime continued the focus on internal affairs begun under Andropov, subtly redefining its economic priorities to include consumer goods issues. While there were no high-level changes among the leadership other than the death of Defense Minister Ustinov, the third round of the succession crisis that would inevitably follow Chernenko's death placed the domestic political agenda and the competition among would-be heirs at center stage.

The impasse in Soviet–U.S. relations that had begun even before Brezhnev's death continued for at least the first half of Chernenko's tenure in office, although there were early hints that the new regime was searching for some formula through which to return to the INF and START talks that had been ended shortly before Andropov's death. Few new initiatives appeared in Soviet dealings with other major problem areas. Overtures to Western Europe were shaped almost totally by Soviet interest in preventing further deployment of U.S. intermediate-range Pershing II and cruise missiles and securing the removal of those weapons now in place; inconclusive talks with the People's Republic of China dragged on; Soviet forces remained tied down in Afghanistan, and there was little visible progress in the negotiations to find an acceptable disengagement; and openings to Third World nations and the Middle East produced few tangible results.

Yet despite these difficulties abroad and the understandable preoccupation with succession politics at home, the new regime succeeded in reopening the arms talks, albeit under the guise of a new format for negotiations. The search for a break in the impasse was not evident in the initial pronouncements of the new regime, which demanded an end to further deployment and the withdrawal of Pershing II and cruise missiles as a precondition for the resumption of talks. Although the new General Secretary's first speeches to the Central Committee plenum that confirmed his selection and to his constituents two weeks later did not fully spell out Soviet demands, his answers in a *Pravda* interview published on April 9, 1984, made it clear that the West "must take steps to restore the situation that existed before the deployment of new American missiles in Western Europe began."[54] The only early break in the Soviet position came in March with the reopening of the Mutual and Balanced Force Reductions talks in Vienna, although no substantive progress emerged from the resumed discussions.[55]

Despite his unyielding position on arms control issues, Chernenko still publicly called for an improvement in Soviet–U.S. relations and reiterated the argument that the deterioration of ties was solely the fault of the Reagan administration. By late spring, it was evident that Moscow's tone was prompted as much by its unwillingness to strengthen the hand of Ronald Reagan's bid for reelection as by its desire to hold firm on the issue of U.S. missiles in Europe. As it had done in connection with the West German elections the year before, it hoped to sway public opinion and affect the outcome of the election. Soviet leaders undoubtedly felt that a prolonged deterioration of bilateral ties and the absence of any progress on arms control would swing public opinion against the incumbent administration, and conversely that any hint of seeming Soviet willingness to reopen the talks under U.S. pressure would suggest that Reagan's unyielding posture had extracted concessions from Moscow.

In addition to its preoccupation with U.S. missiles in Europe and the upcoming U.S. presidential election, the Soviet leadership repeatedly returned to the question of the militarization of space, an issue that had occupied center stage since Reagan's proposal for the so-called "Star Wars" Strategic Defense Initiative (SDI) in March 1983. From the outset, Chernenko repeated his predecessor's call for an agreement to prevent the extension of the arms race into space.[56] Responding to an appeal from U.S. scientists, the General Secretary reiterated the Soviet position in late May, charging that such a system "cannot be regarded as anything but designed for carrying out nuclear aggression with impunity" and warning that "faced with a threat from space, the Soviet Union will be forced to take measures to reliably safeguard its security."[57] He reminded Western audiences that the USSR had unilaterally declared a moratorium on the further development of anti-satellite missiles, in which it was regarded as having a short-term technological lead, and called upon the Americans to take similar action.

Returning to the issue late in June 1984, Chernenko called for a new round of talks on the prevention of the militarization of space, with the first session to be held in September in Vienna, a location suitably removed from the Geneva site of the arms talks Moscow had abandoned over six months previously. The talks would focus on "the complete and mutual renunciation of anti-satellite systems" and would be accompanied by a mutual moratorium on the testing and deployment of such weapons concurrent with the negotiations.[58]

Apparently expecting a quick U.S. rejection of its proposal, which in itself broke no new ground on the issue of space weapons, Moscow was stung by Washington's qualified acceptance. The Reagan administration took the opportunity to suggest that such talks deal not only with anti-satellite systems but also with the whole range of strategic and intermediate-range weapons systems covered by the suspended Geneva negotiations. Moscow now found itself on the horns of a dilemma of its own making. To accept the U.S. proposal for comprehensive talks would be to return to a modified Geneva format without having obtained the withdrawal of Pershing II and cruise missiles from Europe, which had been the oft-repeated precondition for the resumption of talks. Yet to recoil from its own proposal for arms talks of any sort would label the Soviet call for negotiations as ineptly planned and duplicitous, to say nothing of the loss of face among European and other disarmament groups Moscow wished to court. The Soviets escaped from the dilemma by narrowly interpreting their initial summons; according to Moscow, the agenda of the talks was to have been limited to "preventing" the militarization of outer space. Since Washington refused in advance to accept the implication that the only purpose of the negotiations was to prevent the development of anti-missile defensive systems, much less to withdraw its counterproposal that strategic and intermediate-range systems be included, Moscow judged the U.S. response as inadequate and pronounced itself unwilling to meet with U.S. officials.[59]

Soviet behavior at the Stockholm conference on European security also reflected preoccupation with nuclear and space weaponry. Called as a follow-up meeting to the Madrid conference and initially slated to deal with conventional weapons, the Stockholm meetings quickly became a forum for the USSR to press its case for an end to U.S. deployment of intermediate-range weapons in Europe and a prohibition of anti-missile and anti-satellite systems. The latest round of talks, which began in late spring, focused on Soviet demands for agreement on the non-first use of nuclear weapons, a nonaggression pact among conference participants, and a freeze on military expenditures, including funds for nuclear and anti-missile systems. Because of the continuing deadlock in bilateral negotiations on these issues, the talks dragged on inconclusively through the summer.[60]

Chernenko's return to active political life early in September 1984 did little to change the diplomatic stalemate. Proffering an "honest dialogue" with Washington, he repeated the now common charge that the United States had rejected the Soviet call for negotiations on the militarization of space and argued that the current administration was "obsessed by force" and "losing its sense of reality."[61]

The first hint of a break in the impasse came late in September in connection with Foreign Minister Gromyko's trip to the United Nations. While the tone of his comments to that body offered no softening of the Soviet position, his subsequent meeting with Secretary of State Shultz and President Reagan suggested that Moscow at least wished to establish direct contact. His meeting with Walter Mondale, the Democratic candidate for the presidency, revealed that Moscow still held hopes of a change on the Potomac, as did his reference to the presence of some "realistically thinking politicians and statesmen" in the West.[62] Yet Reagan's own more conciliatory comments at the United Nations in which he proposed the creation of "umbrella" talks to combine negotiations on differing weapons systems were labeled mere campaign rhetoric designed to soften his image as a hawk.[63]

Two weeks later, in an interview with the *Washington Post,* Chernenko took the next step. Implying that progress on "at least one of the essential questions" of arms control could lead to improved relations and perhaps a resumption of bilateral talks on strategic and intermediate-range weapons, the General Secretary called for a positive U.S. response on the militarization of space, a mutual freeze on nuclear weapons arsenals, ratification by the United States of the test ban treaty, or a U.S. pledge not to be the first to use nuclear weapons. He offered his strongest endorsement of detente since assuming power, arguing that "there is no sound alternative at all to a constructive development of Soviet–U.S. relations." Although he professed to see no inclination in Washington toward improved ties, he labeled himself an "optimist" and promised that "if what the president has said about readiness to negotiate is not merely a tactical move, I wish to state that the Soviet Union will not be found wanting."[64]

The timing of the General Secretary's comments left open the question of his true intent. While the tone of the interview was more conciliatory than any Soviet pronouncement since the break-up of the Geneva talks, its publication shortly before the Reagan–Mondale debate on foreign policy might also have been intended to suggest that a more forthcoming administration would find the Soviets willing to deal seriously on a wide range of issues. Chernenko's own active role in the proceedings might also have been designed to demonstrate his control in Moscow. Having returned to active political life early in September after a rumored illness, he was described as "fit" and appearing to be in good health by the *Washington Post* interviewer.

The General Secretary's exceptional accessibility to the Western media continued after the U.S. election, which returned Reagan to power. Responding to questions put by an NBC correspondent, he once again promised a positive Soviet response "if the statements that have been made in Washington recently about a desire to resolve questions of arms limitations do not remain merely words. . . ."[65] Arguing that the improved relations of the 1970s had been based on a mutual willingness to restrain the arms race, Chernenko insisted that "broad possibilities" for improved ties would result from an American willingness to respond to the agenda suggested in the *Washington Post* interview. Perhaps as significant was the complete absence of criticism of the re-elected Reagan administration, with which Moscow would have to deal for another four years; the only even moderately negative comments came in Chernenko's insistence that the time was not yet appropriate for a new summit meeting, although "it will not be difficult to set the date" once the logjam had been broken.

Even as he presented his public assurances that the USSR wished to pursue arms talks with Washington, Chernenko privately was urging the Reagan administration to return to the bargaining table. In a message to the White House, the General Secretary proposed another Shultz–Gromyko meeting without insisting on the withdrawal of newly deployed American missiles in Europe or on a moratorium on the testing of space weapons as preconditions. The overture was quickly accepted, and on November 23rd the Soviet media carried the announcement that the foreign ministers would meet in Geneva on January 7–8, 1985, to discuss a new series of talks that would deal with "the entire range of questions relating to nuclear and space arms."[66]

The January meeting produced a new formula for discussions that closely resembled Reagan's proposal for umbrella talks. Three separate negotiating tracks were to be created, each dealing separately with the intermediate-range missiles, strategic weapons systems, and space weapons. Most importantly to the Soviets, the three "tracks" were to be linked, "with all these questions considered and resolved in their interrelationship." The essential unity of the talks was further underscored by the description of the negotiating teams; each side was to be represented by "one delegation" which would be divided into "three groups."[67] From its perspective, the Soviet leadership had secured a forum for the discussion of its most pressing concern, the militarization of space and the U.S. SDI proposals, and made it clear from the pointed references to the "interrelationship" of all issues that progress in areas of greatest concern to the United States — Soviet strength in heavy strategic missiles and the deployment of intermediate-range SS-20s — would be held hostage to forward motion on its priorities. It had also secured the creation of "new" talks, avoiding the embarrassment of returning to the previously separate negotiations that it abandoned shortly before Chernenko assumed power. From the U.S. perspective, Moscow had scrapped all of its preconditions for a resumption of talks and had accepted the umbrella formula suggested by the White House. Moreover, a re-elected and now supremely confident president could easily make the case that his firm treatment of the Soviets had compelled them to return to the bargaining table.

In a lengthy interview five days later, Gromyko drove home the point that the USSR expected serious substantive discussions on all three fronts and not a "seminar" on the technical feasibility of the star wars proposal. Insisting that any agreement that might emerge from the Geneva talks be "interrelated in all three areas," Gromyko hinted that if "the problems of space are considered from the proper angle and if accords in this field make an appearance, it would be possible to make progress on questions of strategic arms as well."[68] The continued deployment of U.S. missiles in Europe was now described merely as making the task of the talks "much, much more complicated" rather than as a reason for their suspension.

In his final public comments — the speech to his constituents read by Grishin on February 22nd — Chernenko took an almost imploring tone to urge the Americans to take the up-coming talks seriously. Referring warmly to the wartime alliance of the two nations, he argued that they could face a common danger such as the threat of nuclear war despite the differences in their social systems. But he also once again underscored the importance of simultaneous progress on all three tracks, which he termed "absolutely necessary to success in this matter."[69]

The Soviet reversal on arms control negotiations marked the most significant change in foreign policy during the brief-lived Chernenko administration. On other fronts, the regime continued initiatives begun by its predecessor, albeit with less vigor and imagination. Moscow's preoccupation with bilateral Soviet–U.S. ties and its tendency to see virtually all other foreign policy issues as derivative of that basic relationship harked back to the mindset of the Brezhnev years, when hopes for better relations on all questions were tied to the never clearly defined nature of detente.

Despite attempts during the Andropov administration to negotiate an acceptable withdrawal of Soviet forces from Afghanistan, Moscow deepened its commitment to that increasingly costly guerrilla war and began to prepare its own public for the sacrifices entailed in a protracted conflict. Although a third round of the so-called "proximity talks" in which United Nations officials shuttled between Afghani and Pakistani negotiating teams was held, there was no progress toward balancing the withdrawal of Soviet troops with a formula to end Pakistani and Western involvement. As the prospects for successful negotiations receded, Soviet authorities signed a new trade and assistance pact with Kabul and deepened the extent of their penetration into and control of the Afghani government.[70] Moscow also intensified its internal press coverage of the twilight war, describing the heroic exploits of Soviet forces and preparing the public to accept the losses inherent in the growing Soviet commitment.[71]

While direct Sino–Soviet negotiations over the normalization of relations continued during the Chernenko interregnum, the overall tone of dealings between the two communist nations deteriorated as both rediscovered that fundamental bilateral issues and long-standing commitments to third parties separated them. Speaking shortly after his elevation to power, the new General Secretary noted the complexity of the relationship:

The normalization of relations with the Chinese People's Republic could, of course, facilitate the enhancement of the role of socialism in international life. We are consistent advocates of such normalization. Political consultations show, however, that there are still differences on a number of fundamental questions. In particular, we cannot enter into any accords that would be detrimental to the interests of third countries. But the exchange of opinions is continuing, and we consider it useful.[72]

Chernenko's references to "differences on a number of fundamental questions" and third-party interests signaled that Moscow was unwilling to compromise on its support of Vietnam's occupation of Kampuchea, its intervention in Afghanistan, or the deployment of its troops on the Sino–Soviet border.[73] Further irritation came from the warming Sino–U.S. relationship, which included visits from President Reagan himself, the chairman of the Joint Chiefs of Staff, and the prospects of U.S. arms sales to the PRC. Similar high-level contacts with Britain and Japan also fueled Soviet suspicions that China was being lured into a de facto anti-Soviet alliance. To signal its displeasure, the new regime abruptly cancelled a visit to Beijing by First Deputy Premier Ivan Arkhipov scheduled for May 1984 and resumed bitterly anti-Chinese commentary in the media. Although the talks eventually were held in December 1984, they produced only a limited agreement on scientific and technical cooperation and improved commercial relations and left untouched the fundamental issues that separated the two nations.[74]

Despite efforts to improve Soviet–Japanese relations, economic and political ties deteriorated during Chernenko's brief tenure. By the early 1980s both trade and joint developmental projects that would have utilized Japanese capital and technology to extract Soviet raw materials had fallen victim to the downturn in the world economy, changing Japanese priorities, and the problems of operating such projects under harsh Siberian conditions, and Japan had slipped from second to fifth place among the USSR's industrialized trading partners.[75] The still unresolved issue of the Kurile Islands remained central to any improvement of relations, and Tokyo's willingness to increase military expenditures under the Nakasone government brought a quick Soviet protest.[76] The October visit of Politburo member Dinmukhamed Kunaev improved the tone of the relationship between the two nations but did little to deal with the substantive issues, leading the Soviet visitor to conclude that "Soviet–Japanese relations have seen better days."[77]

Soviet policy toward Western Europe still remained under the long shadow of missile diplomacy, and Moscow's withdrawal from the talks on strategic and intermediate-range systems and its shorter absence from the Vienna-based talks on conventional weapons did little to improve relations. For its part, the Soviet Union continued its attempts to split the Western allies on the issue of arms talks in general and the further deployment of Pershing II and cruise missiles in particular, but with little result.

Soviet policy toward Britain broke little new ground despite the favorable reception accorded to Margaret Thatcher in her meeting with Chernenko shortly after Andropov's funeral. Yet a routine exchange of visits by First Deputy Foreign Minister Kornienko and British Foreign Secretary Geoffrey Howe produced no positive results in light of the Thatcher government's endorsement of the American position on Euromissiles.[78] British efforts to improve relations throughout the summer and early autumn fell victim to remaining suspicion over Soviet intelligence activities in Great Britain and Moscow's support, both diplomatic and financial, of striking British miners.[79] While Gorbachev's visit to London in December 1984 proved to be a personal success for the ebullient leader, it produced little other than a call for improved commercial and diplomatic relations.[80]

Soviet relations with West Germany deteriorated markedly, largely as a result of Bonn's willingness to deploy

U.S. intermediate-range missiles on its territory. Moscow's earlier attempts to recoup its losses with the Kohl government, whose election it had openly opposed, turned to overt hostility, and the visit of Vice Chancellor and Foreign Minister Hans-Dietrich Genscher to the Soviet capital in May 1984 produced only stern lectures that relations would remain at a low ebb until the American deployment was reversed.[81] By the summer, the Soviet position had hardened even further, and Bonn was accused of violating the spirit of the 1970 nonaggression pact between the two nations.[82] The Soviet media launched an obviously well-orchestrated campaign accusing the Federal Republic of revanchism.[83] Hoping to blunt new West German efforts at building better ties with East Europe, Moscow pressured the East German and Bulgarian governments to reject Bonn's advances, and in September both Erich Honecker and Todor Zhivkov cancelled scheduled visits to the German capital.

Soviet dealings with the Mitterrand government in Paris fared little better. Although the French president visited Moscow in June, his support of the U.S. position on Euromissiles overshadowed all other aspects of the talks. Yet even in condemning the French position, Chernenko attempted to distinguish between the relative guilt of those nations who had merely supported the deployment and those who had permitted the placement of U.S. weapons on their soil. Moscow used the occasion of the visit of a French parliamentary delegation once again to chide Paris for its support of the United States and to charge, in keeping with its campaign against West Germany, that the French government was contributing to the non-nuclear rearmament of their mutual former enemy.[84]

In the Middle East, Soviet diplomacy continued to pursue improved relations with the more moderate Arab states, even at the expense of a cooling of relations with its primary client, Syria. The improvement of relations with Egypt begun under Andropov continued, and new ambassadors were exchanged in the summer, marking the end of a break in full diplomatic relations that resulted from the expulsion of Soviet personnel from Egypt in the early 1970s. Relations with the Saudis also improved, and a high-level Kuwaiti delegation visited Moscow in July to discuss arms purchases.[85] A Soviet trade delegation also visited Jordan in October, and the USSR concluded a 20-year friendship treaty with North Yemen, a moderate nation with strong ties to Saudi Arabia.

At the other end of the Middle East political spectrum, Syrian ties to Moscow were weakened even though Hafez Al-Assad visited the new leadership in October. The Soviet call for an international peace conference that would include the United States ran counter to Syrian wishes, and the resumption of Soviet–Egyptian relations was not well received in Damascus. More importantly, Moscow remained conspicuously aligned with Iraq in its bitter war with Iran, whose most important backing in the region came from Syria. Chernenko also made it clear to Assad that Syria's special relationship with Moscow in terms of military procurement would be ended, with the overall needs of the region now dictating Soviet arms sales decisions.[86]

Soviet successes in the Middle East were not matched by similar events in Africa. Angola and Mozambique, the two principal Soviet clients in the region, had negotiated separate military disengagement pacts with South Africa shortly before Chernenko came to power. The only bright point in Soviet relations with the area came in a marked improvement of ties with the government of Ethiopia, which in September adopted a Leninist-style party structure to consolidate its hold. Mengistu Haile Mariam's December visit to Moscow proved to be a well publicized celebration of that transformation and concluded with the signing of a long-term agreement for closer economic cooperation.[87]

A LESS THAN BIPARTISAN FOREIGN POLICY

While the basic consensus within the Soviet leadership continued during Chernenko's rule, two developments occurred to suggest that some degree of division lay just below the surface. First, the Soviet leadership reversed course on the crucial question of the resumption of arms control talks. While there were few if any visible indications of disagreement within the top circles, the issue of pursuing these once-aborted negotiations must have produced considerable debate. Although we cannot be certain of the divisions, the most likely line-up pitted those who wished to pursue a traditional U.S.-centered notion of detente and arms control against those who sought a more flexible policy toward a wider diversity of Western nations and Japan. Numbered among the former unquestionably were the new General Secretary and probably most of the Brezhnev old guard, who had been closely identified with the improvement of Soviet–U.S. relations and who longed for a return to what had been an intellectually less complex and politically more profitable bilateral thaw between the major superpowers. Among those who sought to differentiate among potential partners in improved relations and to hold forth the prospects of a European oriented version of detente that, however temporarily or permanently, excluded the Americans were included Gorbachev and much of the Andropov entourage. Most difficult to place in this context is Foreign Minister Gromyko himself, who — like the political survivor he has always been — mirrored the existing official line with little variation or nuance. The return to the arms talks clearly signaled the victory of the Chernenko faction and the return of a U.S.-centered foreign policy, no matter how difficult the course. But the conditions and caveats that surrounded the Soviet willingness to return to the bargaining table suggested that those who doubted the prospects for improved ties with Washington had exacted a price for their pro forma support, and doubters such as Gorbachev continued to stress the importance of improved relations with Western Europe completely independent of the fate of Soviet–U.S. dealings.

Second, obvious differences emerged between the military and civilian leadership over key questions such as the Soviet willingness to match the Americans in the development of a new generation of high-technology weapons and the inevitably costly domestic trade-offs that would be required. The dismissal of Marshal Ogarkov in September and the replacement of the deceased Defense Minister Ustinov with the politically insignificant Marshal Sokolov indicated a victory for those who wished, at the least, to postpone a decision about costly new commitments to development of improved weapons systems. Consistent with its own hopes for a return to detente and its consumer priorities at home, the Chernenko regime adhered to a foreign policy line that held forth the possibility that better ties with Washington and a return to meaningful arms control would permit it to shift resources to meet internal needs.

Foreign Minister Gromyko's comments during the brief Chernenko interregnum indicate his general agreement with the official line, at first bitterly condemning the U.S. arms build-up and then cautiously moving toward the possibility of improved ties. The contrast between his comments at the opening of the 39th session of the United Nations General Assembly in late September 1984 and his keynote address at the November 7th celebrations in Moscow suggests the shift. In the former, he reiterated the reasons for the Soviet withdrawal from arms negotiations and portrayed the U.S. intention to develop a star wars defense system as the critical roadblock in an improvement of relations.[88] In the latter, however, he now saw the possibility of "opportunities" for the Reagan administration to prove its good intentions, although he still described Soviet–U.S. relations as being in a state of "disarray."[89] In his election speech for the Russian Republic soviet several months later in February 1985 he voiced a much harsher tone than the general secretary himself, who had implored Washington to take the new arms talks seriously. Instead Gromyko repeated the assertion that the Americans wanted to upset the arms balance and issued a stern warning:

The Soviet Union has bluntly warned the U.S. administration that the implementation of its designs with respect to space [that is, the creation of a comprehensive missile defense system] would mean that there could be no talk about any reduction, not to mention elimination, of nuclear weapons. Moreover, this would open the gates for a further arms race in all directions. . . . [90]

For the time that was left to him during the Chernenko regime — and there is considerable evidence that ill health impaired his ability to function in the fall and winter of 1984

— Defense Minister Ustinov continued to take a predictably hard line and to hint at the need for increased defense expenditures. Accusing Washington of seeking "world domination," Ustinov detailed the Soviet response of positioning additional SS-20 missiles in the German Democratic Republic and Czechoslovakia and missile-bearing submarines closer to American shores.[91] Perhaps understandably, he also took the occasion to call once again for consideration of increased defense expenditures, arguing that the need to strengthen the nation's defense capabilities had acquired "paramount importance."[92]

Mikhail Gorbachev evidenced a modest degree of independence on foreign policy issues, especially on the issue of resumption of improved relations with the West. On the guns and butter issue of investment priorities, he described the worsening of East–West relations as a situation that "diverts a considerable portion of our resources" from peaceful uses, suggesting that they might be applied to better domestic ends, and yet he lamented that in the light of U.S. build-ups, the USSR "cannot act otherwise." But in the same breath, he took the hardline position that Washington was to blame for the impasse and that "imperialist *diktat*" would not force the Soviet Union to return to the bargaining table.[93]

By December 1984, however, his position had softened in connection with the proffered resumption of arms control negotiations, and he returned to the line that detente was a highly selective process. Arguing that "in the 1970s Europe became the cradle of the policy of detente" and that the process of improved relations was only later "joined by the U.S. and Canada, which signed the Helsinki final act," he played upon the theme that "Europe was our common home" to stress the possibility of improved relations with the continent should attempts at arms negotiations with the United States fail. On the question of Soviet–U.S. ties, he offered the balanced assessment that "we continue to believe that there is no sensible alternative to a policy of peaceful coexistence" but also that "the Soviet Union well remembers the words and actions that created the climate of distrust and hostility and led to the destabilization of the international situation." Promising that the United States would find the Soviets to be a "reliable partner" if its intentions were serious, Gorbachev echoed the accepted line that agreement would be possible if all three arenas of arms negotiations "should be considered and resolved as interconnected questions."[94]

By February, when it was apparent that Chernenko's days were numbered, Gorbachev once again stressed his own pro-European sense of detente in his speech before the Russian Republic Supreme Soviet elections. While he averred that the Soviet Union was approaching the new arms control negotiations with "a sincere desire to achieve concrete results," he charged that Washington was "putting out an endless stream of statements sowing skepticism on the success of the talks." Suggesting that Moscow took the broader view, he argued that

while attaching great importance to the normalization of relations with the U.S. and to honest talks with it on all urgent problems of international life, at the same time we do not forget for a minute that the world is not limited to that country — it is much larger. The Soviet Union has devoted and is devoting great and constant attention to its relations with all states that want peace and equal and mutually advantageous cooperation.

Stressing the pro-European theme, Gorbachev continued that

the Soviet people have faith in the common sense of the West Europeans and believe that they have a stake in preventing Europe — our common home — from being turned into a theater of military operations, into a proving ground for testing the Pentagon's doctrines of "limited" nuclear war. We note with satisfaction the desire of many West European states for a political dialogue. For its part, the USSR has adhered and continues to adhere to a policy of good-neighbor relations among all European states.[95]

For his part, Grigorii Romanov, the party secretary in charge of the military-industrial complex and a would-be contender for the highest office, took a harder line in his comments before the republic elections. His tone on the American threat was considerably more foreboding:

Imperialism, above all American imperialism, has conceived the idea of halting the process of social development and the national and social liberation of peoples. The most reactionary, adventuristic circles in the West have made an even more drastic threat: They have decided to seek the restoration of the sway of imperialistic regimes everywhere in the world.[96]

Describing the Soviet response, Romanov promised that the USSR would administer a "resolute rebuff" to U.S. efforts while "at the same time actively striving for the normalization of international relations as a whole," a formulation that suggested that improved relations were a secondary priority. Promising that U.S. efforts were "unable to seriously slow our movement, let alone to force world socialism to retreat," he asserted that "such is the onward march of history. And no one can defeat it." In keeping with his own responsibilities for the military, he told his constituents that

I would like to emphasize . . . that while seeking peace and consistently acting in the name of peace, the party Central Committee and the Soviet government will continue to show tireless concern for the strengthening of the country's defense capability. Soviet people can rest firmly assured that any attempts by imperialism, using military force, to resolve the dispute with socialism in its favor are doomed to failure.[97]

Viktor Grishin had little to say on foreign policy issues during the brief Chernenko interregnum. His criticisms of Washington's foreign policy held closely to the party line, condemning the deployment of missiles in Europe and plans for the "militarization of space."[98] Yet he refused to reject the possibility that the new round of arms talks in Geneva might produce positive results, arguing that only "time will tell" whether the United States would pursue serious arms negotiations. He showed little sympathy with the military's request for additional resources; speaking in Warsaw at the celebration of the liberation of Poland, he claimed that "the Soviet Union and the socialist commonwealth possess sufficient might to uphold their independence and the positions of socialism." Moreover, he implied that even the most aggressive armament program in the West would not deflect the Soviet Union from implementing programs for technological modernization and improving the standard of living, both priorities that would draw resources from the military:

The imperialists' hopes of impeding the successful development of the socialist countries through all kinds of economic pressure, blockades and blackmail are also illusory. Our countries have at their disposal everything necessary, even in the present complex conditions, to move forward, to solve — through collective efforts — urgent problems of economic development and scientific and technical progress, and to carry out planned social programs.[99]

Two days later, speaking to Polish workers, he offered a message about the prospects for East–West ties that was directed more at his counterparts in Moscow than at his present audience. Noting that the "struggle for a turn for the better in international relations ... will be complex and stubborn," he called for the present leadership to evidence "great staying power" in pursuing talks with the Americans, a formulation that suggested that he attached great hopes for a return to detente and all that it implied in terms of domestic priorities.[100]

Whatever their differences on foreign policy, the members of the Politburo could not have been unaware that the next round of succession was close at hand and that once again difficult choices would have to be made about the selection of another interim leader or the promotion of a younger figure whose presence would likely be felt well into the next century.

NOTES

1. *Pravda*, February 11, 1984.
2. Radio Liberty Research Bulletin (hereafter "Radio Liberty"), 105/84, March 7, 1984.
3. Mark Zlotnik, "Chernenko succeeds," *Problems of Communism* 33 (March-April 1984):17–31.
4. Radio Liberty, 105/84, March 7, 1984.
5. *Pravda*, February 8, 1984.
6. Zlotnik, "Chernenko succeeds," p. 20–22.
7. *Pravda*, February 14, 1984.
8. Ibid.

9. *Pravda,* February 14, 1984.
10. Radio Liberty, 119/84, March 15, 1984.
11. *Pravda,* April 11, 1984.
12. Radio Liberty, 150/84, April 17, 1984.
13. Radio Liberty, 104/84, March 8, 1984.
14. Ibid.
15. *Kommunist* (no. 6, 1984); Radio Liberty, 353/84, September 18, 1984.
16. Radio Liberty, 426/84, November 9, 1984.
17. Radio Liberty, 324/84, August 30, 1984, and 457/84, November 29, 1984.
18. Radio Liberty, 387/84, October 9, 1984.
19. *Literaturnaia gazeta,* no. 42, 1984; and Radio Liberty, 422/84, November 2, 1984.
20. *Krasnaia zvezda,* February 17, 1984.
21. *Pravda,* September 5, 1984; and *Krasnaia zvezda,* September 6, 1984.
22. Radio Liberty, 338/84, September 7, 1984.
23. *New York Times,* September 6, 1984.
24. Radio Liberty, 445/84, November 23, 1984.
25. *Kommunist* (no. 3, February 1983).
26. Radio Liberty, 151/84, April 12, 1984, and 439/84, November 16, 1984.
27. *Pravda,* April 12, 1984.
28. Radio Liberty, 151/84, April 12, 1984.
29. Radio Liberty, 102/84, March 29, 1984.
30. Ibid.
31. Radio Liberty, 464/84, December 10, 1984.
32. *Pravda,* October 24, 1984.
33. *Pravda,* October 19, 1984.
34. *Pravda,* December 11, 1984.
35. *Pravda,* December 17 and 19, 1984.
36. Radio Liberty, 24/85, January 25, 1985.
37. Zhores A. Medvedev, *Gorbachev* (New York: Norton, 1986), pp. 127–29.
38. *Observer,* March 17, 1985.
39. Medvedev, *Gorbachev,* pp. 6–11.
40. *Pravda,* February 14, 1984.
41. Ibid.
42. *Pravda,* March 3, 1984.
43. *Pravda,* April 11, 1984.
44. *Pravda,* April 26, 1984.
45. Ibid.
46. *Kommunist* (no. 18, December 1984):4.
47. *Pravda,* November 16, 1984.
48. *Pravda,* February 23, 1985.
49. *Pravda,* August 9, 1984; and *Izvestiia,* July 26, 1984.

50. *Pravda,* November 16, 1984.

51. *Izvestiia,* October 24, 1984.

52. Radio Liberty, 242/84, June 18, 1984; 437/84, November 16, 1984; 476/84, December 12, 1984; and 46/85, February 12, 1985.

53. Radio Liberty, 37/84, February 4, 1984.

54. *Pravda,* April 9, 1984.

55. Radio Liberty, 201/84, May 18, 1984.

56. *Pravda,* March 3 and April 9, 1984.

57. *Pravda,* May 20, 1984.

58. *Pravda,* June 3, 1984.

59. *Pravda,* July 2 and August 6, 1984.

60. Radio Liberty, 209/84, May 23, 1984; and 363/84, September 22, 1984.

61. *Pravda,* September 2, 1984.

62. *Pravda,* September 28 and 29 and October 1, 1984.

63. *Pravda,* September 26, 1984.

64. *Washington Post,* October 17, 1984; and *Pravda,* October 18, 1984.

65. *Pravda,* November 18, 1984.

66. *Pravda,* November 23, 1984.

67. *Pravda,* January 9, 1985.

68. *Pravda,* January 14, 1985.

69. *Pravda,* February 23, 1985. It should be recalled that these comments were probably written by aides of the ailing General Secretary.

70. *Izvestiia,* March 9, 1984; and Radio Liberty, 414/84, October 19, 1984.

71. *Izvestiia,* July 31, 1984; *Komsomolskaia pravda,* September 9, 1984; *Pravda,* September 20, 1984; and *Komsomolskaia pravda,* December 27, 1984.

72. *Pravda,* March 3, 1984.

73. Radio Liberty, 475/84, December 17, 1984.

74. *Pravda,* December 24, 27, and 30, 1984.

75. Radio Liberty, 100/84, March 11, 1984.

76. *Pravda,* August 12, 1984.

77. *Pravda,* October 26, 1984.

78. Radio Liberty, 131/84, March 27, 1984.

79. Radio Liberty, 449/84, November 26, 1984.

80. *Pravda,* December 17, 19, 21, and 22, 1984.

81. *Pravda,* May 22, 1984; and Radio Liberty, 207/84, May 23, 1984.

82. *Izvestiia,* August 11, 1984.

83. Radio Liberty, 38/85, February 5, 1985.

84. *Pravda,* October 26, 1984.

85. Radio Liberty, 275/84, July 17, 1984.

86. Radio Liberty, 401/84, October 18, 1984.

87. *Pravda,* December 18, 1984.

88. *Pravda,* September 28, 1984.

89. *Pravda,* November 7, 1984.
90. *Pravda,* February 20, 1985.
91. *Pravda,* May 21, 1984.
92. *Pravda,* February 23, 1984.
93. *Pravda,* September 9, 1984.
94. *Pravda,* December 19, 1984.
95. *Pravda,* February 21, 1985.
96. *Pravda,* February 15, 1985.
97. Ibid.
98. *Pravda,* January 17, 1985.
99. Ibid.
100. *Pravda,* January 19, 1985.

5   Gorbachev in Power

SETTING THE STAGE FOR THE NEXT SUCCESSION

Throughout the winter of 1984/85, Moscow was once again on a death watch, the third in as many years. The ailing General Secretary, who had returned to active political life in September, slipped from public view amid rumors of his declining health and the possibility of his resignation at the up-coming 27th Party Congress. Although there had been a hint of forceful leadership earlier in the autumn when the regime reversed itself on a return to arms control talks and sacked Marshal Ogarkov, there now remained only a sense of drift. The Politburo deadlock between the Andropov faction, now centered on the rising fortunes of Gorbachev, and the old guard, increasingly supporting the candidacy of Moscow party chief Viktor Grishin, continued; aside from the death of Ustinov, there were no politically significant changes in the Politburo during Chernenko's tenure.

The General Secretary's failing health was confirmed by his repeated absences from important ceremonial occasions. His speech to his constituents just prior to the February 1985 Russian Republic soviet elections was read in his absence by Grishin, and his appearance at an obviously makeshift polling station on election day and then in a brief ceremony accepting his credentials a few days later revealed an ailing and infirm leader whose condition had deteriorated markedly since his last public appearance two months prior.[1] In marked contrast with their behavior during Andropov's long illness, Soviet officials now spoke openly with Western journalists about Chernenko's illness.[2]

Chernenko's declining fortunes sparked a predictable increase in the jockeying among his would-be successors. As they edged closer to another round of succession, the existing leadership could not have missed the obvious point that events were making it increasingly difficult to deal with the question of generational change. Within both the Politburo and the Secretariat — now all the more clearly divided into a coterie of new, younger figures who had been Andropov's protégés, and the older Brezhnev group — the political costs as well as the opportunities were all the more apparent. For younger figures such as Gorbachev, Romanov, Aliev, and even more junior figures waiting in the wings, the succession of yet another member of the old guard would postpone their rise to power, an acceptable state of affairs only if they remained locked in combat with no obvious frontrunner emerging to unite the next generation of Kremlin leaders. Yet for the remaining members of the old guard, it was now all the more difficult to put forth acceptable candidates for the top post. The Politburo was now a very different body of leaders from what it had been even just two years before, and Ustinov's death and Gromyko's seeming willingness to accept the transition with good grace left no members of the inner circle who had dominated the Kremlin in Brezhnev's days to step forward.

In the final months of Chernenko's stay in power, three would-be successors vied for the preeminence needed to succeed him. Gorbachev remained the favored candidate of the Andropov faction and of those members of the old guard who had little to fear from the transition. Already elevated to the status of de facto second secretary, he had held broad responsibilities for party and economic affairs under both Andropov and Chernenko. Set against his preeminence as the heir apparent were the rapid rise of Viktor Grishin and the faltering candidacy of Grigorii Romanov.

Gorbachev's candidacy was by far the strongest in terms of the conventional wisdom of Soviet politics. A member of both the Politburo and the Secretariat, he had been given broad responsibilities for the economy and for party affairs under both Andropov, his former patron who had unsuccessfully tapped him as his chosen heir, and Chernenko, whom he served as second in command on party affairs. He had wisely shed responsibilities for agriculture and had acquired increasing visibility on foreign policy issues, having served as a well-received Soviet emissary to Canada, Italy, and Great Britain. Moreover, he had acquired the all-important portfolio for ideology, which had been held by Andropov and Chernenko prior to their ascension to the top post. In the final months before Chernenko's death, he chaired the Politburo and maintained general oversight over the affairs of the Secretariat; he also apparently played a central role in the Defense Council as it prepared for a new round of negotiations with the Americans. He had spoken third in order of prominence in his speech to his constituents before the Russian Republic soviet election; only Tikhonov and Chernenko himself were accorded more favored positions. Only a day before Chernenko slipped into a coma, he led a Politburo delegation to the celebration of International Women's Day, his name being listed first among Politburo members in attendance.[3]

Gorbachev also seemed to embody the energy, hopes, and aspirations of the next generation of Soviet officials. Pictured both at home and abroad as a vigorous and candid leader, he was known for his straightforward approach to issues, his ability to speak without prepared text on complex and difficult questions, and his penchant for surrounding himself with competent technocrats. He had cultivated ties with the nation's think tanks, and members of reform-oriented institutions such as the Institute of American and Canadian Studies spoke openly to visiting foreigners of their hopes that he would replace Chernenko. He had also been associated with Andropov's brief-lived attempt to bring new blood into the central and regional party apparatus, a role that cast him as the real or potential benefactor of younger cadres whose upward mobility had been delayed by the lack of turnover in higher party posts during Brezhnev's rule.

Yet in some ways, Gorbachev's strengths were also his weaknesses. As the most visible proponent of reform and the renewal of party and state cadres, he became the lightening rod for those who opposed change for whatever reason. Moreover he now held the always dangerous position of the acknowledged frontrunner, making him a natural and tempting target for a coalition of opponents and less prominent also-rans. Among members of the Brezhnev old guard, his recent ascension to the Secretariat and Politburo would weigh against him — he became a member of the former in 1978 and a full member of the latter only in 1980 — as would the lackluster performance of Soviet agriculture under his tutelage. His relatively brief tenure in charge of party cadres under Andropov and Chernenko would have afforded him little opportunity to build an extensive patronage network. While 20 percent of the regional party secretaries and nearly a third of the department heads in the central apparatus had changed hands since Brezhnev's death, any extensive change in the all-important Central Committee — which would confirm the selection of Chernenko's replacement — would have to await the 27th Party Congress; until that time, it would remain a bastion of the middle- and upper-level leaders appointed to and sustained in power by the Brezhnev administration.

Perhaps the greatest weakness of Gorbachev's candidacy came from the likely finality of his rise to power. In both Andropov and Chernenko, the leadership had put forward General Secretaries whose age and poor health would have given them, at best, only a few years in power. But the rise of Gorbachev — or of any other younger figure — portended a consolidation of power that would last perhaps for two decades. For the members of the old guard, the choice was relatively simple: would they accept the inevitability of such change, whatever the political costs, or would they seek to postpone the rise of younger leaders by turning once again to a senior member of the Politburo? But for the younger leadership — which included figures such as Romanov, age 62, and most certainly figures such as Aliev, Ryzhkov, and Vorotnikov, who had risen under Andropov — the question was more complex: would they accept the elevation of one of their own number, knowing that such a selection would likely preclude their own chances for the top post and substantially alter their relationship with the new leader, who would emerge as primus inter pares? Or would they once again acquiesce in the selection of yet another interim General Secretary, hoping that time or the emergence of a cross-generational alliance would improve their own chances?

In the last months of Chernenko's rule, Moscow party secretary Viktor Grishin emerged as the General Secretary's own chosen heir apparent. Rumors were leaked to the Western media that he was "the man to watch," and he appeared prominently with the General Secretary in his few television appearances in February.[4] His selection to deliver Chernenko's election speech was a clear signal of his status and a direct parallel to Andropov's choice of Gorbachev to perform the same role only a year before. Dissident sources such as Zhores Medvedev report that Chernenko planned to resign in Grishin's favor at the 27th Party Congress (which was advanced to November because of the General Secretary's failing health), and that the timetable was then accelerated to stage the resignation at the March Central Committee plenum, which was scheduled to be held, as it turned out, only days after Chernenko's death.[5]

Grishin's candidacy could only have been based on a desire to stop Gorbachev's rise and on the old guard's reluctance to yield power. Age 70 at the time of Chernenko's death, he could have offered little more than another brief interim regime. On the positive side, he had party experience in the demanding post of Moscow party chief, a position that he had held since 1967. In addition, he had been promoted to candidate member of the Politburo in 1961, serving at that time as the Chairman of the All-Union Council of Trade Unions, and then to full member in 1971, four years after his reassignment to the Moscow post. However, he never served on the Secretariat, an experience that usually is regarded as sine qua non for any future General Secretary.

Despite his long experience in party affairs, he had never been a member of Brezhnev's inner circle. While the Soviet capital prospered during the years of his leadership, its good fortune was more attributable to its status as the first city rather than to his tutelage. His own ambitions for the top post were well known, as were his crude attempts to press his candidacy in the last years Brezhnev was in power. Neither a forceful leader in his own right nor a particularly threatening figure to either the old guard or the younger elements who had emerged under Andropov, he was perhaps an ideal interim candidate to block Gorbachev.

None of the other senior members of the Politburo was well positioned to make a bid for power. Nikolai Tikhonov was 79 and in poor health, and his long career in the state economic apparatus had not prepared him for the top party post. Dinmukhamed Kunaev, the Kazakh party secretary, and Vladimir Shcherbitskii, his Ukrainian counterpart, were both non-Russians, a serious impediment to their consideration. Only Andrei Gromyko, the foreign minister, remained a possibility among the old guard. Still vigorous at age 73, he too could have offered the possibility of a brief but respected interim regime. Yet his total preoccupation with foreign affairs and inexperience with domestic economic and political issues made him an unlikely candidate, especially in light of his emergence as a seemingly independent force within the Politburo with whom any future leader would have to reckon.

Grigorii Romanov's position as a serious challenger eroded in the last months of Chernenko's rule. By the February 1985 Russian Republic soviet elections, he had slipped to sixth place in the hierarchy as indicated by the timing of his speech to his constituents. The deterioration of his position was attributable both to his reputation as an authoritarian leader and to his curious position along the spectrum of reformers and conservatives. To the reformers, he was not the logical selection in light of the availability of the younger Gorbachev, even though his forward-looking economic reforms in Leningrad had earned him high marks. His association with the military and defense industries was also problematical; in the Secretariat for only a brief time, he had not been able to build support outside of military and industrial interests, whose own fortunes had declined during Chernenko's rule. To more conservative figures, he was an unlikely first choice as a candidate to block Gorbachev, especially in light of Grishin's availability. He had never been a member of Brezhnev's inner circle and had been kept at arm's length in the Leningrad post until Andropov appointed him to the Secretariat. His own record in Leningrad suggested that he too was intolerant of corruption and inefficiency and would pursue economic reforms with considerably more vigor than had Chernenko. At age 62, he might well hold on to power for a full decade, a prospect that threatened younger leaders hoping to move up the ladder and older members of the Brezhnev group who could be challenged by any leader with so much time to consolidate power and put his policies into action.

GORBACHEV'S RISE TO POWER

Chernenko's death on March 10, 1985, marked the end of Moscow's third death watch and triggered an intense scramble within the Kremlin to choose his successor. Any hopes that the ailing General Secretary would step down in favor of Grishin were ended two days earlier on March 8 when he slipped into a coma, where he remained until his death. The formal announcement of his demise was not made until March 12, a day and a half after the critical Politburo meeting that chose his successor. Breaking precedent, *Pravda* and *Izvestiia* carried the story of Gorbachev's elevation on page one, bannering a report on the Central Committee session held on the 11th that confirmed his selection. Only a brief announcement of the death was carried on the first page; the official obituary, the medical announcement on the cause of death, and a portrait of the fallen leader were bumped to page two. Even in death, Chernenko was accorded second-rate treatment as a footnote in history, while his successor received the more prominent accolades of victory.

The prominence accorded Gorbachev on March 12th concealed the political conflict that surrounded his rise. Despite his preeminence as de facto second secretary and his designation to head the funeral commission, a post held by both Andropov and Chernenko shortly prior to their selection as General Secretary, he encountered last-minute opposition to his elevation to the top post. As had happened twice before, two scenarios emerged within the leadership, one resulting in a minority coalition to block Gorbachev's rise and the other producing a broader majority for the eventual winner.

While the reports are sketchy, it seems likely that Romanov took the lead in attempting to block Gorbachev's selection. According to reports that circulated some months later, after Romanov's dismissal from the Politburo, the former Leningrad secretary nominated Grishin for the top post. As a blocking maneuver, it was intended to capitalize both on Grishin's presumed acceptability to the members of the Brezhnev group and on the possibility that other more junior figures would agree to another interim regime in the hope of improving their chances at the top position. But while the strategy had worked once before at the time of Andropov's death, the situation within the Politburo and the timing of the succession made success unlikely.

By March 1985 the death or dismissal of senior members of the Politburo had made it a very different political body. Now the old guard was virtually equally balanced by more junior figures or by their own contemporaries who owed their recent advancement to Andropov rather than to Brezhnev or Chernenko. Their political weakness was further exacerbated by the absence of Kunaev, who was in Alma Ata at the time of Chernenko's death, of Shcherbitskii, who was leading a Soviet delegation in the United States, and of Vorotnikov, who was in Yugoslavia. At the critical Politburo session late in the evening of March 10th, at which the selection was actually made, it is certain that Shcherbitskii and Vorotnikov had not had time to reach Moscow and it is likely that Kunaev, who rushed back from Central Asia, also missed the vote.[6]

In institutional terms, the Politburo that met to choose Chernenko's successor also was less representative of the Soviet establishment. Absent as full voting members were representatives of the military and the KGB; Defense Minister Sokolov had not yet been elevated to candidate membership and was without significant party experience, and KGB chief Chebrikov was only a candidate member.

Absent also was a representative of heavy industry, although Romanov presumably had ties to the defense sector. Although Gorbachev had held general responsibility for the economy as a whole, he was not a specialist in industrial affairs. Vladimir Dolgikh, a specialist in heavy industry and the energy sector whose bright prospects had begun to tarnish since Brezhnev's death, held only candidate membership on the Politburo in addition to his post on the Secretariat, and Nikolai Ryzhkov, a former First Deputy Chairman of Gosplan with experience in heavy industry, was a newcomer to the Secretariat appointed by Andropov in 1982 to head the program of industrial and managerial reforms.

It also seems unlikely that there was significant support for Grishin's candidacy from the junior members of the Politburo. Aliev owed his elevation to Andropov and likely hoped for further advancement, perhaps to chairman of the Council of Ministers to replace the ailing Tikhonov; in any event, he would have little to gain from Grishin's success and could not hope, because of his nationality, to rise eventually to General Secretary in case of a prolonged deadlock. Solomentsev and Vorotnikov were also unlikely to incline toward Grishin. Each owed his long-overdue elevation to full membership in the Politburo or the rescue of his career to Andropov and doubtless harbored resentments against the old leadership. Moreover, neither was a viable candidate for the top post. Solomentsev's advanced age at 71 made it likely that his present post as chairman of the Party Control Committee would be the apex of his career, and that body would prosper more under Gorbachev's leadership because of its active involvement in rooting out malfeasance within the party. Vorotnikov might aspire to higher office, possibly in competition with Aliev for Tikhonov's slot, and it seemed more likely that Gorbachev would play the role of patron.

The attempt to block Gorbachev also faltered because of Gromyko's crucial role of kingmaker. His selection to nominate Gorbachev at the March 11th Central Committee session probably indicated deference to his senior position rather than, as in the past, his status as the most prominent challenger now compelled to nominate the candidate who had bested him and offer the traditional plea for unity. Whether he strongly backed Gorbachev from the beginning or simply emerged as the consensus builder cannot be determined; his rambling nominating speech had not been carefully drafted in advance and was not immediately published in the Soviet media, perhaps suggesting that he stepped forward at the last minute to play the role of healer.

Whatever Gromyko's initial role, it seems evident that the new General Secretary won the immediate endorsement of at least three of his colleagues — Aliev, Solomentsev, and Gromyko — and may well have picked up the backing of senior figures such as the late-arriving Kunaev, Vorotnikov, and Shcherbitskii, as the Romanov–Grishin coalition fell apart. The initial line-up probably saw a four-to-three split, pitting the votes of Gorbachev, Aliev, Solomentsev, and Gromyko against a Grishin-Romanov-Tikhonov bloc. The political survival of both Kunaev and Shcherbitskii beyond the 27th Party Congress suggests that they quickly fell into line despite their ties to the Brezhnev group, just as the dismissal of Romanov in June and the sacking of Grishin just prior to the congress implies their opposition.

There also is evidence that the Politburo vote was less than unanimous and that opposition carried over into the Central Committee plenum. As Zhores Medvedev has noted, the description of both votes differed slightly from the way in which the Andropov and Chernenko elections had been handled. In the latter cases, the vote was described as *edinoglasno,* which implies that a formal vote has been taken and the decision has been unanimous. But in Gorbachev's case, both Gromyko's description of the Politburo's instructions and the Central Committee vote were described as *edinodushno,* a term used to describe a situation in which there has been overwhelming agreement but not complete unanimity.[7]

The Central Committee meeting on March 11th was initially chaired by Gorbachev himself, following the activist precedent set by Andropov at the time of his ascension to power. Gromyko's nominating speech, given "on instructions" from the Politburo, was a rambling and personalized endorsement of the new leader. Breaking precedent, it was not immediately published in the media, suggesting that the Foreign Minister had spoken extemporaneously, and that time was required to produce an acceptable written text. An obviously edited official version was published weeks later in *Kommunist*.[8]

While Gromyko's comments warmly praised Gorbachev for being a "man of principles" and holding "strong convictions," they made virtually no reference to his policies or to his previous experience other than to note that he had chaired the Politburo in Chernenko's absence and presided over the Secretariat. Perhaps because little could be cited in concrete terms — his years in charge of agriculture had not witnessed outstanding successes, and the economic reforms over which he had presided had produced little result — Gromyko contented himself with lauding the new leader's ability at "grasping the essence" of problems and "organiz[ing] people and finding a common language with them." Perhaps the purpose of his comments was to portray Gorbachev as a strong leader capable of dealing with the nation's many problems, and thus to capitalize on the respect accorded Andropov for a brief attempt at forceful leadership, an interpretation consistent with the likelihood that the edited portions of Gromyko's speech had dealt candidly with the leadership issue.[9]

Gorbachev's first speech to the Central Committee as the newly elected General Secretary was brief and to the point. His references to Chernenko hardly exceeded the cursory review necessary at such an occasion, and his sole concession to mending political fences was to speak of the correctness of party policy "worked out at the 26th congress and at subsequent plenary sessions of the Central Committee, with the active participation of Yuri Vladimirovich Andropov and Konstantin Ustinovich Chernenko," a formulation that muted his past inclination to stress the importance of the November 1982 plenum that elected Andropov.[10]

From the beginning, he made it clear that economic policy would be the central focus of his administration. Calling for "the acceleration of the country's social and economic development," he noted that such a policy required the "transformation of the material and technical base of production" and the "improvement of the system of social relations, economic relations above all." Returning to themes associated with what Soviet theorists have termed the "scientific and technological revolution," Gorbachev called for the nation to place its faith in the development of high technology:

We will have to achieve a decisive turn in switching the national economy onto the tracks of intensive development. We must, we are obliged, in a short time to attain the most advanced scientific and technical positions and to reach the highest world level in the productivity of social labor.[11]

To this end, the General Secretary pledged a thorough review of management, including an expansion of the decision-making powers of individual enterprises and the creation of rewards and incentives that would "give them a greater stake in the final results of their work."

While there was no clear statement of economic priorities in terms of allocations to heavy industry, consumer goods, or the military, the general secretary's comments hinted that the latter two were not at the top of his list. Reversing his predecessor's penchant for consumer goods, he asserted that while the standard of living would rise with the economy as a whole, "the improvement of man's living conditions would be based on his growing contribution to the common cause," that is, on higher productivity within the consumer good sector rather than on greater investment. The military also received only slight attention. While he pledged that it "will continue to have everything necessary" for national defense, he deferred reference to the national security question until near the end of his speech, an obvious signal of the military's decreased status, as was the absence of prominent military figures at the Chernenko funeral.

Striking a new tone, Gorbachev also called for greater "publicity" in the work of party and state organs. Implying both a greater flow of information and candor as well as expanded public discussion of issues, the promise of improved "publicity" would improve the ties between regime and society. "The better informed people are," Gorbachev argued, "the more intelligently they act and the more actively they support the party and its plans and programmatic goals."

On foreign policy, the new General Secretary first turned his attention to China, calling for a "serious improvement" in relations between the two communist states, a goal that was held to be "completely possible" given "reciprocity" on both sides. Noting that the Geneva arms control talks would begin the following day, he reiterated the Soviet desire for a freeze on the growth of nuclear arsenals and for a halt to the deployment of U.S. missiles in Europe, a formulation that omitted a demand for an immediate withdrawal of the already deployed missiles as a precondition for the success of the Geneva talks. He further called for a "real, major reduction in stockpiled arms" and for the prevention of the militarization of space, both stock Soviet responses already articulated before the decision to return to the arms control talks. Taken in toto, his comments merely reflected present Soviet policy, and the moderate tone seemed intended to keep options open in dealing with both Beijing and Washington.

Speaking the following day at Chernenko's burial, Gorbachev returned to the old formulation concerning the emphasis to be placed on past Central Committee plenums. Once again he spoke of the party's policies as flowing from the "26th CPSU congress and the November [1982] and subsequent plenary sessions of the Central Committee," thus establishing a clearer tie to the Andropov period. The diminished status of the military again was underscored by Gorbachev's assertion that "socialism ... will prove its advantages, but it will do so not by force of arms but by force of example in all fields of the vital activity of society — economic, political, and moral."[12]

Gorbachev began his attempts to consolidate power almost immediately. Despite the evident opposition he encountered at the March Politburo and Central Committee sessions, he felt sufficiently in charge the following month to set the date for the 27th Party Congress and to begin a series of important personnel changes. The congress was scheduled to begin on February 25, 1986, a four-month delay beyond the date rumored during Chernenko's last days. The postponement probably was caused by the new regime's need to control the delegate selection process and arrange the election of a new Central Committee. Not accidentally, as a Russian would say, the congress was also timed to coincide with the 30th anniversary of Khrushchev's de-Stalinization speech, a choice heavy with symbolism for the new leadership.[13]

A number of important personnel changes also took place. Viktor Chebrikov, head of the KGB, was promoted from candidate to full membership in the Politburo and Central Committee Secretaries Egor Ligachev and Nikolai Ryzhkov were moved directly to full Politburo membership, bypassing candidate member status. Marshal Sokolov, who had become Defense Minister at the time of Ustinov's death, was promoted to candidate member of the Politburo, and Viktor Nikonov, who had assumed responsibility for agriculture when Gorbachev surrendered that portfolio, was made a member of the Secretariat.[14]

These appointments strengthened Gorbachev's hold and moved partially toward restoring the institutional representation of important power blocs within the Politburo. With the exception of Marshal Sokolov, the new appointees had begun their rise to the party's highest levels during Andropov's tenure. Ryzhkov, who was 56, was a specialist in heavy industry who had successfully held the posts of First Deputy Minister of Heavy and Transport Machine Building and First Deputy Chairman of Gosplan before being appointed to the Secretariat by Andropov in 1982. He had been linked both to Kirilenko and subsequently to Vorotnikov, and his appointment continued Andropov's practice of drawing upon Kirilenko's supporters and solidified ties with Vorotnikov. Moreover, it restored a representative of heavy industry to full membership in the Politburo.[15]

Chebrikov's promotion also solidified ties to the KGB and restored the intelligence and security agency to the status it had held since the 1973 appointment of Andropov to full membership in the Politburo. Lacking the personal ties to the KGB of his former mentor, Gorbachev undoubtedly thought it wise to reassure the agency of its important place within the hierarchy. Chebrikov's promotion was all the more significant in light of Sokolov's elevation only to candidate membership. For the first time since Stalin's rule, the KGB outranked the military in terms of representation on the highest party body.

Ligachev's promotion to full membership in the Politburo signaled the rise of yet another Andropov protégé who had gone over to the Gorbachev camp. He had initially been brought into the Secretariat to handle regional party cadres. His appointment to the Politburo both underscored his new responsibilities for party cadres in general, an extremely significant post in light of the approaching party congress, and suggested that he was soon likely to assume responsibility for ideological affairs, a position consistent with his earlier experience as deputy head of the Central Committee's Department of Agitation and Propaganda. Known to be a strict disciplinarian who had rooted out corrupt local party cadres in his earlier post, Ligachev was now positioned to extend the campaign against malfeasance and corruption to higher levels.[16]

The naming of three new members of the Politburo fundamentally shifted the partisan nature of that body. Six of the current 13 members have been appointed since Brezhnev's death (Aliev, Vorotnikov, Solomentsev, Chebrikov, Ligachev, and Ryzhkov) and with his own vote Gorbachev could, for the first time, form a bare majority without courting votes from among the members of the old guard — assuming that the former Andropov group and Gorbachev's own more recent appointments formed a united front.

Viktor Nikonov's promotion to the Secretariat carried less political significance. Having worked his way up in the agricultural chain of command from a machine tractor station to the post of Russian Republic Minister of Agriculture, he was shifted to the Secretariat to take charge of the agriculture slot vacated by Gorbachev. It is safe to presume that he had been well known to the new General Secretary and probably to Vorotnikov, chairman of the Russian Republic Council of Ministers, suggesting that his appointment may well have been endorsed from both quarters.

The plenum was also significant for what did not happen. Vladimir Dolgikh, director of the Central Committee Department of Heavy and Power Industry and candidate member of the Politburo since 1982, was passed over for full membership in that body, a significant omission and a probable signal that the decline in his political fortunes that began under Andropov would continue, especially in light of Ryzhkov's rapid advancement.

The continuing absence of a representative of the Leningrad party organization among the full members of the Politburo and of its Belorussian counterpart among the candidate members was also strange. In the former case, Lev Zaikov's elevation to the Leningrad secretaryship was difficult to read. He had been promoted over the heads of more senior party figures, suggesting high-level intervention to undercut Romanov's ability to handpick his successor and press for his quick admission to the Politburo. The Belorussian case was even more problematical; there was no apparent reason to delay the appointment of the Belorussian party secretary to candidate membership except for the prospect that Gorbachev simply had more important priorities at this particular Central Committee session involving the promotion of Ryzhkov, Chebrikov, and Sokolov.[17]

Gorbachev's comments at the April plenum were almost exclusively directed at the nation's economic woes. While the details of his criticisms and recommendations will be reviewed below, their urgent tone was an important political message no less significant than the personnel changes seen at the plenum. Even the theme of continuity with the policies of the 26th Party Congress was invested with new meaning:

Today we reaffirm the continuity of the strategic course worked out by the 26th party congress and subsequent plenary sessions of the Central Committee. As Lenin understood it, continuity means unfailing progress, the identification and resolution of new problems, and the elimination of everything that impedes development. We should follow this Leninist tradition unswervingly.... [18]

For the first time in a public forum, the new General Secretary openly criticized his predecessors, under whose leadership "in the past few years unfavorable tendencies have intensified." Noting the sweeping changes in the economic and social profile of society in the last two decades, Gorbachev posed an important question:

What is the reason for the difficulties [in the economy]? The answer to this question, as you realize, is of fundamental importance for the party.

Nature and a number of external factors have had an impact, of course. But the main thing, I think, is that the changes in the objective conditions of the development of production, the need for accelerating its intensification and for changes in the methods of economic management were not properly assessed in good time, and — this is especially important — no perseverance was shown in working out and implementing major measures in the economic sphere. Comrades, we must become thoroughly aware of the existing situation and draw the most serious conclusions. The country's historical destiny and the position of socialism in today's world depend in large part on how we handle matters from now on.[19]

Set forth in terms simpler and bolder than uttered by any other top leader, the message was clear: the need for widespread changes in the economy based on the application of advanced technology and modern managerial practices had been underestimated by past leaders who had lacked the political will to press ahead with economically and politically costly reforms. Even if one allows for Gorbachev's understandable tendency to discount his predecessors' long-standing recommendations for the modernization of industry — the theory of the scientific and technological revolution and its larger embodiment in the concept of developed socialism had addressed these issues — his argument was still well on target. Both the economy and the society as a whole were at an important turning point, not unlike the so-called "second industrial revolution" in more advanced nations, at which commitments to the technological profile of the economy, the nature of the work force, and the style of both economic and political leadership would shape the USSR well into the next century.

Gorbachev also issued a clear challenge concerning the promotion of younger and more energetic officials. In his description of personnel policy, the ritual endorsement of "stability" was quickly followed by a foreshadowing of things to come:

The Politburo deems it fundamentally important to continue to pursue a line aimed at ensuring the stability of party leadership and the correct combination of experienced and young personnel. But this cannot be accompanied by any kind of stagnation in the movement of cadres. In their letters to the Central Committee, communists call attention to the fact that some leaders, holding the same post for a long time, frequently stop seeing new things and get used to shortcomings. This is something to think about; we must look for ways to achieve more active movement among our leadership cadres. It is necessary to more boldly promote women and promising young personnel to responsible posts.[20]

Gorbachev's references to the military also sustained the subtle downgrading of their status seen in earlier pronouncements. Reference to the military came late in the speech, led not only by the General Secretary's central comments on economic reforms but also by discussion of relatively trivial points such as the role of the news media, literature, and the arts. And while the brief reference promised the military "everything necessary for the defense of the motherland," it also labeled Soviet and East European forces as already constituting an "invincible force" in international life, a formulation that implied that an already invincible military establishment would require few additional resources.

Shortly after the April plenum, it became apparent that Ligachev was the most rapidly rising star in the new leadership and that he had assumed key responsibilities for ideology. The protocol line-up of top party figures at the May Day parade positioned this newcomer ahead of more senior figures like Aliev and Vorotnikov, and a few days later at a celebration of the 40th anniversary of the defeat of Nazi Germany, he sat at Gromyko's side close to the center of the Presidium. Less than a week later, he presided over a Central Committee conference on ideology, confirming his rise to the position of de facto second secretary with wide-ranging responsibilities for ideology and cadres.[21]

Ligachev's elevation to the second-ranking post was less significant than it might first seem. Under Gorbachev, the functions of the second secretary have been divided among several claimants, none of whom could even remotely be considered a potential replacement for the General Secretary himself. Ligachev supervised the *nomenklatura* system controlling key appointments to party and state posts — a particularly significant function in light of the approaching party congress — and was responsible for ideology. General oversight of the economy and agriculture, both of which Gorbachev had held for most of the Andropov and Chernenko periods, was divided between Ryzhkov and the newly appointed Nikonov, with military industries still nominally under the control of the soon-to-be-removed Romanov.

Georgii Razumovskii was promoted to direct the Central Committee's Organizational Party Work Department vacated by Ligachev. Past career experiences had tied him to both the new General Secretary and to Vorotnikov; in the early 1980s he had headed the Department for Agroindustrial Complexes of the USSR Council of Ministers, a post that would have been directly under Gorbachev's supervision, and subsequently had been tranferred to first secretary of the Krasnodar party organization when Vorotnikov left that post to become premier of the Russian Republic. Under his brief tutelage, nearly half of the local party and state leaders in Krasnodar were replaced, and Razumovskii became known for his willingness to promote younger technocrats to high posts.[22]

In the larger perspective, the extent to which Gorbachev had moved by mid-summer to consolidate his power at lower levels of the party apparatus, as well as the broader picture of change at this level since Brezhnev's death, can be seen from the turnover rate among regional party secretaries, which constitute the single largest voting bloc within the Central Committee. Under Andropov, 21 percent had been replaced, or 33 out of a total of 157. For most of Chernenko's brief tenure, the rate of replacement fell appreciably; from Andropov's death until December 1984 only an additional seven individuals were replaced, constituting just under six percent of the remaining pool that had not been touched under Andropov. The pace accelerated early in 1985 even before Chernenko's death, probably coinciding with Gorbachev's increasing control over party affairs and the preparations for the 27th Party Congress. From January to June 1985, 18 additional regional secretaries were replaced, or just over 15 percent of the remaining pool. For the group as a whole, this means that 37 percent of the regional party secretaries in power at the time of Brezhnev's death have been replaced. Even more striking is the impact of such changes on the group of regional party secretaries who sit on the Central Committee; of the 80 who were elected at the 26th Party Congress in 1981, 33 have been replaced, constituting just under 41 percent of all regional secretaries on that body.[23]

Gorbachev also moved quickly to make additional changes in the party and state apparatus. In addition to Razumovskii's appointment, changes were made in the Central Committee departments. Boris Eltsin, a former first secretary in Sverdlovsk, was named to head the Construction Department, and Arakdii Volskii, a former aide to Andropov, was placed in charge of the Machine Building Department, a critical post given the leadership's interest in high technology. Nikolai Maltsev, the Minister of the Oil Industry, was "retired" at age 56 and replaced by Vasilii Dinkov, the 63 year old Minister of the Gas Industry, whose record in presiding over increasing gas production far outshined the lackluster performance of the oil industry in recent years. Petr Nepdorozhnyi was retired from the Ministry of Power and Electrification, which had been under public attack for years, and was replaced by Anatolii Maiorets, the minister of the Electrical Equipment Ministry. The Ministry of Transportation Construction, which had been held responsible for critical bottlenecks in the transportation network, saw its former minister, Ivan Sosnov, replaced by Vladimir Brezhnev. Similar changes were made at the republic level; in the Russian Republic, six ministers or heads of state committees were pensioned off by mid-summer.[24]

Sweeping personnel changes continued at the July plenum. Grigorii Romanov, who reputedly led the attempt to block Gorbachev, was removed from the Politburo "for health reasons," although it was apparent that his maladies were more political than physical.[25] The dismissal, which occurred without the customary laudatory reference to his past service, came as no surprise; the former Leningrad party secretary had dropped out of public view since shortly after Gorbachev's election, and it had been rumored that his long-standing problem with alcoholism had worsened.[26]

Eduard Shevardnadze, the Georgian party secretary who had held candidate membership in the Politburo since 1978, was promoted to full membership, a move consistent with his surprise appointment as foreign minister the day following Andrei Gromyko's appointment as chairman of the Presidium of the Supreme Soviet (or "president", i.e., the Soviet head of state).[27] A Georgian with earlier career experiences in Komsomol and police affairs before his elevation to party secretary in his native republic, Shevardnadze had distinguished himself in cleaning up corruption in Georgia. While his early work in the youth organization probably brought him into contact with Gorbachev, who was engaged in similar tasks at that point in his career, and his later police experience and anti-corruption efforts made him a logical ally of Andropov, he had virtually no foreign policy credentials. Although widely travelled in the West, the socialist bloc, and the Third World, he had held no foreign policy post other than a 1958 appointment as a member of the presidium of the Soviet Committee for Solidarity with Asian and African Countries.

Shevardnadze's appointment was meant to convey several messages to both domestic and foreign audiences. Most important was the implication that Gorbachev himself would play the key role in making foreign policy decisions. The transfer of Gromyko to the presidency ended his increasing dominance of foreign policy issues since Brezhnev's death, leaving the new General Secretary better able to put his own stamp on foreign affairs. The appointment of a Georgian foreign minister may also have been aimed at Moscow's growing Third World constituency, among which such a move would be seen as an attempt to appoint someone more sympathetic to their concerns and less likely to reflect the traditional insensitivities of great-Russian chauvinism. In the same vein, his appointment also suggested that Gromyko's preoccupation with East–West relations in general and Soviet–U.S. ties in particular might now yield to a more balanced agenda. And finally, the promotion of a regional party secretary to higher duties continued a trend that was now becoming evident: the new leadership would both seek talent and tend to its political fences by courting support from within the ranks of the party apparatus itself.

It was the plenum and the Supreme Soviet session that followed the next day that saw the transfer of Andrei Gromyko from the Foreign Ministry to the largely ceremonial presidency, although it remained uncertain how much influence he would continue to exercise as an elder statesman and member of the Politburo. Having served as foreign minister since 1957 and a member of the Politburo since 1973, he had clearly become the dominant figure on foreign policy, especially since the death of Ustinov. His role as kingmaker only months earlier at the March plenum probably slaked any animosity that may have separated him from the rising new coterie of leaders, and his endorsement of Gorbachev seemed genuine. Only weeks away from his 76th birthday at the time of the July plenum, he had complained in recent years of the wearisome day-to-day duties of his post. His appointment to the presidency should be seen therefore not only as a recognition of his desire to diminish his responsibilities and a reward for his support during the succession but also as a tacit message to the other senior leaders, who might themselves hope for honorable semi-retirement in return for their endorsement of the new leadership. Moreover, it marked a subtle departure in the pattern of the new leader's consolidation of power. Unlike Andropov and Chernenko, who added the presidency to their list of formal appointments for symbolic reasons because Brezhnev had held the post, Gorbachev felt secure enough to use the office for other political purposes. For Gorbachev, consolidation was to be measured by the already considerable impact of his new appointments throughout the party and state hierarchies and not by the mere accumulation of titles.

Two new members were added to the Secretariat at the July plenum. These were Lev Zaikov, who had replaced Romanov as Leningrad party secretary, and Boris Eltsin, who had only recently been named to head the Construction Department. Zaikov predictably assumed responsibility for defense-related industries, a post consistent with his industrial experience in Leningrad. His appointment may also have been a reward for support at the March plenum and for neutralizing the Leningrad party organization. Eltsin continued for the present to hold responsibility for construction; in political terms, he had been associated with Ryzhkov in Sverdlovsk, and his rapid rise was undoubtedly seconded by the Kremlin's new overseer of the economy.[28]

The next significant change came less than three months later with the resignation, again purportedly for reasons of health, of Nikolai Tikhonov, the aging chairman of the Council of Ministers.[29] A member of Brezhnev's Dnepropetrovsk mafia, he had been named first deputy chairman of the USSR Council of Ministers in 1976 as a counterweight to Alexei Kosygin and had risen to the premiership in 1980 after Kosygin's death. Because of his continuing support for Chernenko and probable endorsement of Grishin at the March plenum, he was an obvious target of the new regime.

Tikhonov was replaced by Nikolai Ryzhkov, the most rapidly rising new star among the Kremlin's economic technocrats. An engineer with long experience in machine building, he had served as the first deputy chairman of Gosplan before his transfer in 1982 to the Secretariat to head the Economic Department. His elevation to full membership in the Politburo at the April plenum undoubtedly was in preparation for his assumption of Tikhonov's duties. In political terms, it also blocked, at least for the immediate future, the further rise of Aliev and Vorotnikov, both of whom were touted as possible candidates for the premiership, and underscored the further decline of Dolgikh's political fortunes. It also marked the further rise of yet another member of the former Kirilenko faction, to which both Andropov and Gorbachev turned for key economic appointments.

Two weeks later Nikolai Baibakov was removed from his duties as chairman of Gosplan.[30] Vacating a post that he had held since 1965, Baibakov was replaced by Nikolai Talyzin, a specialist in telecommunications and military technology who had served as a deputy chairman of the USSR Council of Ministers and as the chairman of the Supreme Soviet's Commission on COMECON Affairs. His appointment brought yet another specialist in high technology and its military applications to the ranks of top economic leadership.

The next blow fell late in December with the dismissal of Viktor Grishin as Moscow city party chief and the subsequent removal a week later of V. F. Promyslov as chairman of the city soviet.[31] Now completing the purge of those who had attempted to block his advancement in March, Gorbachev named Boris Eltsin to the party position. Six weeks later, on the eve of the 27th Party Congress, Grishin's fate was sealed through his dismissal from the Politburo. In keeping with the practice of assuring the city's representation on the Politburo, Eltsin was promoted from candidate to full membership and relieved of his duties on the Secretariat.[32]

During January and early February 1986, the various republics held their separate party congresses in preparation for the All-Union Congress scheduled to convene on February 25th. Some measure of the change that had occurred since Brezhnev's death can be seen from the roster of party first secretaries. Of the 15 republics, including the Russian Republic itself, nine had been given new party leaders since November 1982. Three vacancies had occurred because of the promotion of the incumbents, and three because of their death. Among the all-important second secretaries in the 12 non-Slavic republics — posts that go to Russians or other Slavs for control purposes — eight had been replaced over the same period, with only one post being vacated by the death of the incumbent.[33]

Despite the presence of such striking changes, there were also surprising islands of stability, most notably in the Ukrainian party organization. Even though other union republics had seen a widespread shake-up of regional party secretaries, the Ukrainian congress revealed that all 25 oblast party secretaries and the Kiev city party secretary were returned to office. The surprising durability of these regional cadres as well as the survival of the republic first secretary, Vladimir Shcherbitskii, suggests that he may have backed Gorbachev's appointment once he returned to the country and that his absence from the key Politburo session the day before may have saved him from the necessity of irreversible choice.[34]

Thus on the eve of the 27th Party Congress, Gorbachev could celebrate a seemingly irreversible consolidation of power. With his most immediate challengers now removed from high office and with a solid phalanx of his own appointees and those of his mentor, Yuri Andropov, now behind him, he now faced political realities far different from those which had existed just 11 months prior to his ascension to power. But in that same brief period of rule, he had attempted to bring equal resolution and energy to difficult problems in the economy and foreign affairs, and he had learned, as had virtually all Soviet leaders before him, that the consolidation of political power at the center does not guarantee its effective use at the periphery.

THE ECONOMY

Gorbachev's ascension signaled a return to efforts to revitalize the Soviet economy, although the new leadership moved with caution and circumspection in revealing the changes it would seek. Like all Soviet leaders since the death of Stalin, Gorbachev faced two interlocking dilemmas of reform. On the one hand, he had to address the allocational question of sectoral priorities; the choice of directing new investments into the military, heavy industry, consumer goods, or agriculture, or of altering past commitments to the preferential development of certain regions was a difficult economic and political decision. And on the other hand, he had to deal with the continuing issue of structural and managerial reform; while both of his immediate predecessors had attempted to purge the bureaucracy of inefficiency and corruption and had launched experimental managerial reforms, no coherent agenda had emerged, much less won the support of wide segments of the party and state bureaucracies most directly affected by the changes. Unlike his predecessors, however, Gorbachev was under less pressure to reach his goals during an expected short tenure in office. Both his relative youth and the speed with which he seized the reins of power suggested that he would have many years in which to implement his vision of the future.

His first pronouncements on the economy as General Secretary were hardly revolutionary. While he promised a "decisive turn" in the economy and called for the attainment of "the most advanced scientific and technical positions," he did not go beyond what had become the conventional wisdom of the day concerning reform efforts.[35] He shed somewhat greater light on the question of investment priorities, downplaying his predecessor's emphasis on consumer goods and hinting, as he had done in the past, that new investments in the military were a low priority.

A month later, speaking to a special meeting of economic managers convened at the Central Committee headquarters in Moscow, Gorbachev spoke in greater detail of his strategy for organizational change. Arguing for a judicious combination of improved centralized planning and greater local initiative, the General Secretary averred that

While strengthening centralized planning in the main areas, we propose to continue to expand the rights of enterprises, to introduce genuine economic accountability, and, on this basis, to enhance the responsibility, as well as the material interest, of the collective as a whole and of every worker for the final results. . . .[36]

Undoubtedly anticipating the observation that such reforms had been attempted in the past and resulted in de facto recentralization of authority because of the inability or simple unwillingness of local economic officials to exercise their new powers, Gorbachev acknowledged that "apparently a great many executives have not yet proved to be psychologically prepared" for their new role.

Gorbachev's comments also carried a new sense of urgency. Citing "disorganization, complacency, and . . . irresponsibility" as the causes of poor first-quarter results for the current yearly plan, he returned to a theme common during Andropov's brief rule:

We cannot hope for manna from heaven, so to speak. We need intensive, imaginative, honest and conscientious work from everyone — from worker to minister, from engineer to academician. We must resolutely enhance the responsibility of personnel and improve organization and discipline — moreover, not in words but in deeds. The question of strong discipline must be understood in a broad sense. It includes high production standards; strict technological discipline, on which the level of quality of manufactured articles directly depends; the precise fulfillment by enterprises of plans for output deliveries; and, of course, labor discipline. In the final analysis, everything begins on lofty exactingness toward people, toward executives and toward all of us, comrades.[37]

At the April 1985 plenum, the new General Secretary offered more of his economic program, although no clear picture of the regime's investment priorities emerged. Echoing now familiar themes that the further development of the economy depended on "qualitative changes," "intensive growth," and an "all-out increase in efficiency," Gorbachev assured his listeners that important changes could be accomplished in short order "if we put organizational–economic and social reserves into action and, first of all, energize the human factor, making sure that everyone works conscientiously and at peak efficiency. . . ." But while intensified efforts to wring increased efficiency from existing personnel and resources would provide short-term improvements, the long-term changes sought by the regime could be attained only through "revolutionary changes — a shift to fundamentally new technological systems. . . ."[38] While no concrete goals emerged from the General Secretary's comments, it was clear that key sectors such as machine building, computers, instrument making, and electronics were to receive priority, as was the reequipment and modernization of existing industrial capacity.

The April plenum also shed further light on the regime's plans for restructuring management. Improved centralized planning was to concentrate on "strategic tasks" and "long-range social, economic, scientific, and technical tasks," while an expansion of the rights of enterprises and the further introduction of economic accountability were to permit the individual production units to improve their efficiency. The number of centrally planned production indices was to be reduced, and factories were to make better use of "economic normatives," that is, to measure their success in terms of profitability. "Superfluous" layers of bureaucracy were to be eliminated, suggesting efforts to simplify the multi-level administrative apparatus by doing away with intermediate units.

The plenum also promised the development of a consumer goods program "in the near future," suggesting that no decision had yet been made about the priority to be attached to further improvements in the standard of living. The much touted food program was called upon to "make efficient use of available potential" — a sure signal that no significant increase in investment was intended — and to battle the narrow departmental approach of many of the multitude of agencies responsible for food production, whose lack of coordination was offered as the reason for past shortcomings.

Two months later, at the June 1985 plenum, Gorbachev rejected the preliminary draft of the 12th five-year plan and called for revisions both to raise the level of expectations and to shift investment priorities. Reformulating the traditional call for greater economic growth, he argued that

the Central Committee has in mind not simply an increase in the growth rates of the national economy. What is involved here is a new quality of our development, rapid progress in strategically important areas, the structural reorganization of production, switching to intensive tracks and effective forms of management, and the fuller solution of social problems.[39]

On the question of managerial reorganization, the General Secretary repeated the recommendations of the April plenum that better centralized planning be combined with greater latitude at the enterprise level. Ministries should concentrate on "long-range planning and the large-scale use of innovations," and the branch ministries should "substantially reduce" the managerial apparatus and do away with "superfluous elements." In contrast, the individual enterprises were to become the "center of gravity of day-to-day economic work." For its part, Gosplan was similarly to concentrate on long-range planning and eschew involvement in day-to-day activities, while at the same time playing a greater role in the technological modernization of industry.

The June plenum also signaled the reordering of priorities hinted at by earlier pronouncements. In the future, Gorbachev recommended, "main emphasis should be put on the technical reequipment of enterprises, savings of resources, and ensuring a sharp improvement in output quality." Observing that investments in modernizing existing industrial facilities yielded twice the return of expenditures for new construction, he called for an increase in investment in this area to from one-third to one-half of the total investment for the next few years, even though this would mean mothballing some incompleted projects.

On the touchier question of sectoral allocations, Gorbachev made it clear that he did not approve of increased investment in agriculture, which had been the principal beneficiary of Brezhnev's largess for nearly a decade. According to the new General Secretary, investment in this area had reached "optimum proportions, but the return on it is insufficient as yet." In future, increased production was to come from more efficient utilization of existing resources and from a reorganization of the multitude of state agencies dealing with food production.

As he had suggested at the April plenum, Gorbachev pressed for rapidly increasing investment in machine building and certain key sectors such as microelectronics, computers, instrument making, and information gathering and processing, which were described as the "catalysts of progress." Investment in these areas was to increase by 80 to 100 percent during the next five-year plan, resulting in a 50 to 100 percent increase in overall output.

Gorbachev was less clear about his commitment to the military and to consumer goods production. While he lamented that the international situation "compelled" the USSR to maintain its military strength, he reiterated the priority of his commitment to arms control and said that if such efforts fail, the United States would not be permitted to gain military superiority, a formulation that suggested that he regarded the Soviet Union as in no immediate danger of being surpassed by the American arms build-up. The issue of consumer goods production was completely ignored in the June 1985 plenum, undoubtedly to be reserved for a separate announcement on the new consumer goods program.

The General Secretary offered at best a limited commitment to the development of Siberia, a region that had received preferential treatment during the Brezhnev years. While he promised that "the state will continue to be generous in allocating funds for the development of Siberia, " he asserted that "we have a right to demand that they produce a return. . . . " The new emphasis attached to the modernization of existing industrial capacity also cut against the development of new industries in Siberia and favored the older industrial regions of European Russia, a shift that cannot have gone unnoticed in both quarters.

On the question of funding these new priorities Gorbachev waxed optimistic, although there was an obvious caveat in his remarks:

The basic measures to accelerate scientific and technological progress should pay for themselves. They are being conducted in order to raise labor productivity, and hence, to accelerate the growth of national income. But this will take a certain amount of time, while funds are needed immediately. Here we cannot get along without maneuvering resources and concentrating them in key areas.[40]

Further evidence of who would benefit and who would lose from such "maneuvering" came early in October with the publication of the comprehensive plan for consumer goods production. The program called for a 30 percent increase in the production of consumer goods over the next five-year plan and an 80 to 90 percent jump by the year 2000, with particular attention to improving the quality and diversity of consumer commodities. But on the question of how such increases were to be obtained, the new program reiterated a familiar theme that increased efficiency and better production methods, rather than new investment, were to provide the anticipated gains. Even though the program set forth the image of a Soviet-style consumer society by the beginning of the next century, it scotched any hopes that new investments were in the offing.[41]

Shortly after the June plenum, the regime announced a cautious program to increase the powers of individual enterprises and associations vis-à-vis the parent ministries.[42] The changes, which provided greater powers for factory-level personnel to establish quality control, introduce new products, and plan investment, were consistent with the East German reform model, touted by Soviet authorities, which envisioned gradual reform from the top down. While the measures were obviously intended to simplify factory directors' lives through reducing petty supervision by intermediate administrative levels and providing greater financial incentives to modernize production, they avoided any hint of marketization, the hallmark of the Hungarian reform model that had been recommended by some economists.

Other organizational changes quickly followed both to underscore the new commitment to key high-technology sectors and to wring greater efficiency from agriculture. Early in October 1985, a Bureau for Machine Building was created to coordinate the 11 civilian ministries producing such commodities, making it the first new super-ministry to be created by the new regime.[43] Late in November, similar action was taken to coordinate agricultural production through the creation of the State Agro-Industrial Committee, which took over the functions of previously separate entities dealing with a wide range of agricultural, processing, and support services. Yet even with this attempted consolidation, certain responsibilities remained with other agencies, which were instructed to "closely coordinate" their efforts with the new super-ministry.[44] Given the regime's commitment to downplaying the role of conventional ministries and its need to coordinate widely scattered activities, it is likely that more such agencies will be created for key sectors such as energy, transport, and construction, although the compromises seen in the creation of the new agricultural agency probably will be repeated.

In spite of the General Secretary's call for an extensive revision of the draft five-year plan, the final guidelines published in November 1985 incorporated only a part of his recommendations. The overall annual growth rate for the economy was set at 3.5 to 4 percent, slightly less than the level recommended by Gorbachev.[45] Growth rates for the industrial sector, which were set at 3.9 to 4.4 percent a year for the late 1980s, also were below expectations. The target growth rate for machine building was a modest 7 to 7.7 percent a year. The only real beneficiary in terms of increased investment appeared to be agriculture, whose share of total investments was to increase from 30.7 to 31.6 percent of the total, precisely the reverse of the General Secretary's recommendations.[46]

Measured against the agenda articulated by Gorbachev only months earlier, the goals of the five-year plan seemed to suggest that the new General Secretary was having a difficult time getting his way. To be sure, he had placed his own man, Talyzin, at the head of Gosplan only in mid-October, perhaps too late to accomplish extensive revisions in the general guidelines, although the more concrete one-year plan for 1986 seemingly moved further in the direction of responding to his priorities. But even setting aside the question of timing, it seems likely that Gorbachev was now learning what his predecessors had come to know all too well: the Soviet bureaucracy had grown expert at resisting change and swallowing reforms, despite the best intentions and vigorous advocacy of the supreme leadership.

Despite the seeming resistance of the bureaucracy, the tone that characterized the first year of Gorbachev's rule had resulted in a reinvigoration of the reform debate among economists, who had spoken boldly during Andropov's brief rule and lapsed into understandable silence under Chernenko. Most prominent were Abel Aganbegyan, who moved from the directorship of the Institute of Economics and the Organization of Industrial Production in Novosibirsk to an as yet poorly-defined advisory role in Moscow, and Tatiana Zaslavskaia, who had authored the so-called Novosibirsk Report leaked to the West during Andropov's rule. Aganbegyan's views seemed closest to the conventional wisdom about reform voiced by the present leadership, and Zaslavskaia's encompassed notions about the simplification of administrative structures and the improvement of incentive systems as well as less well accepted ideas about the limited marketization of certain sectors of the economy, especially in the service industries. Even more extreme recommendations, particularly for greater marketization, found publication in the specialized economic journals and in mass circulation media such as *Literaturnaia gazeta,* the weekly journal of literary and social commentary widely read within the intelligentsia. While it was difficult to assess who among these contending voices had found the ear of the new leadership, it was clear that the message had gone out that freer discussion was now permitted.[47]

The economic program of the new regime also could be measured in terms of the reinvigorated campaign for discipline and order as well as a new program to combat the pernicious effects of alcohol. Efforts against corruption and widespread malfeasance in office were once again the priority of the day, and a stream of reports about the dismissal of corrupt or merely inept party and state officials filled the Soviet press. Of the 134 "responsible posts" that make up the full ministerial complement of the USSR Council of Ministers, 48 (36 percent of the total) were replaced between Gorbachev's rise to power in March 1985 and the 27th Party Congress in February 1986, and similar changes shook the party and state apparatus at lower levels.

The regime also launched a serious effort to deal with the economic and social costs of alcoholism. Penalties for absenteeism were increased, and the production and sale of all alcoholic beverages were cut back. Alcoholic beverages were banned at all official functions, and the press debated a total or regional prohibition. While Gorbachev's predecessors had undertaken similar token efforts in the past, always with little success, the new General Secretary pressed the anti-alcohol campaign with unprecedented vigor, although it soon became obvious that wily consumers were resisting the party's call to jump on the new red wagon.[48]

FOREIGN POLICY

Gorbachev's first initiative in foreign policy broke no new ground. On the critical issues of Soviet–U.S. ties and arms control, he reflected the conventional wisdom of his predecessor, whose decision to resume carefully hedged three-part talks in Geneva had ended the deadlock between the two major superpowers. For his part, the new General Secretary cautiously approached these negotiations, which were scheduled to begin only days after his ascension to power. Speaking to the Central Committee on March 11th, he was content to reiterate the oft-heard position that such talks should result in a freeze on the further deployment of U.S. missiles in Europe, major reductions in strategic stockpiles, and — above all — in a prohibition of research and deployment of the anti-missile shield envisioned in Reagan's strategic defense initiative.[49]

A month later, Gorbachev spoke more philosophically about his perception of the USSR's role in the world and the place of Soviet–U.S. bilateral ties. He reiterated the theme that the two nations "will prove by force of example, not by force of arms, which is better," a message directed as much at a domestic audience concerned with economic priorities as at his U.S. counterparts.[50] Despite the arms talks, he described relations between Washington and Moscow as "tense," and pointedly suggested that while relations between the two were an "extremely important factor in international politics," the Soviet leadership "by no means look[s] at the world only through the prism of these relations," a reminder that more flexible Soviet diplomatic initiatives toward Western Europe and Asia might well diminish Moscow's fixation with improved bilateral ties. Once again he proposed a moratorium on the development of space weapons and on a further build-up of offensive armaments, including the continuing deployment of intermediate-range missiles in Europe, to run concurrently with the Geneva talks. By the end of April, Gorbachev's tone had grown more strident. Speaking at the Central Committee plenum, he pointedly mentioned the prospects of improved relations with Western Europe and Japan ahead of his reference to the United States, which he accused of attempting to separate space weapons talks from other issues, a prospect that brought a vague threat of a second Soviet withdrawal from the discussions.[51]

Throughout the late spring and summer of 1985, Soviet authorities attempted to increase pressure on the Reagan administration to back off its support of the strategic defense initiative. The attacks came on two fronts, the first charging the White House with abandoning its commitment to the linkage among strategic, intermediate-range, and space weapons talks at Geneva, and the second offering a series of positive incentives for agreement, including an end to Soviet countermeasures against American intermediate-range missiles in Europe, a nuclear test moratorium, and the prospects for radical reductions, up to 50 percent, of offensive weapons in exchange for a prohibition on the development of a protective umbrella. Charges that the Americans sought first-strike capabilities through the deployment of a protective missile shield alternated with vague Soviet threats about potential countermeasures and a resumption of an unbridled high-technology arms race in space.[52] Particular Soviet concern centered on continuing de facto adherence to the provisions of the unratified SALT II treaty and on seeking a U.S. reaffirmation of the Anti-Ballistic Missile Treaty, which had limited each side to one defensive system and ostensibly proscribed research and development efforts, although the U.S. side held that initial research on the star wars system was permitted. For its part, the Reagan administration countered the Soviet initiatives with mixed and frequently conflicting voices, some advocating serious exploration of Moscow's offer to consider deep cuts in strategic weapons and others arguing for rapid development of SDI.

Although late in the spring of 1985 Moscow pronounced the first round of the Geneva talks as ending on an "unsatisfactory" note, it was soon drawn into both the realities and the atmospherics that surround superpower summitry.[53] Early in July, both capitals announced that Reagan and Gorbachev would meet for a two-day summit in Geneva on November 19th and 20th. While both leaders sought the meeting for domestic as well as foreign policy reasons — it was the first opportunity for the new Soviet leader to occupy the world stage and test his mettle against the arch-anti-communist Reagan, and the president would find the trip to Geneva helpful in quieting his critics on the left — each also hoped that the meeting would emphasize his own version of strategic security in a world of increasingly complex and costly weapons systems. Gorbachev's goal was to convince the U.S. president of his serious intent to reduce overall strategic weapons, including intermediate-range systems in Europe, in exchange for a suspension of SDI, and Reagan hoped to assure the Russians of the essentially defensive nature of his proposals for a nuclear umbrella.

Soviet–U.S. relations further deteriorated over the summer with Washington's announcement that it would proceed with testing an anti-satellite weapons system, allegedly to counter previous Soviet research in the area, and with a brief flurry of concern over allegations that Soviet authorities had used a mysterious and potentially harmful tracking substance dubbed "spy dust" to monitor U.S. diplomats in the Soviet Union. Although the successful test of the anti-satellite system did nothing immediately to upset the Geneva talks and the spy dust controversy eventually ended with a U.S. admission that the danger to U.S. personnel was far less serious than initially imagined, both incidents confirmed Moscow's suspicion that hardliners in Washington were intent on pressing their technological advantage in the development of space weapons and in poisoning Soviet–U.S. relations prior to the autumn summit.

It was against this backdrop that Gorbachev painted a more pessimistic picture of summit prospects in his *Time* interview early in September, although he yielded slightly on the question of star wars research.[54] Describing himself as taking "a more cautious look at the prospects for the Geneva meeting than I did at the time we gave our agreement," he pictured Soviet–U.S. relations as "continuing to deteriorate" because of the U.S. rejection of Soviet proposals for a nuclear test ban and other symbolic steps toward agreement. Gorbachev yielded only slightly on the issue of star wars research, arguing that purely laboratory-bound activities were permissible under the Soviet interpretation of the anti-ballistic missile treaty, a position that he also expressed to visiting U.S. senators. Much of his spontaneous response after the formal question period was devoted to his professed bewilderment and anger at the Reagan administration's tone of hostility toward the USSR despite the president's proffered desire to build better relations. Pointing out that Washington still seemed to be a house divided on the issue of improved relations with Moscow, Gorbachev pictured certain circles in the administration as attempting to sabotage the upcoming talks.

If Moscow's approach to the summit lay along the path of playing the serious, if misunderstood — or purposefully misrepresented — suitor who wished to elevate the issues of space weapons and disarmament to the sine qua non of improved bilateral ties, then Washington's approach took the tack that the discussions must deal with a host of issues, including troublesome regional conflicts and the treatment of dissidents in the USSR itself, and could produce little more than an opportunity for the two leaders to become personally acquainted. Reagan's comments at the 40th anniversary celebration of the creation of the United Nations in October set the tone, promising to raise the issue of regional conflicts to a first-order priority during the talks, as did his interview with Soviet journalists early in November.[55] On the critical issue of the creation of a defensive nuclear umbrella, Reagan interpreted the Geneva talks as a forum within which to seek a "balance of defensive and offensive systems" rather than an outright ban on the creation of further defensive capabilities. He reiterated the U.S. pledge to cut strategic nuclear missiles to 5,000 warheads for each side — a position that had long proven unacceptable to the Soviets because of their heavy reliance on rocket forces to counter the U.S. triad of land-based missiles, submarine launched missiles, and aircraft — and offered either a complete ban on all intermediate-range weapons systems, including the Soviet

SS-20s and U.S. Pershing II and cruise missiles, or an interim partial limit on these weapons substantially below present deployment levels.[56]

A month before the summit, the Soviets tabled a comprehensive disarmament plan at the Geneva forum. The proposal called for "the complete prohibition of space strike arms for both sides" and a "radical reduction, by 50 percent, in nuclear arms capable of reaching each other's territory." Departing from their initial insistence about the coupling of all three aspects of the talks, Moscow now offered to reach a separate accord on intermediate-range systems in Europe and to open bilateral talks with Britain and France on their independent nuclear forces, an offer that was quickly rejected in London and Paris.[57]

Gorbachev's state visit to Paris early in October provided a forum for the General Secretary to press for the new Soviet plan. Although the ostensible purpose of the visit was to improve the state of Franco–Soviet ties, which had deteriorated markedly since Mitterrand's election, the dominant issues were the state of East–West relations in general and the approaching Reagan–Gorbachev summit in particular. While the General Secretary lost no chance to laud the Soviet proposals as a realistic package for disarmament and to point out potential strains between the United States and its European allies, he hedged on the linkage between the prevention of the militarization of space and the proposed 50 percent reduction in strategic arms, suggesting in response to a question from the media that such issues should be left for the Geneva meeting itself.[58]

The summit itself began on November 19th amid considerable confusion about what might be accomplished. During a visit to Moscow shortly before the meeting, Secretary of State Shultz had encountered a firm Soviet insistence to center the talks on the space weapons issue, and the principals arrived in Geneva with no agreement on the agenda or expectation that a final communique would be possible. A further shadow was cast over the talks by the publication in the U.S. press of a secret letter to the president from Secretary of Defense Weinberger warning against entering into any form of arms control agreement with the

USSR. The first hint that the Soviets would back away from their preoccupation with SDI came in Gorbachev's arrival statement at the Geneva airport on November 18th, in which he pointedly omitted any reference to space weaponry.[59]

The talks themselves were more significant for the tone of the exchanges between the two leaders than for any concrete results that emerged from their extended meetings. Reagan and Gorbachev quickly shifted from the formal agenda to a series of long personal meetings without aides and advisors. Although the exchanges were described variously as "candid" and "sharp," they covered a wide agenda ranging from arms control and regional conflicts to scientific and commercial cooperation. Perhaps predictably, both leaders spoke positively of what had been accomplished, Reagan describing a "fresh start" in Soviet–U.S. ties and Gorbachev speaking more cautiously of a "search for new forms of developing bilateral Soviet-American relations. . . . "[60]

The joint statement that was hammered out between the two sides reflected both the compromises and accomplishments of the meeting. Both sides agreed to a moderate statement on the critical question of arms control, stressing their common agreement that "a nuclear war cannot be won and should not be fought."[61] Both spoke in vague terms about their intention "to accelerate" the Geneva talks, especially in the areas of common agreement on the need for 50 percent cuts in strategic weapons (although the problem of defining such weapons and obtaining a proper balance of reductions was left untouched) and an interim agreement on intermediate-range weapons in Europe. However, the two remained at loggerheads on the issue of space weapons, even though the willingness to seek progress on strategic and intermediate weapons and the tacit Soviet acceptance of some research on star wars development suggested that the three elements of the Geneva talks might not be as firmly linked as the Soviets had originally insisted.

On less controversial issues, Reagan and Gorbachev agreed to meet again "in the near future" and to explore the creation of a jointly-manned crisis management center. The summit also cleared the way for the final agreement on a long-suspended cultural exchange treaty, a pact on air safety in the Pacific tacitly designed to defuse the sort of situation that had resulted in the Korean airliner incident, more people-to-people exchanges, a resumption of direct air links between the two nations, and a reactivation of the 1972 agreement on cooperation on environmental and conservation questions.

Gorbachev's account of the meeting offered at a wide-ranging press conference before his departure from Geneva was directed at both a domestic and an international audience. He stressed the importance of personal diplomacy and the five to six hours of private meetings between himself and Reagan, a posture that served to strengthen his image as a forceful leader but also ran the predictable risk of violating the canons of collective leadership. He also directly attacked those who voiced "doubts" about the possible success of such a meeting, a formula typically used to criticize unnamed opponents at home who had opposed the more conciliatory tone taken at the summit.[62] Gorbachev now "optimistically" looked toward the future of bilateral ties, a tone at direct variance with his September pronouncements. On the critical issue of space weapons development, he passed over the question of initial research and took the ambiguous stance that the militarization of space would make restraint of other aspects of the arms race "very, very problematical."

The internal Soviet media coverage of the summit hinted that the meeting was less optimistically received in certain quarters. While commentators in *Pravda* and *Izvestiia* spoke of their "optimism and satisfaction," the "breath of something new in the air," and the "new psychological climate . . . created in Geneva," the military journal *Krasnaia zvezda* was far less enthusiastic. Instead of joining in the endorsement, it repeated the allegation that such summitry was intended to "conceal an intention to upset the existing military–strategic parity" and cited Western press commentary that Weinberger's hardline position in opposing any agreement with the Soviets actually reflected Reagan's true intentions.[63]

Gorbachev's report to the Supreme Soviet a week after the Geneva meeting was more defensive in tone, suggesting that some elements of the Kremlin leadership had been critical of the lack of progress on arms control issues. He offered the more cautious conclusion that "the overall balance sheet of Geneva is positive." He also took pains to justify the decision to meet with Reagan, and although he spoke of the "sham peaceableness" of Washington's pre-summit maneuvers, he argued that "the U.S.'s international behavior ... began to undergo changes, something that, needless to say, we could not fail to take into account in considering the question of a possible summit meeting." He once again stressed the importance of his private conversations with the president, which he described as a "stabilizing factor" in a world filled with conflict. On the critical issue of space weapons, he understandably neglected to mention Moscow's seeming new flexibility on pure research and countered that any attempt to gain advantage through the strategic defense initiative would produce a "response that will be effective, sufficiently quick and, perhaps, less costly than the American program."[64]

A far less positive assessment of the talks was offered by other speakers at the legislative session. Marshal Sergei Akhromaev, chief of the General Staff, ignored the improved atmospherics and the commitment to accelerate the Geneva arms talks and spoke only of Washington's intent to upset the strategic balance. Arguing that "we must not put our minds at ease," he focused on the need to "improve the combat readiness of our army and navy," a none too subtle shot across the bow of a new administration that hoped to reduce expenditures for defense.[65] A similar argument came from Vladimir Shcherbitskii, the Ukrainian party secretary, whose acceptance of the notion that an improvement in Soviet–U.S. ties was possible "in principle" was hedged by a litany of criticisms of U.S. intentions.[66]

Despite the pledge to accelerate the Geneva talks, the coming months brought no sign of motion. The Soviets kept up the pressure on the Reagan administration; in December, Gorbachev offered to extend the test moratorium beyond the January 1, 1986, deadline if the Americans would reciprocate, and one month later he offered a comprehensive disarmament plan to scrap all nuclear weapons by the year

2000.[67] On the central questions of arms control, the proposal offered little that was new, and its release just prior to both the 27th Party Congress and the resumption of the Geneva negotiations suggests that it was meant to portray the new General Secretary as a would-be peacemaker and maintain pressure on the Americans to deal comprehensively with arms control issues. The plan envisioned a three-stage process of arms reductions, the first to cover the next five to eight years in which both sides would reduce by 50 percent their nuclear arms "capable of reaching the other's territory." On the remaining delivery vehicles, each side would maintain no more than 6,000 warheads. "It goes without saying," the proposal continued, "that such a reduction is possible only if the USSR and the US mutually renounce the development, testing and deployment of space strike arms," a formulation that still tacitly envisioned the possibility of laboratory-bound research. During the first stage, both sides would completely eliminate intermediate-range ballistic and cruise missiles "in the European zone," leaving the Soviets free to maintain such weapons in the East.[68]

During the second stage, to begin no later than 1990 and to run for five to seven years, the other nuclear powers would join in the arms reduction process, while the two major superpowers would continue reductions of their strategic and intermediate-range forces and freeze tactical nuclear arsenals. The ban on space weaponry would become multilateral, encompassing all major industrial powers, and all participants would foreswear research on the development of non-nuclear weapons based on "new physical principles." In stage three, which would end at the turn of the century, all remaining nuclear weapons would be destroyed.

Despite the now-familiar ring to the Soviet proposals, two concessions stood out. First, as Gorbachev himself reaffirmed, the USSR was now willing to move more quickly on the elimination of intermediate-range missiles in Europe, thus weakening the presumed linkage among the three elements of the Geneva talks. Such weapons would be removed during the first stage of the Soviet proposal, consistent with the pre-summit offer to negotiate separately not only on the question of U.S. missiles but also to open talks with Paris and London on their independent forces. In the present context, therefore, such missiles would be eliminated long before the proposed 50 percent reduction in strategic weapons had been completed. Second, the Soviet announcement that it would extend the nuclear test moratorium for three months also signaled a new willingness to negotiate on the question of verification, which had always been a stumbling block. For the first time, Moscow publicly spoke of the possibility of on-site inspections in addition to verification by "national technical means"[69] and invited the Americans to enter into talks on verification procedures.

As the 27th Party Congress approached, Gorbachev again underscored his optimism about the improvement in Soviet–U.S. ties. While he professed that "signs are beginning to appear" of a return to detente, he added that "one must be cautious" in dealing with the Americans.[70] In political terms, his caution was well advised on the eve of the party congress. Despite the complete about-face that had brought the Soviets back to the bargaining table and the high-stakes game of personal diplomacy that had been played out at the summit, Moscow had little to show for its efforts, and a new leader who had been so intent on making his mark approached the most critical party congress of his career essentially empty handed. While the atmospherics had improved, deep divisions over arms control still continued, and regional conflicts had not been muted by the November meeting.

Despite the seeming improvement of East–West relations, the Soviet union remained deeply involved in an increasingly costly war in Afghanistan. The United Nations-sponsored proximity talks had yielded no positive results, and although Soviet officials continued to profess their willingness to accept a negotiated political settlement that would end so-called outside interference, they were unyielding on the fundamental issue of a continued Soviet military presence. Throughout the summer of 1985 Soviet forces launched massive offensives to root the Mujahidin out of their valley strongholds, producing at best an inconclusive stalemate amid heavy casualties on both sides. It became apparent that the present Afghani leader, Babrak Karmal, was losing favor in Moscow because of the inability of his government to mount effective attacks on the still-disorganized guerrilla fighters, and speculation grew that he would soon be replaced.[71]

The Geneva summit in November brought a new candor to Soviet comments on their involvement in Afghanistan. Because of the importance of such regional issues in the talks, Soviet spokesmen sought to portray the USSR as anxious to reach agreement for a withdrawal. Officials within Gorbachev's entourage sought out Western media to confess that Moscow was "not happy" with its presence in Afghanistan and that a troop withdrawal was one of the new administration's "top priorities."[72]

In his first comments to the Central Committee as the newly elected General Secretary, Gorbachev stressed the importance he attached to a "serious improvement" in Sino–Soviet ties.[73] While cultural and economic cooperation had expanded under his predecessors, political relations remained at a low ebb. The December 1984 visit to Beijing of First Deputy Premier Ivan Arkhipov had improved the tone and resulted in new agreements for cultural ties and increased trade, but the Chinese leadership spurned a Soviet offer a month later to reestablish direct party-to-party ties, a level of diplomatic exchange considered far more important than regular state-to-state relations.[74]

Beijing initially reciprocated Gorbachev's new initiative. For the first time in a quarter century, Hu Yaobang, the party leader, sent a congratulatory message to the new Soviet leader, and the Chinese press began to refer to Gorbachev as "comrade," a courtesy that had been withheld from his predecessors. Despite the improvement in atmospherics, the next round of Sino–Soviet consultations, held in Moscow in April 1985, produced no improvement in the long-chilled relationship. The Soviets held firm on the three issues that had prevented any reconciliation — Afghanistan, the Vietnamese invasion of Kampuchea, and Soviet military strength along the Sino–Soviet border — and a Chinese effort to break the deadlock in May by suggesting that the Kampuchean issue would be the easiest to resolve fell victim to renewed fighting along the Sino–Vietnamese border.[75]

Throughout the summer, the two sides seemed to be speaking in different languages in describing their relationship. The July 1985 visit to Moscow of a Chinese trade delegation headed by Vice Premier Yao Yilin produced Soviet assurances that both nations were headed toward a normalization of their relationship and firm Chinese reminders that no such denouement was possible as long as the fundamental issues separating them remained unaddressed. The follow-up visit of Soviet Deputy Foreign Minister Mikhail Kapitsa to China in December produced another round of the now-familiar non-dialogue, with his Chinese hosts charging that despite his optimistic tone, he refused to "talk seriously" about the unresolved political issues. Beijing underscored its continued opposition to any normalization a month later by once again refusing to sign a nonaggression pact with Moscow, an agreement that the Soviets had sought since 1974.[76]

Soviet–Japanese relations, which had long been chilled by the Kurile Islands issue and the failure to agree on mutually profitable joint projects to develop Siberian resources, seemed to warm slightly with Gorbachev's ascension to power. In March 1985, Prime Minister Nakasone attended the funeral of Konstantin Chernenko and later met with the new Soviet leader, a significant signal given Andropov's refusal to meet with Nakasone's predecessor in 1982 and the Japanese failure to attend Andropov's funeral in February 1984. Despite the restoration of minimal diplomatic courtesies, the two nations merely reiterated each side's conventional wisdom over the next several months, with the Japanese demanding a settlement on the Northern territories, their name for the Kuriles, and the Soviets objecting that Tokyo was placing "artificial obstacles" in the way of a normalization of relations and succumbing to Washington's pressure to increase the size of the Japanese defense force.[77]

The autumn of 1985 saw the beginnings of a mild thaw between the two nations. Early in September, Deputy Foreign

Minister Kapitsa visited Japan and disclosed that Foreign Minister Shevardnadze would come to Tokyo in the near future. A meeting between the Japanese Foreign Minister, Shintaro Abe, and Shevardnadze later in September while both were at the United Nations General Assembly opening in New York produced signs that Moscow was backing off its harsh rhetoric on the Kurile issue and wished to explore increased cultural contacts, an overture that had been voiced weeks before by the Soviet minister of culture, Petr Demichev, while in Tokyo.

Both sides held great hopes for Shevardnadze's visit to Tokyo, which was scheduled for mid-January 1986. While Nakasone's government continued to insist that the Kurile Islands issue occupy center stage in the talks, it also voiced its hopes for a formal Soviet–Japanese peace treaty and for a visit by the prime minister to Moscow. For its part, Moscow stressed the significance of the visit both in restoring at least a semblance of normal relations and in pressing for its proposal for an Asian security conference, an idea that the Soviets had long touted as a counterbalance to the American military presence in the Pacific.

Not surprisingly, the visit produced no major breakthroughs. The Soviet interpretation of events attempted to picture the talks in the best light, observing that while "Japanese ruling circles" had stressed "unsubstantiated territorial claims against the USSR, "the prime minister had stated his desire for the development of a "wide-ranging dialogue between Japan and the USSR in the economic, cultural and other fields and for reciprocal visits by the two countries' top leaders."[78] The official communique issued at the conclusion of the discussions confirmed the Japanese invitation to Gorbachev to visit Tokyo and provided for regular consultations at the foreign ministers' level. The two also agreed to continue discussions about a peace treaty, to expand economic and trade relations, to seek accord on fishing rights in disputed waters, and to increase cultural relations.[79]

Soviet diplomatic initiatives toward Western Europe proved to be far more diversified and subtle under Gorbachev's leadership, although they produced no major substantive breakthroughs in Moscow's ties with the region. They did, however, confirm the new General Secretary's willingness to depart from the tendency to view the world through the prism of Soviet–U.S. relations and signaled a new level of sophistication in attempting to turn legitimate European concerns with security issues and separate foreign policy aspirations against U.S. influence on the continent. But despite these efforts, Soviet diplomacy met with a number of setbacks. Belgium and Holland went ahead with the deployment of U.S. intermediate-range missiles, despite considerable internal opposition, and both Britain and West Germany agreed to participate in preliminary research on star wars weapons systems. In addition, Gorbachev's first year also saw yet another round of expulsions of Soviet diplomats from Britain, France, and Italy, actions that brought retaliation from Moscow.[80]

Despite the British infatuation with Gorbachev, who had charmed both official and media circles during his visit to London as Chernenko's second-in-command, the Thatcher government held the new Soviet "peace offensive" at arm's length. Moscow's strident opposition to space weapons development was a continuing obstacle to improved relations with the European government that had most strongly endorsed their creation and most enthusiastically entered into joint experimental programs with the Americans. In September, the mutual expulsion of Soviet and British diplomats charged with espionage further poisoned relations, which saw no sign of improvement as Moscow turned its attention to other capitals.[81]

Soviet relations with Bonn similarly remained at a low ebb during Gorbachev's first year. Stung by its failure to forestall the deployment of U.S. intermediate-range missiles on German territory, Moscow tried to soften its efforts to convince the German government to resist involvement in star wars development, warning vaguely of the resurgence of "revanchist circles" and of the negative impact on long-term German–Soviet ties.[82] The highest level contacts occurred in May between the new Soviet leader and Willy Brandt, chairman of the opposition SPD party and the Socialist Internationale. While Brandt predictably voiced his opposition to the U.S. strategic defense initiative, the Kohl government nonetheless pledged itself to participation in preliminary research efforts, producing a sharp condemnation from Moscow.[83]

While French President Mitterrand's June 1984 trip to Moscow had improved the tone of Franco–Soviet relations, which had soured because of the socialist president's endorsement of the deployment of U.S. intermediate-range missiles and strident condemnations of the Soviet invasion of Afghanistan and the suppression of human rights at home, there was no fundamental improvement of substantive issues under the new regime. The French government continued to occupy a middle ground on the star wars question, supporting U.S. research efforts to develop such weapons systems but speaking out against their eventual deployment.

Despite the continuing differences, Moscow had obviously singled out France for special attention in its new "peace offensive," and the French foreign minister, Roland Dumas, was in Moscow preparing the groundwork for Chernenko's reciprocal visit to Paris when the chronically ill leader died in March 1985. Two days later, the new Soviet leader, Gorbachev, had a brief meeting with Mitterrand, who was in Moscow for the funeral, and accepted an invitation to visit the French capital in the near future. The prospects of the future summit were clouded during the summer of 1985 by a scandal over Soviet espionage in France and the growing imbalance in trade between the two nations, which had resulted in a 5.2 billion franc debt to Moscow by the end of 1984, largely because of Soviet natural gas and oil exports to France.[84] On July 3rd Paris and Moscow disclosed that the General Secretary would visit the French capital in October, the announcement occurring on the same day that Soviet and U.S. negotiators confirmed that Reagan and Gorbachev would meet in Geneva in November.

For all of its professed interest in avoiding preoccupation with Soviet–U.S. relations, Moscow treated the Paris summit as a dress rehearsal for the Geneva meeting. Gorbachev's public comments centered on recent Soviet proposals for a prohibition of star wars research and a 50 percent cut in strategic weapons and offered the prospect that a separate deal could be reached on the question of Soviet and U.S. intermediate-range missiles.[85] The sole new initiative that dealt with immediate French concerns came in an offer to negotiate directly with Paris and London over reductions in their independent nuclear arsenals, a suggestion that was quickly rejected by both nations. Despite the continuing deadlock on arms control, the two sides reached an economic and trade agreement that would reduce the trade imbalance.[86]

The Kremlin's new interest in courting European capitals was also evident in its treatment of Italy. In May 1985, Premier Craxi visited Moscow for meetings with the new Soviet leader, the trip constituting a follow-up exchange to Gromyko's earlier journey to Rome shortly before Chernenko's death. Soviet interest in improved relations was keyed to an earlier Italian endorsement of Moscow's proposal for a moratorium on the deployment of intermediate-range missiles on the continent and its lukewarm response to Reagan's star wars proposals.

Moscow's Middle Eastern policies enjoyed modest success following Gorbachev's rise to power. The courtship of conservative Arab states continued; in September 1985 Oman announced that it would establish diplomatic relations with the Soviet Union, and in December the United Arab Emirates took similar action. Political upheavals in South Yemen, a close ally of Moscow, have complicated Soviet efforts to shore up its presence in the region.[87] Tentative efforts were also made to improve relations with Iran. Deputy Foreign Minister Georgii Kornienko visited Teheran in February 1986, but despite a warming of economic and trade ties, the relationship has remained chilled.[88]

Under Gorbachev, Soviet fortunes in Africa increased slightly, due in large part to the increasing intransigence of the South African government. The declaration of a state of emergency in that nation predictably placed strains on the agreements that Pretoria had negotiated with Angola and Mozambique, causing both to move closer to Moscow once again. The Soviet Union has also patched up its relations with Zimbabwe, once again giving it greater influence among the more important black nations.[89]

GORBACHEV'S DIPLOMACY:
STYLE AND SUBSTANCE

Gorbachev's brief stewardship of foreign policy has revealed him to be a leader anxious to reshape the style of Soviet relations with the rest of the world while only marginally altering their content. Many of the substantive policies of his regime were initiated, or at least foreshadowed, by his predecessors. The movement away from a tendency to view the entire spectrum of Soviet relations with the outside world through the prism of East–West ties had begun under Andropov, as had a new round of more sophisticated initiatives in dealing with Western Europe, China, the Middle East, and the Third World. Similarly, it was Chernenko who had found a way out of the impasse in arms control negotiations caused by the Soviet withdrawal from the separate talks because of the U.S. deployment of intermediate-range missiles in Europe.

Yet it would be inaccurate merely to picture Gorbachev's foreign policy merely as old wine in new, more attractive bottles. In a world in which the public and private dimensions of diplomacy are intertwined and in which the appearance of motion and innovation may be as significant as the reality of change or stagnation, the new Soviet leadership has scored important points both for its new diplomatic style and for its seeming flexibility and pragmatism on policy issues.

The appearance of a new diplomatic style may simply have been inevitable with the passing of the older generation of party and foreign policy leaders. The higher level of activism was as much a consequence of the replacement of an aging and infirm leadership with younger and more vigorous figures as it was a conscious decision on the part of the new General Secretary. Yet three elements do stand out in the diplomatic style of Gorbachev and his new circle of foreign policy advisors. The first is the importance attached to personal diplomacy and, in particular, to the role of Gorbachev himself as a vigorous spokesman for Soviet concerns abroad. At both the Paris and Geneva meetings, there was little doubt that the general secretary spoke as the principal representative of the nation. Whatever the surviving realities of collective leadership at home, Gorbachev clearly now speaks as primus inter parus, at least on foreign policy. Having assembled a new diplomatic team of his own making (the extent of these changes will be reviewed below) he has emerged from under the shadow of former Foreign Minister Gromyko and the conventional foreign policy establishment rooted in the Foreign Ministry. Military influence has also remained at a low ebb; Defense Minister Sokolov has remained in the background, a position befitting his apolitical career and his second-class status as a candidate member of the Politburo, and the once vocal Marshal Ogarkov apparently remains on the fringes of the inner circle despite his public reappearance.

Soviet sophistication in managing the public aspects of diplomacy must also be measured as an accomplishment of the new regime. Crude efforts to manage Western public opinion and to affect critical choices such as the West German election have yielded to more polished attempts to present the Soviet case to a wide range of audiences. The "media offensive" at Geneva was only the tip of of the iceberg in terms of overhauling the presentation of Soviet policies; consistent with its attempts to improve the media as an effective tool of governance at home, the new leadership has made extensive changes in its foreign propaganda and information agencies.

Gorbachev has also extensively reshaped the foreign-policymaking apparatus, both to place his own team into positions of power and to restore firm party leadership within the Ministry of Foreign Affairs, which under the powerful Gromyko had become an independent force. Gromyko's departure to the largely ceremonial presidency was followed by significant changes in the ministry. In addition to Shevardnadze's appointment — and it must be remembered that by past career experience he was primarily a party apparatchik rather than a creature of the state bureaucracy — two new deputy foreign ministers were posted. They were Vadim Loginov, former Soviet ambassador to Angola and an expert on Third World affairs, and Valentin Nikiforov, who had previously served as deputy head of the Central Committee's Organizational Party Work Department, which oversees personnel policies. The appointment of the latter as deputy foreign minister for cadres was seen as a move to strengthen central party control over the ministry.[90]

Two holdovers from the Brezhnev era were retired from key Central Committee posts dealing with foreign policy. Konstantin Rusakov, who maintained liaison with governing communist parties, was the first to go, followed by Boris Ponomarev, who was in charge of ties with non-ruling parties and national liberation movements. Perhaps more significantly, Gorbachev sacked Andrei Aleksandrov-Agentov, who had served as the principal advisor on East–West relations to Brezhnev, Andropov, and Chernenko. He was replaced by Anatolii Chernaev, a deputy head of the international department, who rapidly emerged as one of the key players on the new team.

The transfer of Anatolii Dobrynin from the Washington embassy, where he had served for nearly a quarter of a century, to the Secretariat with general responsibilities for foreign policy further confirmed the growing importance of the party apparatus. Although a career diplomat, Dobrynin had no direct ties to any major group within the Foreign Ministry itself, giving him both the independence and political stature to restore party control. He quickly named a former Washington aide, Georgi Kornienko, as his senior deputy; Kornienko surrendered his post as first deputy foreign minister to make the jump to the Secretariat post.

Extensive changes have also taken place in the organization of the foreign policy establishment. In addition to the growing importance of the Secretariat in making overall policy choices, the Foreign Ministry, which is expected to implement party-made policy on a day-to-day basis, has been overhauled. Two new first deputy ministers and six new deputy ministers have been named since Shevardnadze's appointment, new departments have been created to deal with arms control and human rights issues, and major geographic bureaus have been realigned to fit contemporary policy directions. The press department has also been revamped and its former director, Vladimir

Lomeiko, whose hardline polemical bent had made it difficult to deal with Western journalists, has now been replaced by the more approachable Gennadi Gerasimov. Almost to a man, the new department heads have been drawn from the Secretariat apparatus or have had close ties to Dobrynin.[91]

NOTES

1. *New York Times,* February 25, 1985.
2. *New York Times,* January 22, 1985
3. Zhores, A. Medvedev, *Gorbachev* (New York: Norton, 1986), p. 14.
4. *Observer* (London), March 17, 1985.
5. Medvedev, *Gorbachev,* p. 6.
6. Ibid., p. 113.
7. *Pravda,* March 12, 1985; and Medvedev, *Gorbachev,* p. 16.
8. *Kommunist* (no. 5, March 1985).
9. Ibid.
10. *Pravda,* March 12, 1985.
11. Ibid.
12. *Pravda,* March 14, 1985.
13. *Pravda,* April 24, 1985.
14. *Pravda,* August 24, 1985.
15. Radio Liberty Research Bulletin (hereafter "Radio Liberty"), 134/85, April 26, 1985.
16. Ibid.
17. Ibid.
18. *Pravda,* April 24, 1985.
19. Ibid.
20. Ibid.
21. Radio Liberty, 183/85, June 5, 1985.
22. Radio Liberty, 187/85, June 4, 1985.
23. Radio Liberty, 201/85, June 20, 1985.
24. Ibid.
25. *Pravda,* July 2, 1985.
26. Radio Liberty, 218/85, July 3, 1985.
27. *Pravda,* July 2 and 3, 1985.
28. Radio Liberty, 218/85, July 3, 1985.
29. *Pravda,* September 28, 1985.
30. *Pravda,* October 15, 1985.
31. *Pravda,* December 25, 1985; and *Vechernaia Moskva,* January 4, 1986.
32. *Pravda,* February 19, 1986.

33. Radio Liberty, 28/86, January 17, 1986.
34. Radio Liberty, 52/86, January 23, 1986.
35. *Pravda,* March 12, 1985.
36. *Pravda,* April 12, 1985.
37. Ibid.
38. *Pravda,* April 24, 1985.
39. *Pravda,* June 12, 1985.
40. Ibid.
41. *Pravda,* October 9, 1985.
42. *Pravda,* August 4, 1985.
43. *Pravda,* October 18, 1985.
44. *Pravda,* November 23, 1985.
45. *Pravda,* November 9, 1985.
46. Radio Liberty, 68/86, February 11, 1986.
47. Radio Liberty, 291/85, September 4, 1985; and 308/85, September 16, 1985.
48. Radio Liberty, 68/86, February 11, 1986; and *Pravda,* September 9 and October 30, 1985.
49. *Pravda,* March 12, 1985.
50. *Pravda,* April 8, 1985.
51. *Pravda,* April 24, 1985.
52. *Pravda,* May 6, June 6, and June 9, 1985.
53. *Pravda,* May 27, 1985.
54. *Pravda,* September 2, 1985.
55. *Pravda,* October 26 and 27, 1985; and *Izvestiia,* November 5, 1985.
56. *Izvestiia,* November 6, 1985.
57. *Pravda,* October 4, 1985.
58. *Pravda,* October 5, 1985.
59. Radio Liberty, 391/85, November 26, 1985.
60. *Pravda,* November 22, 1985.
61. Ibid.
62. Ibid.
63. *Izvestiia,* November 22, 1985; *Pravda,* November 23, 1985; and *Krasnaia zvezda,* November 24, 1985.
64. *Pravda,* November 28, 1985.
65. *Izvestiia,* November 28, 1985.
66. Ibid.
67. *Pravda,* December 19, 1985 and January 16, 1986.
68. *Pravda,* January 16, 1986.
69. Ibid.
70. *Pravda,* February 8, 1986.
71. Radio Liberty, 307/85, September 11, 1985.
72. Radio Liberty, 391/85, November 26, 1985.
73. *Pravda,* March 12, 1985.
74. Radio Liberty, 103/85, April 3, 1985.

75. Radio Liberty, 335/85, October 4, 1985.
76. Ibid.
77. Radio Liberty, 22/86, January 14, 1985.
78. *Pravda,* January 8, 1986.
79. *Pravda,* January 20, 1986.
80. Radio Liberty, 78/86, February 17, 1986.
81. *Pravda,* September 15, 1985.
82. *Pravda,* April 15, 1985.
83. *Pravda,* December 29, 1985.
84. Radio Liberty, 328/85, October 1, 1985.
85. *Pravda,* October 15, 1985.
86. *Pravda,* October 5, 1985.
87. Radio Liberty, 37/86, January 21, 1986.
88. Radio Liberty, 61/86, February 4, 1986.
89. Radio Liberty, 78/86, February 17, 1986.
90. Radio Liberty, 132/86, March 21, 1986.
91. *New York Times,* August 10, 1986.

6   # The 27th Party Congress and After

THE 27TH PARTY CONGRESS

The 27th Party Congress, which began on February 25, 1986, was an event of great significance for the new administration. As would any new leader, Gorbachev sought to put his stamp on the proceedings, using the congress both to affirm the general policy lines that had been laid down under his direction and to attempt to consolidate his hold on power. In the same vein, the congress was equally important for symbolic reasons. Quite apart from the substantive issues, the tone of realism and "openness" that characterized the General Secretary's narration of past difficulties and his sober plans for the future were intended to send a signal about the style of the new leadership and encourage a perhaps still doubtful party and state apparatus to follow him down the path of candor and open discussion. No less significant was the timing of the meeting. It was hardly accidental, as a Russian would say, that the congress began on the 30th anniversary of Khrushchev's denunciation of Stalin at the 20th Party Congress in 1956. While no one expected such earthshaking developments from the present congress, the timing alone suggested that the new leadership considered it to be a major watershed in the nation's political life.

The congress was also touted as a potential turning point in Gorbachev's consolidation of power. The extensive changes in party and government personnel that occurred since his rise to power had a profound impact on the Soviet establishment, continuing a process of renewal that had begun under Andropov. Perhaps as importantly, the months before the congress were rife with rumors about further impending changes in the leadership, and the last minute dismissal of Viktor Grishin from the Moscow party post fueled the suspicion that the congress would witness a further loosening of the hand of the old guard and the promotion of younger figures presumably philosophically closer to and politically indebted to the General Secretary.

In one important aspect, Gorbachev had reversed the usual pattern by which Soviet leaders consolidate power. In the past, Stalin and Khrushchev had strengthened their support at the grassroots and middle levels of the party, eventually translating such backing into solid majorities within the Central Committee and then using such support to attack real or potential opponents within the Politburo. Brezhnev's experience had only partially fit the pattern, largely due to the political balance that was struck at the time of his appointment. But in Gorbachev's case, change at the top had occurred first. By the time of the congress, the highest levels of party and state leadership had already undergone significant transformation, as had other key elements such as the regional party leadership. The congress itself would provide the first opportunity to reflect such changes in the Central Committee itself, a body that would undoubtedly play a decisive role in any future clash within the leadership and whose membership would be read as a bellwether of future change.

The 27th Party Congress also was slated to approve a new party program, drafting of which began as early as the final years of Brezhnev's rule and extended throughout the uncertain transition that followed. With a new leader in power, the program would be particularly important for three reasons. First, it would be read for any hint of the new regime's confirmation or rejection of what had become the conventional wisdom of the day about the Soviet Union's present status as a developed socialist society and the timely course of its evolution toward communism. Second, it would be read for subtle indications of what might constitute the new leadership's "political formula," that is, the interplay of theoretical and practical issues that would shape the nation's priorities and lend legitimacy and force to a particular strategy of reform and, by implication, to those who advocated such changes. And finally, it would be read for its programmatic content alone, particularly in the areas of economic reform and social issues, which had been the key elements of the new regime's agenda.

On the whole, the congress produced few positive surprises and some disappointments, especially for those who had anticipated that the meeting and new party program would lend even further impetus to reform efforts. While Gorbachev's program clearly remained on track, there were no indications that the congress produced major breakthroughs or reinterpretations. The personnel changes at the top and in the Central Committee were less extensive than anticipated, and there were hints that the new General Secretary was increasingly frustrated by opposition to, and frequent bureaucratic footdragging concerning, his programs.

ELITE POLITICS

In political terms, Gorbachev's speech to the congress broke no new ground. Predictably, the most strongly worded sections dealt with the economy and with the need to proceed with "radical reform," marking the first time the General Secretary departed from his usual practice of calling for a "restructuring" in favor of more strident terminology.[1] Yet despite the stronger rhetoric, the substantive proposals were by now a familiar litany of better centralized planning, greater local initiative, and critical attention to the "human factors" of motivation, rewards, and discipline.

Unlike Khrushchev, who as a new party leader 30 years earlier had condemned his predecessors in the so-called secret speech on the crimes of the Stalin era, Gorbachev was almost gentle in comparison in pointing out the stagnation of the latter years Brezhnev was in power:

For a number of years — not just because of objective factors, but also for reasons that are primarily subjective in nature — the practical actions of party and state agencies lagged behind the demands of the times and of life itself. Problems in the country's development grew faster than they were solved. Sluggishness, ossification of the forms and methods of management, decreased dynamism in work, the growth of bureaucracy — all these things did considerable damage to the cause.[2]

Acknowledging that the party itself had succumbed to the temptation to avoid rigorous self-examination and that it had permitted virtually autonomous and unquestionably corrupt fiefdoms to emerge both at the center and in the provinces — power centers that had been the targets of major purges since Brezhnev's death — Gorbachev demanded greater control and supervision over party and state organizations at all levels. Throughout the hierarchy, leaders and organizations were to be required to file "regular reports" on their activities, and greater supervision would also be exercised by the People's Control committees, by meetings of workers' collectives and the general population, and by the media. "In the party," Gorbachev argued, "there neither are nor should be any organizations that are outside supervision and closed to criticism, and there neither are nor should be any officials who are protected from party responsibility."

Gorbachev also once again stressed the theme of "openness," noting that it was an important "political question" and a "point of departure in the psychological restructuring of our cadres." Particularly at the local level, where decisions reached in the factories and communities touch directly on the lives of the common citizen, such candor was to become an important element in establishing a sense of trust between the leadership and the population. The general secretary also implied that such openness had met opposition from some circles:

Sometimes, when the matter at hand is public openness, one hears appeals for greater caution in talking about our shortcomings and deficiencies, about the difficulties that are inevitable in any vital endeavor. There can be only one answer to this, a Leninist answer: under all circumstances, communists need the truth.[3]

Personnel changes in top party bodies also brought few surprises, in part because of the cumulative changes that had taken place under Andropov and during the pre-congress period under Gorbachev. Only one new full member of the Politburo was named — Lev Zaikov, whose rapid rise from the Leningrad party organization carried him to Politburo status without the customary apprenticeship as a candidate member. He retained his membership in the Secretariat, where since July 1985 he exercised responsibility for military related industries. Since that time his duties have been broadened to include supervision of the economy as a whole, placing him in line for the de facto senior secretary post vacated by Nikolai Ryzhkov.

With Zaikov in place, the Politburo now contained only four holdovers who had been appointed under Brezhnev. These included Gorbachev himself, Andrei Gromyko, who had been elevated to the largely ceremonial presidency, and the Ukrainian and Kazakh party leaders, Vladimir Shcherbitskii and Dinmukhamed Kunaev, whose regions had enjoyed remarkable stability despite the sweeping changes initiated by the new leadership. The remaining eight new members had all been appointed since Brezhnev's death late in 1982. Their average age was 64, six years younger than the average age of Politburo members at the time of Brezhnev's death.[4]

Zaikov's appointment also helped at least partially to restore the pattern of institutional representation characteristic of the Politburo during the Brezhnev years. In such terms, Politburo membership now included representatives of the KGB (Chebrikov), the Foreign Ministry (Shevardnadze), the economic apparatus (both civilian and military represented by Zaikov, although Ryzhkov also clearly continued to have special responsibility for this area), the Party Control Committee (Solomentsev), internal party and cadre affairs (Ligachev), the central government apparatus (Ryzhkov as chairman of the Council of Ministers and, to a lesser extent, Aliev as first deputy chairman), and three regional leaders (Shcherbitskii and Kunaev from the Ukrainian and Kazakh party organizations and Vorotnikov, who serves as chairman of the Russian Republic Council of Ministers). Only one — Gromyko — failed to represent a major constituency, a political reality explained as much by his status as elder statesman as by the expediency involved in his "promotion" from the Foreign Ministry.

Two candidate members of the Politburo were shunted off into honorable retirement, and two were added to the new leadership team. Retired were Vasilii Kuznetsov, who had functioned since 1977 as the deputy head of state largely to reduce the work load of the already ailing Brezhnev, and Boris Ponomarev, who had headed the Central Committee's department that dealt with nonruling communist parties and national liberation movements. The new appointees were Nikolai Sliunkov, who had served as first secretary in Belorussia from January, 1983, and Yurii Solovev, the new Leningrad party secretary.

Of the seven candidate members named at the congress, only two — Demichev and Dolgikh — were holdovers from the Brezhnev period. The remaining five had all been appointed during Gorbachev's tenure. Most significant in political terms was the continued candidate member status of Marshal Sokolov, whose role as minister of defense would have entitled him to full membership in the Politburo under Brezhnev, and the appointment of Nikolai Talyzin, the new technocratic chief of Gosplan, an agency slated for greater power and status under Gorbachev.

More extensive changes were seen in the Secretariat, which consisted of seven members, only one of whom dated to the Brezhnev era. Two long-time Brezhnev associates whose careers had plummeted since their patron's death were removed from the body. The most important was Ivan Kapitonov, who was transferred to the party's watchdog agency, the Central Auditing Commission. He had been a member of the Secretariat since the mid-1960s, with principal responsibility for the Organizational Party Work Department, which handles personnel appointments throughout the party apparatus. Having been moved to the far less important secretarial post in charge of light industry when Andropov appointed his own man, Igor Ligachev, to handle cadres, Kapitonov now slid further from the center of power. The other dismissals were that of 81 year old Boris Ponomarev, whose loss of candidate membership in the Politburo also signaled his retirement from the Secretariat, and Konstantin Rusakov, who had headed the Department of Liaison with Communist and Workers' Parties in Socialist Countries.[5]

Several new appointments to the Secretariat strengthened the hand of the new leader and conveyed open messages about the regime's future policies. Georgii Razumovskii, the present head of the Organizational Party Work Department, joined the body. He had replaced Ligachev as supervisor of cadres assignments in 1985 in connection with the latter's promotion to de facto second secretary, making his appointment to the Secretariat a certainty. Having spent most of his career in agricultural work and subsequently as party first secretary in the Krasnodar region, he undoubtedly was already well known to Gorbachev at the time of his transfer to Moscow in 1985.

A surprising new appointment to the Secretariat was Anatolii Dobrynin, who had served as Moscow's ambassador to Washington since 1962. Named to oversee the International Department, Dobrynin subsequently expanded the functions of this once-limited office to include general overview of Soviet foreign policy, with particular attention to Soviet–U.S. relations. His appointment was further confirmation of Gorbachev's desire to shift the focus of foreign policy formation from the Foreign Ministry itself into Central Committee staff hands.

For the first time since Khrushchev's tenure, a woman was named to a major national party office. Aleksandra Biriukova was appointed to the Secretariat, with particular responsibility for light industry, a traditional stepchild in the Soviet economy. A textile engineer with long experience as a trade union activist, she had risen to the post of deputy chairman of the All-Union Central Council of Trade Unions prior to her elevation to the Secretariat.

Two additional appointments were made to the Secretariat. These were Vadim Medvedev, who was named by Andropov in 1983 to head the Science and Education Department, and Aleksandr Yakovlev, who was tapped by

Gorbachev to head the Propaganda Department the previous year. Medvedev was a former academician and economist who had served as the rector of the Academy of Social Sciences, and Yakovlev was a former propaganda and media specialist who had been shunted off to the Soviet embassy in Canada in 1973. His career had been rescued by Andropov, who brought him back to Moscow in 1983 to head the troubled Institute of World Economics and International Relations. His appointment to the propaganda post was all the more surprising because of the continued presence of Mikhail Zimianin as a fellow member of the Secretariat. Under Brezhnev, the latter had been the faithful spokesman of the regime, a post that he presumably now yields to Yakovlev, who is reputedly close to Gorbachev.

The turnover within the Central Committee was far less than had been anticipated, suggesting that Gorbachev either chose to proceed cautiously or did not have the political strength (or the political will) to impose more extensive changes. Sixty percent of those members who were elected at the 26th Party Congress in 1981 were reelected at the 27th congress, to which should be added the 23 candidate members elected in 1981 who have now been promoted to full membership.[6] While this rate falls below the reelection figures for the Brezhnev years, which saw 80 percent on average returned to the Central Committee, it must be noted that the former General Secretary accomplished such stability only through the gradual expansion of the body. In contrast, the 27th congress witnessed a slight reduction in the number of full members, which fell from 319 elected in 1981 to the present 307.

Some indication of the relative stability can be seen in the average age of full members, which fell from 63 at the time of the 26th congress to 61 at the 27th congress, hardly suggesting that the next generation had made significant inroads against the old guard. Moreover, some highly visible political holdovers from previous administrations remained on the body despite their retirement from important posts. Among these were Nikolai Tikhonov, the former Chairman of the Council of Ministers, Admiral Sergei Gorshkov, former head of the Soviet navy, and Nikolai Baibakov, former director of Gosplan.

The proportional distribution of Central Committee posts among the various professional and occupational groups also remained relatively unchanged. Among full members, 44.5 percent were drawn from the party apparatus (compared with 41.3 percent in 1981), 28.3 percent from the state apparatus (31.1 percent in 1981), 7.5 percent from the military (7.2 percent in 1981), with similar proportions found among smaller groups.[7]

THE ECONOMY

Gorbachev's comments on the economy also broke little new ground beyond the programs that had been articulated since his rise to power and, in some cases, dating back to the reform initiatives of the Andropov period. The economic priorities of the 12th five-year plan, which had provoked much evident debate throughout 1985, reflected a more cautious approach than suggested by the General Secretary's first pronouncements, and the allocation of scarce capital indicated that concessions had been made to more conventional time-honored priorities, especially in agriculture. While the long-term goals advocated at the congress differed little from the reform agenda with which Gorbachev had been associated, the short-term policies consisted of the more conventional wisdom of greater discipline, less waste, and greater productivity from the existing industrial capacity and work force.[8]

More candidly than at any other point in his address, Gorbachev spoke of the "difficulties" that had emerged in the economy in the 1970s. While he admitted that certain objective problems were beyond the control of economic and political leaders, he confessed that they were "not decisive" in causing the malaise. "The main thing," he continued, "is that we did not make a timely political evaluation of the change in the economic situation, that we did not realize in full the critical and urgent need to shift the economy to intensive methods of development and make active use . . . of the achievements of scientific and technical progress."

Gorbachev's formula for correcting these ills was a now familiar call for the "acceleration" of economic development, broadly defined to include increasing growth rates, the rapid introduction of advanced technology, the preferential development of key high-technology industries, especially in electronics and machine building, the "restructuring" of economic management, and social measures designed to produce a better trained and more responsible workforce. In overall terms, national income was slated to increase by almost 100 percent by the end of the century, with labor productivity growing by 130 to 150 percent, and energy consumption down by almost 30 percent.

The regime's investment priorities were reflected both in Gorbachev's remarks and in Ryzhkov's more detailed speech on the economy several days later.[9] Apparently there had been further reworking of the five-year plan since the guidelines had been published in November; the critical change came in overall investment levels, which had increased from an anticipated 3.4 to 3.9 percent annual growth rate in the guidelines to a higher growth rate of 4.6 percent as stated in Ryzhkov's speech. The new figures suggested that the regime had also backed off its willingness to reduce investment in agriculture, which was to continue to receive about one-third of total investment. Predictably, certain areas such as machine building also received favorable treatment, as did the reequipment and modernization of existing industrial capacity. The former was to receive an 80 percent expansion of total investment and would increase its output by 40 percent over the five year period, while the latter was to receive half of all new investment, compared to a mere 35 percent in 1984. What was less clear was which sectors were to suffer cuts, although it is safe to assume that the regime hoped to lessen the impact of such reallocations through increased labor productivity.

On the critical issue of managerial reform, the General Secretary promised a gradual "step by step" transformation of planning mechanisms. Clearly both the central planners in Gosplan and the enterprises and factories themselves were to be the major beneficiaries of reforms that would, on the one hand, improve the quality of central planning through more scientific procedures and, on the other, give the production level units more autonomy in determining output. The losers were to be the branch ministries, which would drop by the wayside either through the creation of functionally integrated superministries for whole sectors of the economy or through the formation of a two-tier management system linking central planners with enterprise and factory officials. Consistent with these reforms, the price system would be overhauled to permit more rational choice, direct contractual arrangements among enterprises would be encouraged, especially in the wholesale trade of machinery and other producer goods, and incentive systems would be redesigned to link the quality and marketability of production to bonuses for workers and managers — all familiar themes in virtually all previous reform attempts since the mid-1960s.

In agriculture, Gorbachev once again called for greater use of the work brigade system with which he had long been identified, suggesting that the family unit might provide the appropriate work team. Collective and state farms were to be given stable five-year production targets and were to be free to dispose of above-plan production as they saw fit. The General Secretary also raised the economically successful if politically suspect specter of the New Economic Policy of the 1920s in referring to the possible use of a food-products tax as a means of raising revenue from the agricultural sector.

Gorbachev hinted at the existence of resistance to his economic reforms in confessing that there was a "widespread" view that "any change in the economic mechanism is perceived as all but a retreat from the principles of socialism. . . . " Yet he was blunt in warning the doubters about his intention to proceed with reforms:

It is difficult to understand those who take a wait-and-see attitude or, like the Gogol character who organized all kinds of harebrained schemes, for all practical purposes do nothing and change nothing. No peace is envisaged with the position taken by managers of this sort. We and they are simply not moving in the same direction. This applies especially to those who hope that everything will calm down and return to the old rut. That's not going to happen, comrades![10]

FOREIGN POLICY

Gorbachev's comments on foreign policy comprised the least forceful element of his five hour address, perhaps predictably in light of the nature of his audience and his understandable preoccupation with domestic questions.[11] On the whole, his tone on the critical question of Soviet–U.S. ties was hopeful; although he repeated the now-familiar litany of charges against the Reagan administration and the "right-wing groupings" that dominated Washington's thinking, he noted that there were now "signs of a change for the better . . . in Soviet–American relations. . . . " In substantive terms, however, he merely repeated the Soviet proposal first offered in mid-January linking an American abandonment of the development of the strategic defense initiative with the promise of significant cuts in strategic weapons and a separate deal on intermediate-range missiles in Europe. Gorbachev urged that a second summit meeting could be arranged in the near future to ratify such an agreement on Euromissiles and to confirm a mutual pledge to end nuclear testing.

Despite the prominence accorded Soviet-U.S. relations and disarmament issues, Gorbachev reiterated the position that "one cannot confine oneself solely to relations with any one country, even if it is a very important one." In order of precedence within the General Secretary's comments, Afghanistan was mentioned second only to Soviet-U.S. ties. He described the continued fighting there as a "bleeding wound" and expressed a desire to withdraw Soviet forces "in the very near future" if a political settlement could be reached concerning "armed interference" from abroad.

Surprisingly, West Europe received only brief attention in Gorbachev's speech. In a one paragraph reference, the General Secretary contented himself with calling for continued collaboration and the creation of "mature detente" within the region. No individual nation was singled out for special attention. In contrast, Gorbachev devoted even greater attention to the Asian and Pacific areas, which were described as of growing importance. Reflecting Soviet initiatives in the region, his comments called for closer political ties and measures to "take the edge off" military confrontation. Gorbachev was particularly pleased with improved Soviet–Chinese relations, although he passed over in silence the remaining political difficulties that prevented a further normalization of relations.

Problems in the Middle East, Africa, and Central America were lumped together in one brief paragraph that advocated "collective searches" for ways of defusing such conflicts. The "disgusting face of terrorism" was also briefly condemned, and Gorbachev promised measures to protect Soviet "lives, honor, and dignity" abroad, not a surprising reference in light of the fact that the USSR had begun to experience the first instances of violence against its citizens in the Middle East.

Particular attention was also given to Soviet–East European relations, an area that has grown in importance under Gorbachev. The Polish leader, General Jaruzelski, was accorded a particularly visible role at the congress, signaling Soviet approval of his suppression of the Solidarity movement and sending a clear message to other East European leaders about Moscow's limited tolerance for deviation and experimentation. Emphasis was also placed on the further economic integration of the COMECON nations, a measure that would link the Soviet economy to some of its more technologically advanced East European counterparts and stabilize raw material and finished product trade. Conspicuously absent, however, were the calls to examine East European experience for possible models for Soviet reforms that had been typical under Andropov.

THE NEW PARTY PROGRAM

The 27th Party Congress also approved a new party program to replace the 1961 document. Unlike Khrushchev's overly optimistic program, which called for the transition to communism to begin by the 1980s, the new version was a more cautious and realistic pronouncement that envisioned a gradual transition to the highest stage of the dialectic only in the distant — and cautiously undated — future.

Yet in several important aspects, the program bore the stamp of the new leadership and functioned, as had all its predecessors, as both a statement of current realities and a political formula linking the present with the future. Two things were significant about its tone and content. First, it offered a definition of the current tasks facing Soviet society that mirrored the leadership's reform program and justified its call for economic and social change. The sections dealing with the economy and society repeated in virtually identical detail the provisions of the current five- and fifteen-year plans calling for the accelerated development of science and technology and the preferential development of the high-technology sectors of the economy.

Second, the program cautiously moved away from earlier assertions offered by theorists in the Brezhnev years on the eventual transition to communism and subtly redefined the nature of the current era. Under the former leader, the Soviet Union had been described as having entered into the phase of "developed socialism," that is, a technologically and socially more mature phase of socialism vaguely resembling Western notions of post-industrial society. To be sure, at best the model was only partially accurate. Like all such formulations, it was intended both to celebrate the obvious advances that had occurred (with a considerable amount of exaggeration and self-congratulation, as was typical under Brezhnev) and to lay out a plan for future development consistent with the further technological modernization of the economy and the professionalization of party and state leadership. Theory aside, the political realities of the Brezhnev era dictated that little of that plan was translated into reality, especially in terms of internal party and state reforms. But the model remained the benchmark against which the evolution of Soviet society would be measured and the framework within which the new leadership would have to cast its programs.

The new party program seemingly departed from the Brezhnev formulation in two ways. First, it deemphasized the significance of the concept of developed socialism, which had been the theoretical cornerstone of the Brezhnev era. The draft program, published in October, 1985, even introduced a new definition of the current phase of the dialectic, terming it "integral socialism" rather than developed socialism.[12] Although not directly defined, the concept was introduced after a brief description of the economic, social, political, and cultural changes that were to result from the "acceleration of the country's social and economic growth." Thus integral socialism seemed to indicate an even higher stage of developed socialism in which the disjointed and uneven advances over the last two decades were to be correlated into a coherent whole:

The result of these transformations will be a qualitatively new stage of soviet society — in Lenin's words, "integral socialism" — that will fully disclose the enormous advantages of the new system [of economic and social changes] in all spheres of life. Thereby, an historic step forward will be taken on the path to the highest phase of communism.[13]

The introduction of this new concept in the draft program is difficult to interpret, especially in light of its omission in the final document approved only months later at the congress. In substantive terms, the content of the doctrine remained almost identical to that of the notion of developed socialism, save only the stress now placed on the acceleration of the pace of change. Perhaps the new leadership simply wished to place its own mark on theory, both to add a new sense of urgency to its reform efforts and to discover a new theoretical peg on which to hang its interpretation of current reality. Or perhaps the invention of integral socialism was but another signal that the new regime wished to break with the past in theory as well as practice.

Despite the clear indication in the draft program that the Soviet Union was entering into a new historical phase, the congress itself scrapped the notion of integral socialism and returned to the more comfortable definition of developed socialism, albeit with qualifications. Gorbachev's speech to the congress confirmed that the Soviet Union had "entered the stage of developed socialism" and revealed that the discussion of the draft provisions on integral socialism had caused considerable debate within the party, with "some people suggest[ing] that the provisions on developed socialism be completely removed from the program. . . . " Yet he made it clear that his real objection to the theory lay in its political misuse rather than in its admittedly progressive content:

At the same time, it is appropriate to recall that the thesis concerning developed socialism became widespread in our country as a reaction to simplified notions about the ways and timetables for accomplishing the tasks of communist construction [that is, in response to Khrushchev's overly optimistic program approved by the 22nd congress]. But later on, the accents in the interpretation of developed socialism were gradually shifted. Frequently the matter was reduced solely to the registering of successes, while many burning problems relating to switching the economy onto the tracks of intensification, increasing labor productivity, improving supply to the population and overcoming negative phenomena were neglected or not given proper attention. Willy-nilly, this served as an excuse of sorts for sluggishness in the accomplishment of urgent tasks.[14]

The final draft of the program reiterated previous conventional wisdom that the country "has entered into the phase of developed socialism" and completely dropped reference to the idea of integral socialism.[15] Yet developed socialism was mentioned only once at the beginning of the program in connection with the delineation of the many stages through which the nation has passed on its way to communism; the sections on economic, political, and social change ignored both the old and new formulations and instead mirrored the new regime's call for an acceleration in the pace of development in all spheres.

The second way in which the new party program differed from the conventional interpretation of developed socialism au courant during the Brezhnev years lay in the description of the transition from socialism to communism. The new program held that

Socialism and communism are two successive phases of the single communist formation. There is no sharp boundary between them: the development of socialism, the ever fuller disclosure of its possibilities and advantages, and the strengthening of its inherent general communist principles signify the actual movement of society toward communism.[16]

The political significance of this formulation becomes apparent when one realizes the implications for the regime's reform efforts. Under Brezhnev, reformers were exhorted "not to put the cart before the horse" and to attempt the creation of economic and social conditions that would be appropriate to the more advanced stage of communism while the Soviet Union remained in the less mature stage of developed socialism. But under the new formulation, the two stages are intertwined, justifying bolder measures to move society forward along the dialectic. While the new program cautioned against the temptation to ignore the "objective laws of development" — the reference seems more aimed at Khrushchev's "subjective" attempt to build communism within his lifetime — it also warned against "sluggishness in carrying out transformations whose time has come. . . . "

In political terms, the new program offered no surprises. The party remained the leading core of all economic, social, and political institutions, its role justified both by its special mastery of Marxist-Leninist theory, its role in the "deepening" of Soviet democracy, and its integrative role as a supra-political agency knitting together the diverse strands of an increasingly complex social and political order. Special importance was attached to increased intra-party democracy and the supervision of all levels of party leadership to prevent the emergence of autonomous centers of power and corruption, a clear indictment of the Brezhnev era. The program reaffirmed the "principle of collectivity" and "public openness" as key elements of party leadership, although it curiously omitted any direct reference to the notion of collective leadership at the top.

Taken in toto, the program still clearly revealed its philosophical roots in the Brezhnev years, with a few special twists to justify the current regime's reform efforts and a bow toward establishing Gorbachev's legitimacy as a theorist. The scientific and technological revolution remained the driving force of history, and the Soviet Union was still poised on the edge of the massive transformations in all aspects of economic, political, and social life. And caution was still the word of the day — but not so much caution that immediate reforms were to be prevented. But programs are like leaders; they evolve and change in response to the political realities that surround them and their own visions of the future, and the new program, unlike Khrushchev's precise timetable for the building of communism, was sufficiently vague to permit a multitude of alternative futures.

FROM THE CONGRESS INTO THE FUTURE

While an important event in its own right, the 27th Party Congress did not mark the final consolidation of Gorbachev's power or assure the successful implementation of his policies. Like all Soviet leaders before him, the new General Secretary is now and will until the end of his days in office be engaged in a constant political struggle to exercise power as first among equals within the Politburo and to secure approval for his policies. Always more than a mere powerbroker among the conflicting interests and power centers within the bureaucracy, he must also emerge as a leader in two senses of the term. As George Breslauer has perceptively noted in his study of Khrushchev and Brezhnev, a Soviet leader must both consolidate power in the conventional sense of building a coalition of supporters within party and state — although the precise composition of that coalition may vary from time to time — and also establish an aura of legitimacy surrounding his leadership.[17] The first task involves the conventional process of building ties to important constituencies and placing one's supporters in important positions throughout the nomenklatura. While the extensive turnover of personnel in both party and state would suggest that Gorbachev has been well positioned to accomplish this task, two caveats are in order. First, much of the new leadership team owes its rise to national prominence first to Andropov, as did Gorbachev himself; such leaders would be disposed to view the new General Secretary at best as a first among equals rather than as a supreme leader with unquestioned powers of patronage. Second, in an increasingly complex and specialized political order, position within the institutional structure is as significant as initial political ties in determining policy preferences, especially as the first rush of personnel changes winds to an end and the processes of institutional socialization and identification take hold.

The question of consolidating power aside, the second task of establishing legitimacy is equally difficult for any new leader, for it is linked to the dual problems of articulating seemingly viable solutions to the nation's problems and seeing to their implementation through the hands of an always cumbersome bureaucracy. In one sense, the first task is easier, for it involves merely (merely?) the need to define the nation's problems in ways amenable to solution by the social and political resources at hand and mobilizing support for the leader's particular vision of the future. In this regard, Gorbachev has not proven to be particularly imaginative or innovative. Despite the efforts to scrap the notion of developed socialism, his solutions to economic and social problems are cut whole-cloth from the pattern offered in the early 1970s. What is new is his approach to the second dilemma — the implementation of these reforms throughout the ossified and inherently conservative institutional order. There he has relied not only on a massive shake-up of institutions and people but also on the creation of a more open and candid political process, one stressing the constant review of leadership at all levels of the system.

In the months that followed the congress, evidence emerged that the new leader was increasingly frustrated by the lagging pace of reforms and the inertia of the party and state apparatus. His comments at the June 1986 Central Committee plenum were filled with references to attempts to block economic reforms and to "take a wait-and-see attitude. . . ."[18] Observing that "old approaches pull us back, and inertia is strong," he called for increasingly vigorous party leadership, especially at the regional and local levels, to translate policy pronouncements into concrete achievements. At one point, the general secretary hinted at continuing opposition within the Central Committee itself, referring to the measures that had been worked out as having been approved *edinodushno* rather than *edinoglasno,* (i.e., broad consensus but less than unanimity). It should be recalled that Gorbachev's own election as general secretary had been described as occurring *edinodushno,* suggesting that whatever opposition that existed in March 1985 may still remain within the Central Committee.[19]

Whatever his frustrations, and whatever the level of open or covert opposition that presently exists to his reform-oriented leadership, Gorbachev faces a number of serious obstacles to implementing his programs. One of the most intractable is inherent to the Soviet bureaucratic order itself. In the past, most efforts to restructure the administrative apparatus or to alter its modus operandi have faltered because of the persistence of narrow "departmental interests" and the unwillingness of administrative cadres to alter their perceived role in society. Only Khrushchev was even marginally successful in altering the institutional order, however, temporarily, and he paid the ultimate political price for his efforts.

Adding to this dilemma is the nature of the reform proposals themselves. No matter how cloaked in the rhetoric of "developed" or "integral" socialism, they offer a clear sense of déjà vu. Economic reforms calling for improved central planning, greater independence and initiative at the enterprise level, and improved incentive and price systems have been attempted since the mid-1960s — and all have fallen wide of the mark because of the failure of political leadership and the opposition of important segments of the bureaucracy. In substantive terms, the "new" proposals offer little that is in fact new. Their only hope lies in the possibility that the political will now exists to force them on a reluctant bureaucracy, no matter what the costs in terms of the disruption of existing power centers, the dismissal and replacement of leadership cadres, and the sacrifices required of the population in general, which must once again postpone increases in the standard of living for the sake of technological modernization.

Gorbachev also faces several political dilemmas of his own making. As we have noted above, the Central Committee underwent far less extensive change at the 27th Party Congress than had been expected, and there are indications that some elements continue to oppose the new leadership. Given the critical role of that body in resolving disputes that might break out among members of the Politburo, it seems likely that the new General Secretary would proceed cautiously to build consensus within top party circles rather than risk the creation of internal conflicts that might spread to such an uncertain court of appeals. Such political realities suggest that Gorbachev will emerge as a consensus-oriented leader, a posture consistent with the consolidation and maintenance of power but perhaps not with the implementation of bold reforms.

The Politburo itself is hardly a creature of the General Secretary's making. Of the 12 full members of that body, only two — Lev Zaikov and Eduard Shevardnadze — owe their rise to national power solely to Gorbachev. While Chebrikov, Ligachev, and Ryzhkov were promoted to full membership during his tenure, their political ascendence began under Andropov, as did that of Aliev, Solomentsev, and Vorotnikov. Indeed, Gorbachev's selection of Ryzhkov to replace Tikhonov as Chairman of the Council of Ministers blocked the further advancement of Aliev and Vorotnikov, each of whom was touted as a possible replacement. The situation is somewhat better among the non-voting candidate members: Elstin, Solovev, and Talyzin are clear beneficiaries of Gorbachev's rise. Yet the continued membership of Dolgikh, whose hopes for advancement began to slip under Andropov and were dashed by his successors, and of Marshal Sokolov, the Minister of Defense, suggest the presence of potential opposition at this level as well.

But there is also a brighter side to the situation facing Gorbachev. Given the malaise and stagnation that existed in the last years of Brezhnev's rule, even the slightest breath of fresh air will draw forth an enormous reserve of goodwill and hopefulness from all levels of Soviet society. In one sense, the Soviet Union (and Tsarist Russia as well) have always been governable because their people were never very demanding. There is little to suggest that the new leadership will have to produce on all of its promises in the near future. Slight improvements in the economy, a sense of forward motion toward building a modern and competitive industrial society, a feeling of new openness and candor in the political process, and a perception that the old leadership is yielding place to a new generation — all of these will be welcomed by the elite and the common people. Gorbachev's greatest danger lies not in a public backlash against a leader who promised more than he could deliver but in the mismanagement of the political and administrative dilemmas inherent in his reform program. Khrushchev rushed forward with little regard for such realities, and Brezhnev yielded to political expediency at the expense of substantive change. Gorbachev's task will be to find the middle ground.

NOTES

1. *Pravda,* February 26, 1986.
2. Ibid.
3. Ibid.
4. Radio Liberty Research Bulletin (hereafter "Radio Liberty"), 111/86, March 6, 1986.
5. Ibid.
6. Radio Liberty, 106/86, March 10, 1986.
7. Radio Liberty Supplement 1/86, July 8, 1986; and Radio Liberty, 139/86, March 27, 1986.
8. *Pravda,* February 26, 1986.
9. Ibid.; and *Pravda,* March 4, 1986.
10. *Pravda,* February 26, 1986.
11. Ibid.
12. *Pravda,* October 26, 1985.
13. Ibid.
14. *Pravda,* February 26, 1986.
15. *Pravda,* March 7, 1986.
16. Ibid.
17. George W. Breslauer, *Khrushchev and Brezhnev as Leaders: Building Authority in Soviet Politics* (London: George Allen and Unwin, 1982), pp. 3–22.
18. *Pravda,* June 17, 1986.
19. Radio Liberty, 232/86, June 18, 1986.

Bibliographic Essay

While much of the preceding study has been based on original Russian-language materials, there are several sources of information available to a non-Russian speaking audience. Most widely available is the *Current Digest of the Soviet Press*, which publishes both translations and abstracts from leading Soviet newspapers and journals. Similar materials encompassing both print and broadcast media are available from the Foreign Broadcast Information Service. More recently, a verbatim facsimile translation of *Pravda* has begun to be published.

The most valuable source of timely commentary on Soviet affairs may be found in the Radio Liberty Research Bulletins, which cover virtually all aspects of political, social, cultural, and international topics. Among the academic journals, *Problems of Communism, Survey,* and *Orbis* offer the best sources of current analysis.

A number of valuable background works deal either with the last years of the Brezhnev administration or the general features of the succession. Usually written before Brezhnev's death in November 1982, they predictably hedge on the exact shape of the coming changes and instead spell out the problems and political issues that shape any succession crisis. These works include:

Bialer, Seweryn. *Stalin's Successors: Leadership, Stability, and Change in the Soviet Union.* Cambridge, Mass.: Cambridge University Press, 1980.

Breslauer, George W. *Khrushchev and Brezhnev as Leaders: Building Authority in Soviet Politics.* London: George Allen and Unwin, 1982.

Brucan, Silviu. *The Post-Brezhnev Era: An Insider's View.* New York: Praeger, 1983.

Byrnes, Robert F., ed. *After Brezhnev.* Bloomington: Indiana University Press, 1983.

Hoffmann, Erik P., ed. *The Soviet Union in the 1980s.* New York: Proceedings of The Academy of Political Science, 1984.

Hough, Jerry F. *Soviet Leadership in Transition.* Washington, D.C.: The Brookings Institution, 1980.

Kelley, Donald R. *The Politics of Developed Socialism: The Soviet Union as a Post-Industrial State.* New York: Greenwood, 1986.

Kelley, Donald R., ed. *Soviet Politics in the Brezhnev Era.* New York: Praeger, 1980.

McCauley, Martin, ed. *The Soviet Union after Brezhnev.* New York: Holmes and Meier, 1983.

Nogee, Joseph, ed. *Soviet Politics: Russia After Brezhnev.* New York: Praeger, 1985.

Sonnenfeldt, Helmut, ed. *Soviet Politics in the 1980s.* Boulder: Westview, 1985.

Works that deal with events since Brezhnev's death are few in number and either have been rushed into print and are essentially journalistic in style and content or have emerged from the pens of emigré authors, whose unnamed sources cannot be verified through independent channels. These works include:

Butson, Thos. G. *Gorbachev: A Biography.* New York: Stein and Day, 1985.

Medvedev, Zhores A. *Andropov.* New York: Norton, 1983.

Medvedev, Zhores A. *Gorbachev.* New York: Norton, 1986.

Schmidt-Hauer, Christian. *Gorbachev: The Path to Power.* Topsfield, Mass.: Salem House, 1986.

Solovyov, Vladimir, and Elena Klepikova, *Yuri Andropov: A Secret Passage into the Kremlin.* New York: Macmillan, 1983.

Steele, Jonathan, and Eric Abraham. *Andropov in Power: From Komsomol to Kremlin.* Garden City: Anchor, 1984.

Zemtsov, Ilya. *Andropov: Policy Dilemmas and the Struggle for Power.* Jerusalem: Israel Research Institute of Contemporary Society, 1983.

Index

Abegenian, Abel, 135
Academy of Sciences, 56
Administrative Organs Department, 24
Afanasev, Viktor, 120, 121
Afghanistan, 14, 88, 95, 97, 136, 143, 144, 199, 200
Aganbegyan, Abel, 188–89
Akhromaev, Sergei, 125, 197
Aleksandrov-Agentov, Andrei M., 36, 116, 208
Al-Assad, Hafez, 147
Aliev, Geidar, 49, 56–57, 58–59, 68, 98, 107, 113, 126, 158, 160, 165, 171, 174, 179, 216, 232
American and Canadian Studies Institute of the Soviet Academy of Sciences, 42, 159
Andropov, Yuri Vladimirovich: 46, 47, 49, 50, 107, 11, 115–17, 120–21, 125, 127, 129, 134, 143, 146, 158, 159, 162–64, 166, 171, 208, 212, 218, 230, 232; administration, 55, 61, 63, 66; agricultural reform, 59, 60, 76–88; campaign platform for general secretaryship, 40–42; in Central Committee Department for Liaison with Socialist Nations, 27; chairman of

the Presidium of the Supreme Soviet, 50, 63–64, 120; chairmanship of the Defense Council, 50, 63; corruption, 42, 51, 60–61, 74, 78–79, 129; death of, 74, 98, 105–6, 136, 175–76; diplomatic work, 27; disassociation with KGB, 32; discipline campaigns, 83; economic reform, 50, 52, 61, 63, 76–88; election to the general secretaryship, 44, 49; first party post, 26; foreign policy, 41, 88–102; industrial reform, 76–88; ill health, 54, 58, 68, 70, 75, 92; KGB chief, 10, 20, 27–28, 31, 41, 47; leadership style, 51; military policy, 41–42, 53; party aparatus, 53, 66; Politburo member, 30; in power, 44–102; promotion to Secretariat, 34–35; pursuit of general secretaryship, 40–42; Reagan, 93; reform efforts, 69; rise of, 18–42, 46
Angola, 14, 98, 147, 207
Anti-Ballistic Missile Treaty, 191
anti-corruption campaign, 31, 54, 57, 60, 69, 78–79, 129, 177
apparatchiki, 111

About the Author

DONALD R. KELLEY is professor and chairman of the Department of Political Science at the University of Arkansas, Fayetteville. He has edited and contributed to *Soviet Politics in the Brezhnev Era* (Praeger, 1980) and is author of *The Solzhenitsyn–Sakharov Dialogue: Politics, Society, and the Future* (Greenwood, 1982) and *The Politics of Developed Socialism: The Soviet Union as a Post-Industrial State* (Greenwood, 1986). He has also contributed to numerous anthologies and journals on Soviet affairs.